Betty Crocker

the big book of cakes

HMH

General Mills

Food Content and Relationship Marketing Director: Geoff Johnson

Food Content Marketing Manager: Susan Klobuchar

Editor: Grace Wells

Kitchen Manager: Ann Stuart

Senior Food Editor: Andrea Bidwell

Recipe Development and Testing: Betty Crocker Kitchens

Photography: General Mills Photography Studios and Image Library

Photographer: Val Bourassa

Food Stylists: Carol Grones, Karen Linden and Jerry Dudycha

Houghton Mifflin Harcourt

Publisher: Natalie Chapman

Editorial Director: Cindy Kitchel

Executive Editor: Anne Ficklen

Senior Editor: Adam Kowit

Editorial Associate: Heather Dabah

Senior Production Editor: Marina Padakis Lowry

Cover Design: Suzanne Sunwoo

Interior Design and Layout: Holly Wittenberg

Manufacturing Manager: Kevin Watt

The Betty Crocker Kitchens seal guarantees success in your kitchen. Every recipe has been tested in America's Most Trusted Kitchens™ to meet our high standards of reliability, easy preparation and great taste.

FIND MORE GREAT IDEAS AT
Betty Crocker.com

For information about permission to reproduce selections from this book, write to Permissions, Houghton Mifflin Harcourt Publishing Company, 215 Park Avenue South, New York, New York 10003.

www.hmhbooks.com

Library of Congress Cataloging-in-Publication Data:

Crocker, Betty.
  The big book of cakes / Betty Crocker
      pages cm
  At head of title: Betty Crocker.
  Includes index.
  ISBN 978-1-118-36403-1 (pbk.); 978-1-118-36385-0 (ebk.); 978-1-118-36404-8 (ebk.); 978-1-118-36405-5 (ebk.);
  1. Cake. I. Title. II. Title: Betty Crocker, the big book of cakes.
  TX771.C6975 2013
  641.86'53—dc23

                    2012030910

Manufactured in the United States of America

DOC 10 9 8 7 6 5 4 3 2 1

Cover photos: Top (left to right): Chocolate Malt Ice Cream Cake; Spicy Mexican Brownie Cake; Cookies 'n' Cream Sports Ball Cake Pops; Vanilla Cake with Fondant Ribbons
Bottom (left to right): Raspberry-Laced Vanilla Cake; Marzipan Princess Cake

Dear Friends,

Maybe it's the nostalgia that comes with a favorite birthday cake, or perhaps it's a special feeling when you serve something beautiful and indulgent at the end of a meal. Whatever the reason, cakes hold a special place in our hearts—they're sweet, delicious and just perfect for any occasion. And baking a cake instead of picking it up at the bakery, whether it's simple or elaborate, makes the experience even more personal and wonderful.

Home-baked cakes made with scratch ingredients top the list, and you'll find a delicious variety of recipes to try in this cookbook. But the clever use of a cake mix can get you to home baked too, so look for those recipes that focus on convenient mixes to get you started. Whatever you are looking for, there's sure to be a cake that will suit your mood and occasion perfectly!

So in *The Big Book of Cakes,* get ready for fabulous cakes of all kinds—layer cakes, tube cakes, sheet cakes, angel food cakes and even cheesecakes are included. There's also a fun chapter filled with tiny cakes of all kinds. You'll find favorites like Red Velvet Cake and Sour Cream Spice Cake, plus new flavor combinations such as Chocolate Stout Cake with Caramel Frosting and Chipotle Devil's Food Bites.

If you like decorating, there are lots of great ideas to inspire you—from cakes for children's parties to elegant creations for special occasions. And we provide directions every step of the way.

So browse through this beautiful book filled with delicious cakes—then start baking!

Sincerely,
Betty Crocker

Contents

Baking Cakes

Tips for Perfect Cakes

❋ Heat the oven to the correct temperature. If the oven is too cold, the cake will not rise; if it is too hot, the cake might over bake. Turn the oven on 10 to 15 minutes before you plan to bake so that it can heat to the baking temperature.

❋ Measure ingredients accurately and add them in the order listed in the recipe. Be accurate— if directions are not followed carefully, the cake may not rise or bake properly.

❋ Use butter for the best results. If you choose to use margarine, use one that has at least 65% fat. Do not use reduced-fat butter or whipped products.

❋ Bake cakes on the oven rack in the center of the oven unless noted otherwise in the recipe.

❋ Follow directions for cake cooling and pan removal. If a cake is left in the pan too long, it can stick. If this happens, try reheating it in the oven for about 1 minute.

❋ Cool cakes on cooling racks to allow for air circulation.

About Cake Pans

❋ Use the pan size called for in the recipe. How do you determine size? Measure the length and width from inside edge to inside edge. If the pan's too big, your cake may be flat and dry; too small and it will bulge or overflow the pan.

❋ For tender, light cakes, use shiny pans, which reflect heat. Dark pans or pans with nonstick coating may absorb heat faster than shiny pans and can cause too much browning.

❋ If you use dark, nonstick or glass baking pans, follow the manufacturer's directions, which may call for reducing the baking temperature by 25 degrees because these pans absorb heat and cakes will bake and brown faster.

Dark pan with nonstick coating

Shiny pan

Easy Cake Removal

To easily remove cake layers from pans, cool in pans on wire cooling racks for 10 minutes. Run a dinner knife around the side of each pan to loosen the cake. Place a cooling rack on top of each cake layer in the pan; turn upside down as a unit and remove pan. Then, place a rack, top side down, on bottom of cake layer; turn over both racks so the layer is right side up. Let layers cool completely on racks.

Grease and flour pans as directed in recipe.

Place cooling rack on top of cake; turn over and remove pan.

Place cooling rack on cake layer; turn both racks over so layer is right side up.

Splitting Cake Layers

Mark middle points on sides of cake layer with toothpicks. Using picks as a guide, cut through the layer with a long thin sharp knife.

Frosting Cakes

Frosting and Decorating Cakes

Dollop, swirl and pipe to your heart's content! It's fun to frost and decorate when you have the right equipment at your fingertips. Decoration essentials to have on hand include:

* Small spatulas for spreading frosting.

* Pastry bags or as a quick substitute use resealable food-storage bags—just snip a small corner and squeeze the frosting onto the cake. There's no tip required!

* Decorating tips sold individually or in sets. They come in a variety of shapes and sizes to make different designs with frosting.

* Decorating icing in assorted colors available in aerosol cans at the grocery store.

* Food colors made from liquid, gel or paste. Paste food color makes the most vivid colored frosting.

* Assorted colored sugars, edible glitters and pearls.

* Assorted candy sprinkles in a variety of colors and shapes.

* Assorted premade decors made from sugar including flowers, hearts, stars, etc.

Frosting a Layer Cake

Brush any loose crumbs from cake layer. Place 4 strips of waxed paper around edge of plate. Place layer, rounded side down, on plate.

Spread ⅓ to ½ cup frosting over top of first layer to within about ¼ inch of edge.

Place second cake layer, rounded side up, on frosted first layer. Coat side of cake with a very thin layer of frosting to seal in crumbs.

Frost side of cake in swirls, making a rim about ¼ inch high above top of cake. Spread remaining frosting on top, just to the built-up rim. Carefully remove waxed-paper strips.

Making and Drizzling Glaze

Making the glaze. Glaze should be consistency of thick syrup.

Drizzling the glaze. With spoon, drizzle glaze over top of cake.

Using Ganache

For a perfect ganache. Ganache is ready to use when it is fairly thick and mounds slightly when dropped from a spoon.

Spreading ganache. Pour ganache carefully onto center of cake; spread to cover top and down side of cake.

Storing Cakes

AT ROOM TEMPERATURE: Cool unfrosted cakes completely before covering and storing to keep the top from becoming sticky. Store either frosted or unfrosted cakes loosely covered at room temperature up to 2 days. To loosely cover, place foil, plastic wrap or waxed paper over the cake without sealing it around the edges so air can circulate. You can also use an inverted bowl with a knife under one edge for air circulation.

IN THE REFRIGERATOR: Store cakes with whipped cream toppings, cream cheese frosting or cream fillings in the refrigerator.

IN THE FREEZER: Unfrosted or frosted cakes can be tightly covered and frozen for up to 2 months. Loosen wrap on frozen unfrosted cakes and thaw at room temperature 2 to 3 hours. Loosen wrap on frosted cakes and thaw overnight in the refrigerator.

Don't Smash the Frosting!

Want to cover a frosted cake with foil? Just create a foil tent by placing several toothpicks partway into the top of the cake. The foil will rest on the toothpicks and not touch the frosting.

Flavor Peek!

After frosting your cake, sprinkle or decorate the top with some of the ingredients from the cake. Sprinkle with a little of the spice that's used, chocolate chips or additional chopped nuts or dried fruit. It lets people know what flavors they can expect.

Decorating Cakes

Simple Ways to Make a Cake Look Fabulous

Turn a plain frosted cake into a masterpiece with one of these easy toppers:

* Fresh fruit such as berries, kiwifruit or star fruit added just before serving adds a pop of color.

* Candies such as fruit slices, gummy candies, colorful chocolate-filled candy pieces and marzipan.

* Cookies such as animal crackers, pirouette cookies or mini sandwich cookies can add interest.

* Edible flowers, candied violets or rose petals are great additions. Be sure they are food-safe and grown without pesticides.

* Nuts such as pecans, cashews or walnuts, or even chocolate-covered nuts or coffee beans.

* Coconut, either shredded or flaked.

* Chocolate curls (see opposite) or shavings, or chopped chocolate.

Add Some Bling!

Instead of just frosting your cake, sprinkle decorator sugar crystals of the same color (or clear) over the frosting to add extra glitz to the top.

Top with Curls!

Create chocolate curls to make any cake look special: Press a swivel-headed vegetable peeler firmly against a bar of chocolate, white chocolate or chocolate after-dinner mints (for striped curls), pulling toward you in long thin strokes. Then pile them on top of your frosted cake or cupcakes—as many as you like! Here's a little food-styling secret: If they break when you pick them up, use a toothpick to lift them.

Just a Sprinkle Does It!

A nice way to decorate is to sprinkle powdered sugar or cocoa on like snow. It's an easy way to decorate frosted cakes or cupcakes—but do it just before serving. Here's how: Place sugar or cocoa in a small mesh strainer and tap the edge of the strainer with a spoon to sprinkle it evenly over the top. Or to make designs on unfrosted cake, place a doily or stencil lightly on top of the cake and carefully remove after sprinkling.

chapter 1

Basic Cakes

Chocolate Cake

Prep Time: 20 minutes * Start to Finish: 2 hours 15 minutes * **12 SERVINGS**

2¼ cups all-purpose flour or 2½ cups cake flour

1⅔ cups sugar

¾ cup butter, softened

⅔ cup unsweetened baking cocoa

1¼ cups water

1¼ teaspoons baking soda

1 teaspoon salt

1 teaspoon vanilla

¼ teaspoon baking powder

2 eggs

Fudge Frosting (page 25) or Fluffy White Frosting (page 26), if desired

1 Heat oven to 350°F. Grease bottom and side of 2 (9-inch) or 3 (8-inch) round pans with shortening; lightly flour.

2 In large bowl, beat all ingredients except frosting with electric mixer on low speed 30 seconds, scraping bowl constantly. Beat on high speed 3 minutes, scraping bowl occasionally. Pour into pans.

3 Bake 30 to 35 minutes, or until toothpick inserted in center comes out clean. Cool 10 minutes; remove from pans to cooling rack. Cool completely, about 1 hour.

4 Fill and frost with Fudge Frosting.

1 Serving: Calories 330; Total Fat 13g (Saturated Fat 6g; Trans Fat 0.5g); Cholesterol 65mg; Sodium 430mg; Total Carbohydrate 48g (Dietary Fiber 2g); Protein 5g **Exchanges:** 2 Starch, 1 Other Carbohydrate, 2½ Fat **Carbohydrate Choices:** 3

Change the Pan Size

Follow the recipe as directed and pour batter into 13 x 9-inch pan; bake 40 to 45 minutes.

Starlight Yellow Cake

Prep Time: 10 minutes * Start to Finish: 2 hours * **12 SERVINGS**

2¼ cups all-purpose flour
1½ cups sugar
3½ teaspoons baking powder
 1 teaspoon salt
½ cup butter, softened
1¼ cups milk
 1 teaspoon vanilla
 3 eggs
   Chocolate Buttercream
   Frosting (page 24)

1 Heat oven to 350°F. Grease bottom and side of 2 (9-inch) or 3 (8-inch) round pans with shortening; lightly flour.

2 In large bowl, beat all ingredients except frosting with electric mixer on low speed 30 seconds, scraping bowl constantly. Beat on high speed 3 minutes, scraping bowl occasionally. Pour into pans.

3 Bake 25 to 30 minutes, or until toothpick inserted in center comes out clean or cake springs back when touched lightly in center. Cool 10 minutes; remove from pans to cooling rack. Cool completely, about 1 hour.

4 Fill and frost with Chocolate Buttercream Frosting.

1 Serving: Calories 290; Total Fat 10g (Saturated Fat 4.5g; Trans Fat 0g); Cholesterol 75mg; Sodium 420mg; Total Carbohydrate 45g (Dietary Fiber 0g); Protein 5g **Exchanges:** 2 Starch, 1 Other Carbohydrate, 1½ Fat **Carbohydrate Choices:** 3

Starlight Cherry Cake:
Stir in ½ cup dried cherries after beating batter in Step 2. Frost with Cherry-Nut Frosting (page 26).

Starlight Peanut Butter Cake: Substitute peanut butter for the butter. Frost with Fudge Frosting (page 25).

Change the Pan Size
Follow the recipe as directed and pour batter into 13 × 9-inch pan; bake 35 to 40 minutes.

Silver White Cake

Prep Time: 10 minutes ✳ **Start to Finish:** 2 hours 5 minutes ✳ **12 SERVINGS**

2¼ cups all-purpose flour
  or 2½ cups cake flour
1⅔ cups sugar
3½ teaspoons baking powder
1 teaspoon salt
⅔ cup shortening
1¼ cups milk
1 teaspoon vanilla or almond
  extract
5 egg whites
  **Fluffy White Frosting
  (page 26) or Chocolate
  Buttercream Frosting
  (page 24), if desired**

1 Heat oven to 350°F. Grease bottom and side of 2 (9-inch) or 3 (8-inch) round pans with shortening; lightly flour.

2 In large bowl, beat all ingredients except egg whites and frosting with electric mixer on low speed 30 seconds, scraping bowl constantly. Beat on high speed 2 minutes, scraping bowl occasionally.

3 Beat in egg whites on high speed 2 minutes, scraping bowl occasionally. Pour into pans.

4 Bake 9-inch pans 30 to 35 minutes, 8-inch pans 23 to 28 minutes, or until toothpick inserted in center comes out clean or until cake springs back when touched lightly in center. Cool 10 minutes; remove from pans to cooling racks. Cool completely, about 1 hour.

5 Fill and frost with Fluffy White Frosting.

1 Serving: Calories 320; Total Fat 12g (Saturated Fat 3g; Trans Fat 2g); Cholesterol 0mg; Sodium 370mg; Total Carbohydrate 47g (Dietary Fiber 0g); Protein 5g **Exchanges:** 2 Starch, 1 Other Carbohydrate, 2 Fat **Carbohydrate Choices:** 3

Marble Cake: Before pouring batter into pan(s), remove 1¾ cups of the batter; reserve. Pour remaining batter into pan(s). Stir 3 tablespoons unsweetened baking cocoa and ⅛ teaspoon baking soda into reserved batter. Drop chocolate batter by tablespoonfuls randomly onto white batter. Cut through batters with knife for marbled design. Bake and cool as directed in Step 4.

Chocolate Chip Cake: Fold ½ cup miniature or finely chopped regular semisweet chocolate chips into batter just before pouring into pans.

Cookies 'n' Cream Cake: Stir 1 cup crushed chocolate cream sandwich cookies into batter after beating in egg whites. Bake as directed. Frost with Fluffy White Frosting; garnish with chocolate cream sandwich cookies.

Marble Cake

Change the Pan Size
Follow the recipe as directed and pour batter into 13 x 9-inch pan; bake 40 to 45 minutes.

Buttermilk Spice Cake

Prep Time: 10 minutes * Start to Finish: 1 hour 55 minutes * **15 SERVINGS**

2½ cups all-purpose flour
   or cake flour
 1 cup granulated sugar
 ¾ cup packed brown sugar
 ½ cup shortening
1⅓ cups buttermilk
 1 teaspoon baking powder
 1 teaspoon baking soda
 1 teaspoon salt
 ¾ teaspoon ground cinnamon
 ¾ teaspoon ground allspice
 ½ teaspoon ground cloves
 ½ teaspoon ground nutmeg
 3 eggs
   Caramel Frosting
   (page 26)

1 Heat oven to 350°F. Grease bottom and sides of 13 × 9-inch pan with shortening; lightly flour.

2 In large bowl, beat all ingredients except frosting with electric mixer on medium speed 30 seconds, scraping bowl constantly. Beat on high speed 3 minutes, scraping bowl occasionally. Pour batter into pan.

3 Bake 40 to 45 minutes or until toothpick inserted in center comes out clean. Cool completely, about 1 hour.

4 Frost with Caramel Frosting.

1 Serving: Calories 260; Total Fat 9g (Saturated Fat 2.5g; Trans Fat 1g); Cholesterol 45mg; Sodium 310mg; Total Carbohydrate 42g (Dietary Fiber 0g); Protein 4g **Exchanges:** 1 Starch, 2 Other Carbohydrate, 1½ Fat **Carbohydrate Choices:** 3

Change the Pan Size

Follow the recipe as directed and pour batter into 2 (9-inch) round pans; bake 35 to 40 minutes. Cool 10 minutes; remove from pans to cooling rack. Cool completely, about 1 hour.

Pound Cake

Prep Time: 20 minutes * Start to Finish: 4 hours * **24 SERVINGS**

3 cups all-purpose flour
1 teaspoon baking powder
¼ teaspoon salt
2½ cups granulated sugar
1 cup butter, softened
1 teaspoon vanilla or almond extract
5 eggs
1 cup milk or evaporated milk
Powdered sugar, if desired

1 Heat oven to 350°F. Generously grease bottom, side and tube of 10-inch angel food (tube) cake pan or 12-cup fluted tube cake pan with shortening; lightly flour.

2 In medium bowl, mix flour, baking powder and salt; set aside. In large bowl, beat granulated sugar, butter, vanilla and eggs with electric mixer on low speed 30 seconds, scraping bowl constantly. Beat on high speed 5 minutes, scraping bowl occasionally. Beat flour mixture into sugar mixture alternately with milk on low speed, beating just until smooth after each addition. Pour into pan.

3 Bake 1 hour 10 minutes to 1 hour 20 minutes, or until toothpick inserted in center comes out clean. Cool 20 minutes; remove from pan to cooling rack. Cool completely, about 2 hours. Sprinkle with powdered sugar.

1 Serving: Calories 230; Total Fat 9g (Saturated Fat 4.5g; Trans Fat 0g); Cholesterol 65mg; Sodium 115mg; Total Carbohydrate 33g (Dietary Fiber 0g); Protein 3g **Exchanges:** 1 Starch, 1 Other Carbohydrate, 2 Fat **Carbohydrate Choices:** 2

Toasted Almond Pound Cake: Substitute almond extract for the vanilla. Fold 1½ cups slivered almonds, toasted*, into batter. Drizzle with Chocolate Glaze (page 27) or Vanilla Glaze (page 27), if desired.

*To toast almonds, heat oven to 350°F. Spread almonds in ungreased shallow pan. Bake uncovered 6 to 10 minutes, stirring occasionally, until light brown.)

Lemon–Poppy Seed Pound Cake: Substitute 1 teaspoon lemon extract for the vanilla. Fold 1 tablespoon grated lemon peel and ¼ cup poppy seed into batter.

Orange-Coconut Pound Cake: Fold 1⅓ cups coconut and 2 tablespoons grated orange peel into batter.

Change the Pan Size
Follow the recipe as directed and pour batter into 2 (9 x 5-inch) loaf pans; bake 55 to 60 minutes.

Angel Food Cake

Prep Time: 20 minutes * Start to Finish: 3 hours 25 minutes * **12 SERVINGS**

1½   cups egg whites (about 12)
1½   cups powdered sugar
 1   cup cake flour
1½   teaspoons cream of tartar
 1   cup granulated sugar
1½   teaspoons vanilla
 ½   teaspoon almond extract
 ¼   teaspoon salt
     Chocolate Glaze (page 27)
     or Vanilla Glaze (page 27),
     if desired

Cherry Angel Food Cake:
Gently fold ⅓ cup chopped, very
well-drained maraschino cherries
into batter in Step 3. Continue as
directed.

**Chocolate-Cherry Angel
Food Cake:** Stir 2 oz grated
semisweet baking chocolate into
powdered sugar and flour in Step
2. Continue as directed. Gently
fold ⅓ cup chopped, very well-
drained maraschino cherries into
batter in Step 3. Continue as
directed.

**Chocolate Confetti Angel
Food Cake:** Stir 2 oz grated
semisweet baking chocolate into
powdered sugar and flour in Step
2. Continue as directed.

**Espresso Angel Food
Cake:** Stir 2 tablespoons
instant espresso coffee powder
or granules into powdered sugar
and flour in Step 2. Continue as
directed.

1 Let egg whites stand at room temperature for 30 minutes. Room
temperature egg whites will have more volume when beaten than cold
egg whites. Move oven rack to lowest position. Heat oven to 375°F.

2 In medium bowl, mix powdered sugar and flour; set aside. In large,
clean, dry bowl, beat egg whites and cream of tartar with electric mixer
on medium speed until foamy. Beat in granulated sugar, 2 tablespoons
at a time, on high speed, adding vanilla, almond extract and salt with
the last addition of sugar. Continue beating until stiff and glossy. Do
not underbeat.

3 Sprinkle powdered sugar–flour mixture, ¼ cup at a time, over egg
white mixture, folding in with rubber spatula just until sugar–flour mixture
disappears. Push batter into ungreased 10-inch angel food (tube) cake pan.
Cut gently through batter with metal spatula or knife to break air pockets.

4 Bake 30 to 35 minutes or until cracks feel
dry and top springs back when touched lightly.
Immediately turn pan upside down onto heatproof
bottle or funnel. Let hang about 2 hours or until
cake is completely cool.

5 Loosen side of cake with knife or long metal spatula; remove from
pan. Spread or drizzle Chocolate Glaze over top of cake.

1 Serving: Calories 180; Total Fat 0g (Saturated Fat 0g; Trans Fat 0g); Cholesterol 0mg; Sodium 100mg;
Total Carbohydrate 41g (Dietary Fiber 0g); Protein 4g **Exchanges:** 1½ Starch, 1 Other Carbohydrate
Carbohydrate Choices: 3

Chocolate-Cherry Angel Food Cake

Lemon Chiffon Cake

Prep Time: 20 minutes * Start to Finish: 3 hours 35 minutes * **12 SERVINGS**

2	**cups all-purpose flour or 2¼ cups cake flour**
1½	**cups sugar**
3	**teaspoons baking powder**
1	**teaspoon salt**
¾	**cup cold water**
½	**cup vegetable oil**
2	**teaspoons vanilla**
1	**tablespoon grated lemon peel**
7	**egg yolks (if using all-purpose flour) or 5 egg yolks (if using cake flour)**
1	**cup egg whites (about 8)**
½	**teaspoon cream of tartar Lemon Glaze (page 27), if desired**

1 Move oven rack to lowest position. Heat oven to 325°F.

2 In large bowl, mix flour, sugar, baking powder and salt. Beat in water, oil, vanilla, lemon peel and egg yolks with electric mixer on low speed until smooth.

3 Wash and dry mixer beaters. In large bowl, beat egg whites and cream of tartar with electric mixer on high speed until stiff peaks form. Gradually pour egg yolk mixture over beaten egg whites, folding in with rubber spatula just until blended. Pour into ungreased 10-inch angel food (tube) cake pan.

4 Bake about 1 hour 15 minutes or until top springs back when touched lightly. Immediately turn pan upside down onto heatproof bottle or funnel. Let hang about 2 hours or until cake is completely cool.

5 Loosen side of cake with knife or long metal spatula; remove from pan. Spread glaze over top of cake, allowing some to drizzle down side.

1 Serving: Calories 300; Total Fat 12g (Saturated Fat 2.5g; Trans Fat 0g); Cholesterol 125mg; Sodium 360mg; Total Carbohydrate 42g (Dietary Fiber 0g); Protein 6g **Exchanges:** 2 Starch, 1 Other Carbohydrate, 1 Fat **Carbohydrate Choices:** 3

Orange Chiffon Cake: Omit vanilla. Substitute 2 tablespoons grated orange peel for the lemon peel. Spread with Orange Glaze (page 27), if desired.

Peppermint Chiffon Cake: Omit vanilla; add ½ teaspoon peppermint extract with water and oil in Step 2. Spread with Vanilla or Chocolate Glaze (page 27), if desired.

Spiced Chiffon Cake: Add 1 teaspoon ground cinnamon and ¼ teaspoon each ground nutmeg, allspice and cloves with flour and sugar in Step 2. Spread with Vanilla or Browned Butter Glaze (page 27), if desired.

Jelly Roll

Prep Time: 30 minutes ✳ Start to Finish: 1 hour 15 minutes ✳ **10 SERVINGS**

3 eggs
1 cup granulated sugar
⅓ cup water
1 teaspoon vanilla
¾ cup all-purpose flour
1 teaspoon baking powder
¼ teaspoon salt
   Powdered sugar
   About ⅔ cup jelly or jam

Chocolate Cake Roll:
Increase eggs to 4. Beat in ¼ cup unsweetened baking cocoa with the flour. If desired, fill cake with ice cream instead of jelly or jam. Spread 1 to 1½ pints (2 to 3 cups) slightly softened ice cream over cooled cake. Roll up cake; wrap in plastic wrap. Freeze about 4 hours or until firm.

Lemon Curd Cake Roll: Make jelly roll cake as directed, adding 2 teaspoons grated lemon peel to batter with flour. Omit jelly and spread cake with ⅔ cup purchased lemon curd. Roll as directed. Store covered in refrigerator.

Whipped Cream Cake Roll:
Make jelly roll cake as directed, substituting ½ teaspoon almond extract for the vanilla. In small bowl, whip ½ cup whipping cream, 2 teaspoons powdered sugar and ¼ teaspoon almond extract to stiff peaks. Spread over cake and roll as directed. Store covered in refrigerator.

1 Heat oven to 375°F. Line 15 × 10 × 1-inch pan with waxed paper, foil or cooking parchment paper; generously grease waxed paper or foil with shortening.

2 In medium bowl, beat eggs with electric mixer on high speed about 5 minutes or until very thick and lemon colored. Gradually beat in granulated sugar. Beat in water and vanilla on low speed. Gradually add flour, baking powder and salt, beating just until batter is smooth. Pour into pan, spreading to corners.

3 Bake 12 to 15 minutes or until toothpick inserted in center comes out clean. Immediately loosen cake from sides of pan and turn upside down onto towel generously sprinkled with powdered sugar. Carefully remove paper. Trim off stiff edges of cake if necessary. While cake is hot, carefully roll cake and towel from narrow end. Cool on cooling rack at least 30 minutes.

4 Unroll cake and remove towel. Beat jelly slightly with fork to soften; spread over cake. Roll up cake. Sprinkle with powdered sugar.

1 Serving: Calories 200; Total Fat 1.5g (Saturated Fat 0.5g; Trans Fat 0g); Cholesterol 65mg; Sodium 135mg; Total Carbohydrate 42g (Dietary Fiber 0g); Protein 3g **Exchanges:** 1 Starch, 2 Other Carbohydrate **Carbohydrate Choices:** 3

Cake Frostings

Peppermint Frosting, page 26

Fluffy White Frosting, page 26

Fudge Frosting, page 25

Caramel Frosting, page 26

Lemon Frosting, page 24

Maple-Nut Frosting, page 24

Creamy Cocoa Frosting, page 24

Cherry-Nut Frosting, page 26

Orange Frosting, page 24

Vanilla Buttercream Frosting, page 24

Peanut Butter Frosting, page 24

Browned Butter Frosting, page 24

Cream Cheese Frosting, page 25

Vanilla Buttercream Frosting

Prep Time: 10 minutes * Start to Finish: 10 minutes *
12 SERVINGS (1¾ CUPS FROSTING)

- 3 cups powdered sugar
- ⅓ cup butter, softened
- 1½ teaspoons vanilla
- 1 to 2 tablespoons milk

1 In large bowl, mix powdered sugar and butter with spoon or electric mixer on low speed until blended. Stir in vanilla and 1 tablespoon of the milk.

2 Gradually beat in just enough remaining milk to make frosting smooth and spreadable. If frosting is too thick, beat in more milk, a few drops at a time. If frosting becomes too thin, beat in a small amount of powdered sugar.

3 Frost 13 × 9-inch cake, or fill and frost 8- or 9-inch two-layer cake (see tip opposite).

1 **Serving:** Calories 170; Total Fat 5g (Saturated Fat 2.5g; Trans Fat 0g); Cholesterol 15mg; Sodium 35mg; Total Carbohydrate 30g (Dietary Fiber 0g); Protein 0g **Exchanges:** 2 Other Carbohydrate, 1 Fat **Carbohydrate Choices:** 2

Browned Butter Frosting: In 1-quart saucepan, heat ⅓ cup butter (do not use margarine or vegetable oil spreads) over medium heat just until light brown, stirring constantly. Watch carefully because butter can brown and then burn quickly. Cool butter. Use browned butter instead of softened butter in recipe.

Lemon or Orange Frosting: Omit vanilla. Substitute lemon or orange juice for the milk. Stir in 1 teaspoon grated lemon or orange peel.

Maple-Nut Frosting: Omit vanilla. Substitute 1 to 2 tablespoons real maple syrup or maple-flavored syrup for the milk. Stir in ¼ cup finely chopped nuts.

Peanut Butter Frosting: Substitute creamy peanut butter for the butter. Increase milk to about ¼ cup, adding more if necessary, a few drops at a time.

Chocolate Buttercream Frosting

Prep Time: 15 minutes * Start to Finish: 15 minutes *
12 SERVINGS (2 CUPS FROSTING)

- ⅓ cup butter, softened
- 3 oz unsweetened baking chocolate, melted and cooled at least 5 minutes
- 3 cups powdered sugar
- 2 teaspoons vanilla
- 3 to 4 tablespoons milk

1 In large bowl, beat butter and chocolate with spoon or electric mixer on low speed until blended. Gradually beat in powdered sugar on low speed until blended.

2 Gradually beat in vanilla and just enough milk to make frosting smooth and spreadable. If frosting is too thick, beat in more milk, a few drops at a time. If frosting becomes too thin, beat in a small amount of powdered sugar.

3 Frost 13 × 9-inch cake, or fill and frost 8- or 9-inch two-layer cake (see tip opposite).

1 **Serving:** Calories 210; Total Fat 9g (Saturated Fat 5g; Trans Fat 0g); Cholesterol 15mg; Sodium 35mg; Total Carbohydrate 32g (Dietary Fiber 1g); Protein 0g **Exchanges:** ½ Starch, 2 Other Carbohydrate, 1½ Fat **Carbohydrate Choices:** 2

Creamy Cocoa Frosting: Substitute ⅓ cup unsweetened baking cocoa for the chocolate.

Mocha Frosting: Add 2½ teaspoons instant coffee granules or crystals with the powdered sugar.

White Chocolate Frosting: Substitute 2 oz white chocolate baking squares or bars, melted and cooled at least 5 minutes, for the chocolate. Do not use white vanilla baking chips because they will add a grainy texture.

Fudge Frosting

Prep Time: 10 minutes * Start to Finish: 55 minutes *
12 SERVINGS (3½ CUPS FROSTING)

2 cups granulated sugar
1 cup unsweetened baking cocoa
1 cup milk
½ cup butter, cut into pieces
¼ cup light corn syrup
¼ teaspoon salt
2 teaspoons vanilla
2½ to 3 cups powdered sugar

1 In 3-quart saucepan, mix granulated sugar and cocoa. Stir in milk, butter, corn syrup and salt. Heat to boiling, stirring frequently. Boil 3 minutes, stirring occasionally. Cool 45 minutes.

2 Beat in vanilla and enough powdered sugar for spreading consistency.

3 Frost 13 × 9-inch cake, or fill and frost 8- or 9-inch two-layer cake.

1 Serving: Calories 170; Total Fat 4.5g (Saturated Fat 3g; Trans Fat 0g); Cholesterol 10mg; Sodium 35mg; Total Carbohydrate 32g (Dietary Fiber 1g); Protein 1g **Exchanges:** 2 Other Carbohydrate, 1 Fat **Carbohydrate Choices:** 2

SWEET TIPS For enough Vanilla Buttercream Frosting to fill and frost an 8-inch three-layer cake, use 4½ cups powdered sugar, ½ cup butter, 2 teaspoons vanilla and about 3 tablespoons milk.

For enough Chocolate Buttercream Frosting to fill and frost an 8-inch three-layer cake, use ½ cup butter, 4 oz chocolate, 4½ cups powdered sugar, 1 tablespoon vanilla and about ¼ cup milk.

Cream Cheese Frosting

Prep Time: 10 minutes * Start to Finish: 10 minutes *
12 SERVINGS (2½ CUPS FROSTING)

1 package (8 oz) cream cheese, softened
¼ cup butter, softened
2 to 3 teaspoons milk
1 teaspoon vanilla
4 cups powdered sugar

1 In large bowl, beat cream cheese, butter, milk and vanilla with electric mixer on low speed until smooth.

2 Gradually beat in powdered sugar, 1 cup at a time, on low speed until frosting is smooth and spreadable.

3 Frost 13 × 9-inch cake, or fill and frost 8- or 9-inch two-layer cake.

1 Serving: Calories 260; Total Fat 10g (Saturated Fat 6g; Trans Fat 0g); Cholesterol 30mg; Sodium 80mg; Total Carbohydrate 40g (Dietary Fiber 0g); Protein 2g **Exchanges:** 1 Starch, 1½ Other Carbohydrate, 2 Fat **Carbohydrate Choices:** 2½

Chocolate Cream Cheese Frosting: Add 2 oz unsweetened baking chocolate, melted and cooled 10 minutes, with the butter.

SWEET TIP This is the perfect frosting for carrot cake and spice or applesauce cakes. Be sure to refrigerate the frosted cake since cream cheese is perishable.

Extra Frosting

If you have leftover frosting, glaze or ganache, it can be tightly covered and refrigerated for up to 5 days for most frostings and frozen for up to 1 month. (Do not freeze glazes or ganache.) Let frozen frosting stand 30 minutes at room temperature to soften; stir before using.

Caramel Frosting

Prep Time: 10 minutes * Start to Finish: 40 minutes *
12 SERVINGS (2 CUPS FROSTING)

- ½ cup butter
- 1 cup packed brown sugar
- ¼ cup milk
- 2 cups powdered sugar

1 In 2-quart saucepan, melt butter over medium heat. Stir in brown sugar. Heat to boiling, stirring constantly; reduce heat to low. Boil and stir 2 minutes. Stir in milk. Heat to boiling; remove from heat. Cool to lukewarm, about 30 minutes.

2 Gradually stir in powdered sugar. Place saucepan of frosting in bowl of cold water. Beat with spoon until frosting is smooth and spreadable. If frosting becomes too stiff, stir in additional milk, 1 teaspoon at a time, or heat over low heat, stirring constantly.

3 Frost 13 × 9-inch cake, or fill and frost 8- or 9-inch two-layer cake.

1 Serving: Calories 220; Total Fat 8g (Saturated Fat 4g; Trans Fat 0g); Cholesterol 20mg; Sodium 60mg; Total Carbohydrate 38g (Dietary Fiber 0g); Protein 0g Exchanges: 2½ Other Carbohydrate, 1½ Fat Carbohydrate Choices: 2½

SWEET TIP For a richer frosting, use whole milk or half-and-half.

Fluffy White Frosting

Prep Time: 25 minutes * Start to Finish: 55 minutes *
12 SERVINGS (3 CUPS FROSTING)

- 2 egg whites
- ½ cup sugar
- ¼ cup light corn syrup
- 2 tablespoons water
- 1 teaspoon vanilla

1 Let egg whites stand at room temperature for 30 minutes. Room temperature egg whites will have more volume when beaten than cold egg whites. In medium bowl, beat egg whites with electric mixer on high speed just until stiff peaks form.

2 In 1-quart saucepan, stir sugar, corn syrup and water until well mixed. Cover and heat to rolling boil over medium heat. Uncover and boil 4 to 8 minutes, without stirring, to 242°F on candy thermometer or until small amount of mixture dropped into cup of very cold water forms a firm ball that holds its shape until pressed. For an accurate temperature reading, tilt the saucepan slightly so mixture is deep enough for thermometer.

3 Pour hot syrup very slowly in thin stream into egg whites, beating constantly on medium speed. Add vanilla. Beat on high speed about 10 minutes or until stiff peaks form.

4 Frost 13 × 9-inch cake, or fill and frost 8- or 9-inch two-layer cake.

1 Serving: Calories 60; Total Fat 0g (Saturated Fat 0g; Trans Fat 0g); Cholesterol 0mg; Sodium 15mg; Total Carbohydrate 14g (Dietary Fiber 0g); Protein 0g Exchanges: 1 Other Carbohydrate Carbohydrate Choices: 1

Butterscotch Frosting: Substitute packed brown sugar for the sugar. Decrease vanilla to ½ teaspoon.

Cherry-Nut Frosting: After stiff peaks form, stir in ¼ cup chopped candied cherries, ¼ cup chopped nuts and, if desired, 6 to 8 drops red food color.

Peppermint Frosting: After stiff peaks form, stir in ⅓ cup coarsely crushed hard peppermint candies or ½ teaspoon peppermint extract.

Chocolate Ganache

Prep Time: 5 minutes * Start to Finish: 10 minutes *
12 SERVINGS (1¼ CUPS GANACHE)

- ⅔ cup whipping cream
- 6 oz semisweet baking chocolate, chopped

1 In 1-quart saucepan, heat whipping cream over low heat until hot but not boiling; remove from heat.

2 Stir in chocolate until melted. Let stand about 5 minutes. Ganache is ready to use when it mounds slightly when dropped from a spoon. It will become firmer the longer it cools.

3 Glaze 13 × 9-inch cake or top and side of 8- or 9-inch two-layer cake. Pour ganache carefully onto top center of cake; spread with large spatula so it flows evenly over top and down to cover side of cake.

1 Serving: Calories 120; Total Fat 8g (Saturated Fat 5g; Trans Fat 0g); Cholesterol 15mg; Sodium 5mg; Total Carbohydrate 9g (Dietary Fiber 0g); Protein 0g **Exchanges:** ½ Other Carbohydrate, 1½ Fat **Carbohydrate Choices:** ½

Vanilla Glaze

Prep Time: 5 minutes * Start to Finish: 5 minutes *
12 SERVINGS (1 CUP GLAZE)

- ⅓ cup butter
- 2 cups powdered sugar
- 1½ teaspoons vanilla
- 2 to 4 tablespoons hot water

1 In 1½-quart saucepan, melt butter over low heat; remove from heat. Stir in powdered sugar and vanilla.

2 Stir in hot water, 1 tablespoon at a time, until glaze is smooth and has the consistency of thick syrup.

3 Glaze one 12-cup fluted tube cake, 10-inch angel food or chiffon cake or top of an 8- or 9-inch layer cake.

1 Serving: Calories 130; Total Fat 5g (Saturated Fat 3g; Trans Fat 0g); Cholesterol 15mg; Sodium 35mg; Total Carbohydrate 20g (Dietary Fiber 0g); Protein 0g **Exchanges:** 1½ Other Carbohydrate, 1 Fat **Carbohydrate Choices:** 1

Browned Butter Glaze: Brown the butter as directed in Browned Butter Frosting (page 24). Continue as directed in Step 1.

Lemon or Orange Glaze: Stir 1 teaspoon grated lemon or orange peel into melted butter. Omit vanilla. Substitute lemon or orange juice, heated, for the hot water.

Chocolate Glaze

Prep Time: 5 minutes * Start to Finish: 15 minutes *
12 SERVINGS (½ CUP GLAZE)

- ½ cup semisweet chocolate chips (3 oz)
- 2 tablespoons butter
- 2 tablespoons light corn syrup
- 1 to 2 teaspoons hot water

1 In 1-quart saucepan, heat chocolate chips, butter and corn syrup over low heat, stirring frequently, until chocolate chips are melted. Cool about 10 minutes.

2 Stir in hot water, 1 teaspoon at a time, until glaze is smooth and has the consistency of thick syrup.

3 Glaze one 12-cup fluted tube cake, 10-inch angel food or chiffon cake or top of an 8- or 9-inch layer cake.

1 Serving: Calories 70; Total Fat 4g (Saturated Fat 2g; Trans Fat 0g); Cholesterol 5mg; Sodium 20mg; Total Carbohydrate 7g (Dietary Fiber 0g); Protein 0g **Exchanges:** ½ Other Carbohydrate, 1 Fat **Carbohydrate Choices:** ½

Dark Chocolate Glaze: Substitute dark chocolate chips for the semisweet chocolate chips.

Milk Chocolate Glaze: Substitute milk chocolate chips for the semisweet chocolate chips.

Mint Chocolate Glaze: Substitute mint-flavored chocolate chips for the semisweet chocolate chips.

White Chocolate Glaze: Substitute white vanilla baking chips for the semisweet chocolate chips.

chapter 2

One-Layer Cakes

White Texas Sheet Cake

Prep Time: 30 minutes * Start to Finish: 2 hours * **24 SERVINGS**

cake

- **3 oz white chocolate baking bars or squares, chopped**
- **2 tablespoons whipping cream**
- **1 box white cake mix with pudding**
- **1 cup sour cream**
- **½ cup vegetable oil**
- **3 eggs**

frosting

- **3 oz white chocolate baking bars or squares, chopped**
- **3 tablespoons whipping cream**
- **½ cup butter, softened**
- **3 cups powdered sugar**

garnish

- **½ cup chopped pecans, toasted * if desired**

1 Heat oven to 350°F (325°F for dark or nonstick pan). Spray bottom and sides of 15 × 10 × 1-inch pan with baking spray with flour.

2 In small microwavable bowl, microwave 3 oz white chocolate and 2 tablespoons whipping cream uncovered on High 1 minute, stirring every 30 seconds, until smooth. Cool 10 to 15 minutes.

3 In large bowl, beat cake mix, sour cream, oil, eggs and chocolate mixture with electric mixer on low speed 30 seconds, then on medium speed 2 minutes, scraping bowl occasionally. Pour into pan.

4 Bake 21 to 25 minutes or until toothpick inserted in center comes out clean. Cool completely, about 1 hour.

5 In small microwavable bowl, microwave 3 oz white chocolate and 3 tablespoons cream uncovered on High 1 minute, stirring every 30 seconds, until smooth. Cool 10 to 15 minutes.

6 In medium bowl, beat butter and 2 cups of the powdered sugar with electric mixer on medium speed until blended. Add white chocolate mixture; blend well. Add remaining powdered sugar; beat until smooth. Spread frosting over cake; sprinkle with pecans. Store loosely covered.

To toast pecans, heat oven to 350°F. Spread pecans in ungreased shallow pan. Bake uncovered 6 to 10 minutes, stirring occasionally, until light brown.

1 Serving: Calories 280; Total Fat 15g (Saturated Fat 7g; Trans Fat 0g); Cholesterol 45mg; Sodium 180mg; Total Carbohydrate 35g (Dietary Fiber 0g); Protein 2g **Exchanges:** ½ Starch, 2 Other Carbohydrate, 3 Fat **Carbohydrate Choices:** 2

SWEET TIP **Toasting pecans or other nuts intensifies their flavor.**

Coconut Cake with White Chocolate Frosting

Prep Time: 25 minutes ✳ Start to Finish: 2 hours ✳ **15 SERVINGS**

cake

- 1 **can (14 oz) coconut milk (not cream of coconut)**
- 1 **box white cake mix with pudding**
- ¼ **cup water**
- 3 **egg whites**
- ¾ **cup flaked coconut**

frosting

- 1 **cup white vanilla baking chips (6 oz)**
- 1¾ **cups powdered sugar**
- ⅓ **cup butter, softened**
- ½ **teaspoon vanilla**

1 Heat oven to 350°F (325°F for dark or nonstick pan). Spray bottom only of 13 × 9-inch pan with baking spray with flour. Reserve ⅓ cup coconut milk for frosting.

2 In large bowl, beat cake mix, remaining coconut milk (1⅓ cups), the water and egg whites with electric mixer on low speed 30 seconds, then on medium speed 2 minutes, scraping bowl occasionally. Stir in ½ cup of the coconut until well combined. Pour into pan.

3 Bake as directed on box for 13 × 9-inch pan. Cool completely; about 1 hour.

4 Meanwhile, in 2-quart bowl, microwave vanilla baking chips uncovered on High about 30 seconds or until melted. Stir; if chips are not completely melted, microwave 15 seconds longer, then stir until all chips are melted. Stir in powdered sugar, butter, reserved ⅓ cup coconut milk and the vanilla. Cover; refrigerate 30 to 60 minutes. (If frosting becomes too firm to spread, microwave uncovered on High 10 to 15 seconds to soften; stir until smooth.)

5 Spread frosting over cake. Immediately sprinkle top with ¼ cup coconut. Store loosely covered.

1 Serving: Calories 330; Total Fat 13g (Saturated Fat 10g; Trans Fat 0g); Cholesterol 10mg; Sodium 310mg; Total Carbohydrate 51g (Dietary Fiber 0g); Protein 3g **Exchanges:** 1 Starch, 2½ Other Carbohydrate, 2½ Fat **Carbohydrate Choices:** 3½

SWEET TIP **Shredded coconut can be used instead of flaked.**

Candied Nut–Topped Texas Sheet Cake

Prep Time: 20 minutes * Start to Finish: 2 hours * **12 SERVINGS**

cake

- **1 box devil's food cake mix with pudding**
- **2 tablespoons unsweetened baking cocoa**
- **1¼ cups buttermilk**
- **½ cup vegetable oil**
- **3 eggs**

frosting and topping

- **½ cup butter**
- **1 cup packed brown sugar**
- **¼ cup milk**
- **2 cups powdered sugar**
- **½ cup chocolate-covered cashews**
- **½ cup coarsely chopped cashews**
- **½ cup coarsely chopped candied pecans**

1 Heat oven to 350°F (325°F for dark or nonstick pan). Spray bottom only of 13 × 9-inch pan with baking spray with flour.

2 In large bowl, beat cake ingredients with electric mixer on low speed 30 seconds, then on medium speed 2 minutes, scraping bowl occasionally. Pour into pan. Bake as directed on box for 13 × 9-inch pan. Cool completely, about 1 hour.

3 Meanwhile, in 2-quart saucepan, melt butter over medium heat. Stir in brown sugar. Heat to boiling, stirring constantly. Reduce heat to low; boil and stir 2 minutes. Stir in milk; return to boiling. Remove from heat. Cool to lukewarm, about 30 minutes.

4 Gradually stir powdered sugar into brown sugar mixture. Place saucepan of frosting in bowl of cold water; beat with spoon until smooth and spreadable. If frosting becomes too stiff, stir in additional milk, 1 teaspoon at a time, or heat over low heat, stirring constantly. Frost cake. Sprinkle evenly with cashews and pecans. Store loosely covered.

1 Serving: Calories 590; Total Fat 29g (Saturated Fat 10g; Trans Fat 0g); Cholesterol 75mg; Sodium 420mg; Total Carbohydrate 74g (Dietary Fiber 2g); Protein 6g **Exchanges:** 1½ Starch, 3½ Other Carbohydrate, 5½ Fat **Carbohydrate Choices:** 5

SWEET TIP The original Texas sheet cake is a chocolate cake made with buttermilk. The church-supper favorite is frosted with chocolate frosting and sprinkled with cashews and candied pecans.

Chocolate Chip–Caramel Poke Cake

Prep Time: 30 minutes * Start to Finish: 2 hours 35 minutes * **15 SERVINGS**

1 box devil's food cake mix with pudding
1¼ cups buttermilk
½ cup vegetable oil
3 eggs
1 bag (12 oz) semisweet chocolate chips (2 cups)
1 cup caramel topping
½ cup vanilla creamy ready-to-spread frosting (from 1-lb container)

1 Heat oven to 350°F (325°F for dark or nonstick pan). Spray bottom only of 13 × 9-inch pan with baking spray with flour.

2 In large bowl, beat cake mix, buttermilk, oil and eggs with electric mixer on low speed 30 seconds. Beat on medium speed 2 minutes, scraping bowl occasionally. Pour into pan. Sprinkle with chocolate chips; press gently into batter.

3 Bake 35 to 43 minutes or until toothpick inserted in center comes out clean. Cool 30 minutes. Spray meat fork or other long-tined fork with cooking spray. Poke warm cake every inch with fork tines. Pour caramel topping over cake. Cool completely, about 1 hour.

4 In medium microwavable bowl, microwave frosting 15 to 30 seconds; stir until very soft. Spoon frosting into 1-quart resealable food-storage plastic bag. Cut tiny tip off one bottom corner of bag. Drizzle frosting across top of cake. Store covered at room temperature.

1 Serving: Calories 450; Total Fat 20g (Saturated Fat 7g; Trans Fat 1g); Cholesterol 45mg; Sodium 410mg; Total Carbohydrate 63g (Dietary Fiber 2g); Protein 5g **Exchanges:** 1 Starch, 3 Other Carbohydrate, 4 Fat **Carbohydrate Choices:** 4

Chocolate Chip Swirl Cake

Prep Time: 15 minutes * **Start to Finish:** 1 hour 55 minutes * **15 SERVINGS**

¾ cup miniature semisweet
  chocolate chips
1 box white cake mix with
  pudding
  Water, vegetable oil and
  egg whites called for on
  cake mix box
¼ cup chocolate-flavor syrup
1 container vanilla creamy
  ready-to-spread frosting
  Additional chocolate-flavor
  syrup, if desired

1 Heat oven to 350°F (325°F for dark or nonstick pan). Generously grease, or spray with baking spray with flour, bottom only of 13 × 9-inch pan.

2 In small bowl, toss ½ cup of the chocolate chips with 1 tablespoon dry cake mix. Make cake mix as directed on box, using remaining cake mix, water, oil and egg whites. Stir in the ½ cup coated chocolate chips. Reserve 1 cup of the batter. Pour remaining batter into pan. Stir chocolate syrup into reserved batter. Drop by tablespoonfuls randomly in 8 mounds in pan. Cut through batters in S-shaped curves. Turn pan one quarter turn; repeat.

3 Bake 34 to 38 minutes or until toothpick inserted in center of chocolate comes out almost clean. Run knife around sides of pan to loosen cake. Cool completely, about 1 hour. Stir remaining ¼ cup chocolate chips into frosting. Spread frosting over top of cake; drizzle with additional chocolate syrup. Store loosely covered.

1 Serving: Calories 340; Total Fat 13g (Saturated Fat 4g; Trans Fat 2g); Cholesterol 0mg; Sodium 290mg; Total Carbohydrate 53g (Dietary Fiber 1g); Protein 2g **Exchanges:** ½ Starch, 3 Other Carbohydrate, 2½ Fat **Carbohydrate Choices:** 3½

SWEET TIP **For the best results when making this cake, use miniature chocolate chips because regular-size chips might sink.**

Chocolate Rum Cake

Prep Time: 15 minutes * Start to Finish: 4 hours * **15 SERVINGS**

cake

- 1 **box devil's food or dark chocolate cake mix with pudding**
- 1 **cup water**
- ⅓ **cup vegetable oil**
- 3 **eggs**
- 1 **cup whipping cream**
- 1 **cup whole milk**
- 1 **can (14 oz) sweetened condensed milk**
- ⅓ **cup rum**

topping

- 1 **cup whipping cream**
- 2 **tablespoons rum or 1 teaspoon rum extract**
- ½ **teaspoon vanilla**
- 1 **cup flaked coconut, toasted***
- ½ **cup chopped pecans, toasted****

1 Heat oven to 350°F (325°F for dark or nonstick pan). Grease or spray bottom only of 13 × 9-inch pan with cooking spray.

2 In large bowl, beat cake mix, water, oil and eggs with electric mixer on low speed 30 seconds, then on medium speed 2 minutes. Pour into pan.

3 Bake 30 to 38 minutes or until toothpick inserted in center comes out clean. Let stand 5 minutes. In large bowl, mix 1 cup whipping cream, the whole milk, condensed milk and ⅓ cup rum. Pierce top of hot cake every ½ inch with long-tined fork, wiping fork occasionally to reduce sticking. Carefully pour whipping cream mixture evenly over top of cake. Cover and refrigerate about 3 hours or until chilled and most of whipping cream mixture has been absorbed into cake.

4 In chilled large bowl, beat 1 cup whipping cream, 2 tablespoons rum and the vanilla on high speed until soft peaks form. Frost cake with whipped cream mixture. Sprinkle with coconut and pecans. Store covered in refrigerator.

To toast coconut, heat the oven to 350°F. Spread coconut in ungreased shallow pan. Bake uncovered 5 to 7 minutes, stirring occasionally, until golden brown.

**To toast pecans, heat oven to 350°F. Spread pecans in ungreased shallow pan. Bake uncovered 6 to 10 minutes, stirring occasionally, until light brown.*

1 Serving: Calories 430; Total Fat 24g (Saturated Fat 12g; Trans Fat 0g); Cholesterol 90mg; Sodium 330mg; Total Carbohydrate 43g (Dietary Fiber 1g); Protein 6g **Exchanges:** 1½ Starch, 1½ Other Carbohydrate, 4½ Fat **Carbohydrate Choices:** 3

Chewy Turtle Snack Cake

Prep Time: 15 minutes ✳ Start to Finish: 2 hours 25 minutes ✳ **16 SERVINGS**

cake

- ¾ **cup sugar**
- 6 **tablespoons butter, softened**
- 2 **oz sweet baking chocolate, melted, cooled**
- 1 **cup all-purpose flour**
- ½ **teaspoon baking soda**
- ⅛ **teaspoon salt**
- ½ **teaspoon vanilla**
- 6 **tablespoons buttermilk**
- 3 **tablespoons water**
- 2 **eggs**

topping

- ½ **cup butter**
- 1 **bag (14 oz) caramels, unwrapped**
- 1 **can (5 oz) evaporated milk**
- 1 **bag (11.5 to 12 oz) semisweet chocolate chunks (2 cups)**
- ½ **cup chopped pecans**

1 Heat oven to 350°F. Grease bottom and sides of 13 × 9-inch pan with shortening; lightly flour.

2 In large bowl, beat sugar and 6 tablespoons butter with electric mixer on high speed about 3 minutes, scraping bowl occasionally, until fluffy. Beat in melted chocolate, flour, baking soda, salt, vanilla, buttermilk, water and eggs on medium speed 2 minutes, scraping bowl occasionally. Pour into pan.

3 Bake 20 minutes or until toothpick inserted in center comes out clean.

4 Meanwhile, in 2-quart saucepan, heat ½ cup butter, the caramels and evaporated milk over medium heat, stirring constantly, until smooth. Spread over hot cake. Sprinkle with chocolate chunks and pecans. Bake 20 minutes longer or until chocolate is melted. Cool completely, about 1 hour 30 minutes.

1 Serving: Calories 440; Total Fat 24g (Saturated Fat 13g; Trans Fat 0g); Cholesterol 55mg; Sodium 230mg; Total Carbohydrate 51g (Dietary Fiber 2g); Protein 5g **Exchanges:** 1½ Starch, 2 Other Carbohydrate, 4½ Fat **Carbohydrate Choices:** 3½

SWEET TIP **No buttermilk on hand?** Place 1¼ teaspoons lemon juice or white vinegar in a measuring cup, then add 6 tablespoons milk and stir. Let stand a few minutes before adding to the other ingredients.

Fudge Lover's Strawberry Truffle Cake

Prep Time: 25 minutes * Start to Finish: 2 hours 50 minutes * **12 SERVINGS**

cake

- **1 box chocolate fudge cake mix with pudding**
- **Water, vegetable oil and eggs called for on cake mix box**

ganache filling and topping

- **2 packages (8 oz each) semisweet baking chocolate, finely chopped**
- **1⅓ cups whipping cream**
- **¼ cup butter (do not use margarine)**
- **2 cups cut-up fresh strawberries**

garnish

- **6 fresh strawberries, cut in half lengthwise through stem**
- **¼ cup white vanilla baking chips**
- **½ teaspoon vegetable oil**

1 Heat oven to 350°F (325°F for dark or nonstick pan). Make and bake cake as directed on box for 13 × 9-inch pan. Cool completely, about 1 hour.

2 Meanwhile, in large bowl, place chopped chocolate; set aside. In 2-quart saucepan, heat whipping cream and butter over medium heat, stirring occasionally, until butter is melted and mixture comes to a boil. Pour cream mixture over chocolate; stir until smooth.

3 Line bottom of 9-inch springform pan with waxed paper. Cut cake into 1-inch cubes. In large bowl, beat half of the cake cubes on low speed until cake is crumbly. Add remaining cake cubes and 1¾ cups of the ganache (reserve remaining ganache for topping). Beat on low speed 30 seconds, then on medium speed until well combined (mixture will look like fudge). Fold in 2 cups cut-up strawberries. Spoon mixture into springform pan; smooth top. Cover with plastic wrap; freeze about 45 minutes or until firm enough to unmold.

4 Run knife around side of pan to loosen cake. Place serving plate upside down on pan; turn pan and plate over to remove cake. Frost side and top of cake with reserved ganache. Arrange strawberry halves on top of cake.

5 In small microwavable bowl, microwave baking chips and ½ teaspoon oil uncovered on High 45 seconds, stirring every 15 seconds, until melted. Place in small resealable food-storage plastic bag; cut off tiny corner of bag. Drizzle over top of cake. Refrigerate until ready to serve. Best served the same day.

1 Serving: Calories 610; Total Fat 38g (Saturated Fat 19g; Trans Fat 0.5g); Cholesterol 100mg; Sodium 380mg; Total Carbohydrate 59g (Dietary Fiber 3g); Protein 6g **Exchanges:** 2 Starch, 2 Other Carbohydrate, 7½ Fat **Carbohydrate Choices:** 4

SWEET TIP **You can bake the cake ahead. Store the completely cooled and tightly covered cake for up to 2 months in the freezer.**

Chocolate-Fig Cake with Mascarpone Frosting

Prep Time: 30 minutes ✳ Start to Finish: 3 hours 15 minutes ✳ **16 SERVINGS**

cake

- 1 cup diced Calimyrna figs, stems removed (6 oz)
- 1 cup dry red wine (such as Merlot or Cabernet Sauvignon) or water
- 1 cup butter, softened
- 1 cup granulated sugar
- 2 eggs
- 1 teaspoon vanilla
- 1¾ cups all-purpose flour
- 2 tablespoons unsweetened regular or dark baking cocoa
- 1 teaspoon baking soda
- 4 oz semisweet baking chocolate, melted, cooled

frosting

- 1 container (8 oz) mascarpone cheese
- 2½ cups powdered sugar
- ½ teaspoon vanilla

garnish, if desired

- 1 bar (1.55 oz) milk chocolate

1 Heat oven to 350°F (325°F for dark or nonstick pan). Grease bottom and side of 9- or 10-inch springform pan with shortening; lightly flour. In 1½-quart saucepan, combine figs and wine. Bring to a boil over medium-high heat. Remove from heat and cool while preparing batter.

2 In large bowl, beat butter and granulated sugar with electric mixer on medium speed until creamy. Add eggs and 1 teaspoon vanilla. Beat at medium speed until thick and creamy, scraping bowl occasionally. Add flour, cocoa and baking soda. Beat at low speed until moistened, scraping bowl occasionally. Add melted chocolate, figs and wine. Beat at low speed until mixed. Spread in pan.

3 Bake 55 to 60 minutes or until toothpick inserted in center comes out clean. Cool in pan on cooling rack until completely cooled, about 2 hours. Remove side of pan.

4 In medium bowl, beat mascarpone cheese, powdered sugar and ½ teaspoon vanilla at low speed until mixed. Beat at medium speed until thick and creamy. Frost side and top of cake.

5 To make garnish, pull vegetable peeler along edges of chocolate bar to form curls. (If curls crumble, slightly warm chocolate bar with hand.) Garnish cake with chocolate curls. Store in refrigerator.

1 Serving: Calories 380; Total Fat 19g (Saturated Fat 12g; Trans Fat 0g); Cholesterol 65mg; Sodium 190mg; Total Carbohydrate 47g (Dietary Fiber 2g); Protein 3g **Exchanges:** 3 Other Carbohydrate, ½ Medium-Fat Meat, 3½ Fat **Carbohydrate Choices:** 3

SWEET TIP **For large chocolate curls, melt 1½ ounces of semisweet baking chocolate with 1 teaspoon shortening. Spread on the back of a smooth cookie sheet in 6 × 3-inch strip. Cool until set. Starting at one end, push flat metal spatula under chocolate to form ½-inch-wide curls.**

Heavenly Chocolate Soufflé Cake

Prep Time: 30 minutes ✳ Start to Finish: 1 hour 25 minutes ✳ **12 SERVINGS**

cake

- 1⅔ **cups semisweet chocolate chunks**
- ½ **cup butter**
- ½ **cup all-purpose flour**
- 4 **eggs, separated**
- ¼ **teaspoon cream of tartar**
- ½ **cup granulated sugar**

sauce

- ⅓ **cup semisweet chocolate chunks**
- 3 **tablespoons granulated sugar**
- ¼ **cup evaporated fat-free milk**
- ½ **teaspoon butter**

whipped cream

- 1 **cup whipping cream**
- 2 **tablespoons powdered sugar**
- 1 **teaspoon vanilla**

    Crushed hard peppermint candies, if desired

1 Heat oven to 325°F. Grease bottom and side of 9-inch springform pan with shortening. In 2-quart heavy saucepan, heat 1 cup of the chocolate chunks and ½ cup butter over medium heat, stirring occasionally, until melted. Cool 5 minutes. Stir in flour until smooth. Stir in egg yolks until well blended.

2 In large bowl, beat egg whites and cream of tartar with electric mixer on high speed until foamy. Beat in ½ cup granulated sugar, 1 tablespoon at a time, until soft peaks form. Fold about one-quarter of the egg whites into chocolate mixture; fold chocolate mixture into egg whites. Spread in pan. Sprinkle ⅔ cup chocolate chunks evenly over top.

3 Bake 35 to 40 minutes or until toothpick inserted in center of cake comes out clean (top will appear dry and cracked). Cool 10 minutes. Remove side of pan; leave cake on pan bottom. Cool completely on cooling rack.

4 Just before serving, in 1-quart saucepan, heat ⅓ cup chocolate chunks, 3 tablespoons granulated sugar and the milk over medium heat, stirring constantly, until chocolate is melted and mixture boils. Remove from heat; stir in ½ teaspoon butter.

5 In chilled small bowl, beat all whipped cream ingredients with electric mixer on high speed until stiff peaks form. Place cake on serving plate. Drizzle servings of cake with sauce. Serve with whipped cream. Sprinkle with candies.

1 Serving: Calories 390; Total Fat 25g (Saturated Fat 15g; Trans Fat 0.5g); Cholesterol 110mg; Sodium 105mg; Total Carbohydrate 36g (Dietary Fiber 2g); Protein 4g **Exchanges:** 1½ Starch, 1 Other Carbohydrate, 5 Fat **Carbohydrate Choices:** 2½

SWEET TIP **Instead of peppermint candies, use chopped toffee candy bars.**

Triple-Chocolate Cake

Prep Time: 15 minutes * Start to Finish: 2 hours * **12 SERVINGS**

cake

1½ **cups semisweet chocolate chips**

½ **cup butter**

½ **cup all-purpose flour**

4 **eggs, separated**

½ **cup sugar**

2 **tablespoons butter**

2 **tablespoons corn syrup**

glaze

¼ **cup white vanilla baking chips**

1 **teaspoon shortening**

1 Heat oven to 325°F. Grease bottom and side of 9-inch round pan. In 2-quart heavy saucepan, melt 1 cup of the chocolate chips and ½ cup butter over low heat, stirring constantly; cool 5 minutes. Stir in flour until smooth. Stir in egg yolks until well blended.

2 In large bowl, beat egg whites with electric mixer on high speed until foamy. Beat in sugar, 1 tablespoon at a time, until soft peaks form. Fold chocolate mixture into egg whites. Spread in pan.

3 Bake 30 to 35 minutes or until toothpick inserted in center comes out clean (top will appear dry and cracked). Cool 10 minutes. Run knife around edge of pan to loosen; remove cake from pan to cooling rack. Cool completely, about 1 hour. Place cake on serving plate.

4 In 1-quart saucepan, heat remaining ½ cup chocolate chips, 2 tablespoons butter and the corn syrup over low heat, stirring constantly, until chocolate chips are melted. Spread over top of cake, allowing some to drizzle down side.

5 In 1-quart saucepan, melt glaze ingredients over low heat, stirring constantly. Drizzle over top of cake.

1 Serving: Calories 320; Total Fat 19g (Saturated Fat 12g; Trans Fat 0g); Cholesterol 90mg; Sodium 120mg; Total Carbohydrate 32g (Dietary Fiber 1g); Protein 4g **Exchanges:** 1½ Starch, ½ Other Carbohydrate, 3½ Fat **Carbohydrate Choices:** 2

SWEET TIP **Top this pretty cake with white chocolate curls for a finishing touch. Make the curls by pulling a vegetable peeler toward you across a white baking bar. Press firmly, using long, thin strokes.**

Spicy Mexican Brownie Cake

Prep Time: 30 minutes * Start to Finish: 3 hours * **15 SERVINGS**

cake

1¼	cups butter, softened
¾	cup unsweetened baking cocoa
4	eggs
2	cups granulated sugar
1½	cups all-purpose flour
1½	teaspoons baking powder
1	teaspoon ground cinnamon
¼	teaspoon plus ⅛ teaspoon ground red pepper (cayenne)
¼	teaspoon salt
½	cup milk
1	tablespoon vanilla

frosting

⅓	cup butter, softened
⅓	cup crema (Mexican-style cream) or sour cream
¼	teaspoon ground cinnamon
¾	teaspoon vanilla
4	cups powdered sugar
1	to 2 teaspoons milk
	Unsweetened baking cocoa, if desired

1 Heat oven to 350°F. Grease bottom and sides of 13 × 9-inch pan with shortening; lightly flour. In small bowl, stir 1¼ cups butter and ¾ cup cocoa until blended. In large bowl, beat eggs with electric mixer on high speed 3 minutes. On low speed, beat in remaining cake ingredients and cocoa mixture, just until blended. Spread in pan.

2 Bake 35 to 40 minutes or until top edge of cake just begins to pull away from sides of pan. (Top may appear irregular with slight dips in some spots.) Cool completely in pan on cooling rack, about 2 hours.

3 In large bowl, beat ⅓ cup butter with electric mixer on medium speed until fluffy. Beat in crema, ¼ teaspoon cinnamon and ¾ teaspoon vanilla until light and fluffy, scraping bowl frequently. On low speed, add powdered sugar, 1 cup at a time, scraping bowl occasionally. Stir in milk, 1 teaspoon at a time, until smooth and spreadable. Frost cake. Sprinkle lightly with cocoa. Store in refrigerator.

1 Serving: Calories 510; Total Fat 23g (Saturated Fat 14g; Trans Fat 1g); Cholesterol 105mg; Sodium 290mg; Total Carbohydrate 72g (Dietary Fiber 2g); Protein 4g **Exchanges:** 1 Starch, 4 Other Carbohydrate, 4½ Fat **Carbohydrate Choices:** 5

SWEET TIP **Crema is a full-bodied, rich-flavored sour cream sold in a jar in the dairy case. There are two types you can buy—we like the "agria" variety for this recipe.**

Candy Bar–Peanut Butter Cake

Prep Time: 15 minutes ✳ **Start to Finish:** 1 hour 15 minutes ✳ **8 SERVINGS**

1½ cups all-purpose flour
¾ cup sugar
⅓ cup peanut butter
¼ cup butter, softened
¾ cup milk
2 teaspoons baking powder
¼ teaspoon salt
2 eggs
½ cup coarsely chopped 1-inch chocolate-covered peanut butter cup candies

1 Heat oven to 350°F. Grease bottom and sides of 8-inch square pan with shortening; lightly flour.

2 Beat all ingredients except candies in medium bowl with electric mixer on low speed 30 seconds, scraping bowl constantly. Beat on high speed 3 minutes, scraping bowl occasionally. Pour into pan. Sprinkle with candies.

3 Bake 35 to 40 minutes or until toothpick inserted in center comes out clean. Serve warm or cool.

1 Serving: Calories 410; Total Fat 19g (Saturated Fat 7g; Trans Fat 0g); Cholesterol 65mg; Sodium 390mg; Total Carbohydrate 50g (Dietary Fiber 2g); Protein 9g **Exchanges:** 2 Starch, 1½ Other Carbohydrate, ½ Medium-Fat Meat, 3 Fat **Carbohydrate Choices:** 3

Change the Pan Size
Follow the recipe as directed and pour batter into 9-inch round cake pan; bake as directed.

Butternut Squash Cake

Prep Time: 20 minutes ✳ **Start to Finish:** 2 hours ✳ **15 SERVINGS**

cake

¾	cup butter, softened
1½	cups granulated sugar
3	eggs
1½	teaspoons baking powder
½	teaspoon baking soda
½	teaspoon salt
½	teaspoon ground ginger
½	teaspoon ground cinnamon
¼	teaspoon ground nutmeg
2½	cups all-purpose flour
¾	cup buttermilk
2	cups shredded peeled butternut squash (1 small)
½	cup chopped walnuts

frosting

½	cup butter, softened
1	package (3 oz) cream cheese, softened
4	cups powdered sugar
2	to 4 tablespoons milk
1½	teaspoons maple flavor
½	cup chopped walnuts

1　Heat oven to 350°F. Spray bottom only of 13 × 9-inch pan with cooking spray.

2　In large bowl, beat ¾ cup butter and the granulated sugar with electric mixer on medium speed until light and fluffy. Beat in eggs until fluffy. Beat in baking powder, baking soda, salt, ginger, cinnamon and nutmeg. Add flour alternately with buttermilk, scraping side of bowl. Beat 1 minute. Stir in squash and ½ cup walnuts. Spread in pan.

3　Bake 30 to 40 minutes or until toothpick inserted in center comes out clean. Cool completely.

4　In medium bowl, beat ½ cup butter and the cream cheese with electric mixer on medium speed until light and fluffy. Add powdered sugar, 2 tablespoons milk and the maple flavor. Beat until smooth and creamy, adding additional milk if needed. Frost cake. Sprinkle with ½ cup walnuts. Cover and refrigerate.

1 Serving: Calories 530; Total Fat 24g (Saturated Fat 12g; Trans Fat 0.5g); Cholesterol 90mg; Sodium 320mg; Total Carbohydrate 72g (Dietary Fiber 1g); Protein 6g **Exchanges:** 1½ Starch, 3½ Other Carbohydrate, 4½ Fat **Carbohydrate Choices:** 5

SWEET TIP **A box grater or the shredding blade of a food processor works well for shredding the squash.**

Sweet Potato Cake with Maple Frosting

Prep Time: 30 minutes * Start to Finish: 2 hours * **15 SERVINGS**

cake

2½ cups all-purpose flour
1¼ cups granulated sugar
1½ teaspoons baking soda
1 teaspoon baking powder
1 teaspoon salt
1 teaspoon ground cinnamon
1 teaspoon ground nutmeg
½ teaspoon ground cloves
1½ cups mashed cooked dark orange sweet potatoes (2 medium)
½ cup butter, softened
½ cup buttermilk
1 teaspoon vanilla
2 eggs

frosting

4 cups powdered sugar
½ cup butter, softened
3 to 4 tablespoons milk
2 teaspoons maple flavor

1 Heat oven to 350°F. Grease bottom and sides of 13 × 9-inch pan with shortening or cooking spray; lightly flour. In large bowl, beat all cake ingredients with electric mixer on low speed, scraping bowl occasionally, until blended. Beat on high speed 3 minutes, scraping bowl occasionally. Pour into pan.

2 Bake 35 to 40 minutes or until golden brown and toothpick inserted in center comes out clean. Cool completely in pan on cooling rack, about 1 hour.

3 In medium bowl, beat frosting ingredients, adding enough milk until frosting is smooth and spreadable. Frost cake.

1 Serving: Calories 420; Total Fat 14g (Saturated Fat 8g; Trans Fat 0.5g); Cholesterol 60mg; Sodium 450mg; Total Carbohydrate 71g (Dietary Fiber 1g); Protein 4g **Exchanges:** 1½ Starch, 3 Other Carbohydrate, 2½ Fat **Carbohydrate Choices:** 5

SWEET TIP It's easy to cook the sweet potatoes in the microwave. Pierce whole potatoes with a fork; place on microwavable paper towels. Microwave on High 9 to 11 minutes, or until tender. Cover; let stand 5 minutes. When cool enough to handle, cut each potato lengthwise. Scoop out flesh into bowl; mash with fork and cool.

Butter Rum–Glazed Applesauce Cake

Prep Time: 20 minutes * Start to Finish: 1 hour 25 minutes * **9 SERVINGS**

cake

- ⅓ cup butter (do not use margarine)
- ¾ cup granulated sugar
- 1 cup applesauce
- 1 teaspoon vanilla
- 1½ cups all-purpose flour
- 1 teaspoon baking soda
- 1 teaspoon ground cinnamon
- ½ teaspoon salt

glaze

- 2 tablespoons butter (do not use margarine)
- 1 cup powdered sugar
- 3 to 4 teaspoons half-and-half or milk
- ½ teaspoon rum extract

1 Heat oven to 350°F. Grease bottom and sides of 8-inch square pan with shortening or cooking spray.

2 In 1½-quart saucepan, melt ⅓ cup butter over medium heat. Cook 2 to 2½ minutes, stirring occasionally, until butter just begins to brown. Immediately remove from heat. Stir in granulated sugar, applesauce and vanilla.

3 In large bowl, mix flour, baking soda, cinnamon and salt. Stir in applesauce mixture. Pour batter into pan.

4 Bake 30 to 35 minutes or until toothpick inserted in center comes out clean.

5 In 1½-quart saucepan, melt 2 tablespoons butter over medium heat; cook about 3 minutes or until butter just begins to brown. Immediately remove from heat. Stir in remaining glaze ingredients until smooth and spreadable. Pour over warm cake. Cool 30 minutes. Serve warm.

1 Serving: Calories 300; Total Fat 10g (Saturated Fat 6g; Trans Fat 0g); Cholesterol 25mg; Sodium 340mg; Total Carbohydrate 51g (Dietary Fiber 1g); Protein 2g **Exchanges:** 1½ Starch, 2 Other Carbohydrate, 2 Fat **Carbohydrate Choices:** 3½

SWEET TIP **After adding the glaze, sprinkle the top of the warm cake with a bit of cinnamon, if desired.**

Applesauce-Oatmeal Cake with Broiled Coconut Topping

Prep Time: 20 minutes * Start to Finish: 1 hour 50 minutes * **9 SERVINGS**

cake

1¼	**cups applesauce**
1	**cup old-fashioned oats**
½	**cup butter, softened**
1	**cup granulated sugar**
1	**teaspoon vanilla**
2	**eggs**
1½	**cups all-purpose flour**
1	**teaspoon baking soda**
½	**teaspoon ground cinnamon**
½	**teaspoon ground nutmeg**
¼	**teaspoon salt**

topping

¾	**cup flaked coconut**
½	**cup packed brown sugar**
⅓	**cup chopped pecans or walnuts**
¼	**cup butter, melted**
3	**tablespoons milk**

1 In 1-quart saucepan, heat applesauce to boiling over medium-high heat. Stir in oats. Let stand 20 minutes.

2 Heat oven to 350°F. Grease bottom and sides of 9-inch square pan with shortening or cooking spray. In large bowl, beat ½ cup butter and the granulated sugar with electric mixer on medium speed until light and fluffy. Beat in vanilla and eggs until fluffy. Beat in applesauce mixture just until mixed. Stir in flour, baking soda, cinnamon, nutmeg and salt, scraping bowl once, just until blended. Pour into pan.

3 Bake 40 to 50 minutes or until toothpick inserted in center comes out clean.

4 Meanwhile, in small bowl, mix topping ingredients until well blended. Spread topping over hot cake. Broil cake with top 6 inches from heat 1 to 2 minutes or until top is golden and bubbly. Cool 30 minutes. Serve warm.

1 Serving: Calories 500; Total Fat 23g (Saturated Fat 13g; Trans Fat 0.5g); Cholesterol 85mg; Sodium 380mg; Total Carbohydrate 67g (Dietary Fiber 3g); Protein 5g **Exchanges:** 1½ Starch, 3 Other Carbohydrate, 4½ Fat **Carbohydrate Choices:** 4½

Gingerbread Poke Cake

Prep Time: 15 minutes * Start to Finish: 2 hours * **12 SERVINGS**

3½ cups all-purpose flour
2 tablespoons chopped crystallized ginger
1 tablespoon ground ginger
2 teaspoons ground cinnamon
½ teaspoon salt
1 cup molasses
1 cup sugar
1 cup canola oil
2 eggs
1 cup boiling water
1 tablespoon baking soda
1 cup whipping cream
4 pasteurized egg yolks*
¼ cup sugar
Whipped cream (page 55), if desired

1 Heat oven to 350°F. Spray 13 x 9-inch pan with cooking spray. In large bowl, mix flour, crystallized ginger, ground ginger, cinnamon and salt; set aside.

2 In medium bowl, mix molasses, 1 cup sugar and the oil with wire whisk until blended. Add eggs, one at a time, stirring with whisk until blended. Add molasses mixture to flour mixture, stirring with whisk until blended. In small bowl, mix boiling water and baking soda until soda is dissolved. Add to batter, stirring until blended. Pour into pan. Bake 40 to 45 minutes or until toothpick inserted in center comes out clean.

3 In 1-quart saucepan, heat whipping cream to simmering. In small bowl, mix pasteurized egg yolks and ¼ cup sugar; add to cream, stirring with whisk. Strain mixture through fine strainer. Poke warm cake every inch with wooden skewer halfway into cake. Slowly drizzle cream mixture over top of cake. Cool completely, about 1 hour. Store covered in refrigerator. Garnish with whipped cream.

1 Serving: Calories 550; Total Fat 28g (Saturated Fat 7g; Trans Fat 0g); Cholesterol 120mg; Sodium 450mg; Total Carbohydrate 68g (Dietary Fiber 1g); Protein 5g **Exchanges:** 1½ Starch, 3 Other Carbohydrate, 5½ Fat **Carbohydrate Choices:** 4½

Pasteurized eggs are uncooked eggs that have been heat-treated to kill bacteria that can cause food poisoning and gastrointestinal distress. Because the egg yolks in this recipe are not cooked, be sure to use pasteurized eggs. They can be found in the dairy case at large supermarkets.

Gingerbread with Lemon Sauce and Whipped Cream

Prep Time: 20 minutes * Start to Finish: 1 hour 5 minutes * **9 SERVINGS**

gingerbread

2⅓ cups all-purpose flour
½ cup shortening
⅓ cup granulated sugar
1 cup molasses
¾ cup hot water
1 teaspoon baking soda
1 teaspoon ground ginger
1 teaspoon ground cinnamon
¾ teaspoon salt
1 egg

sauce

½ cup granulated sugar
2 tablespoons cornstarch
¾ cup water
1 tablespoon grated lemon peel
¼ cup lemon juice
2 tablespoons butter

whipped cream

1 cup whipping cream
2 tablespoons powdered sugar
1 teaspoon vanilla

1 Heat oven to 325°F. Grease bottom and sides of 9-inch square pan with shortening; lightly flour. In large bowl, beat gingerbread ingredients with electric mixer on low speed 30 seconds, scraping bowl constantly. Beat on medium speed 3 minutes, scraping bowl occasionally. Pour into pan.

2 Bake 50 to 55 minutes or until toothpick inserted in center comes out clean.

3 Meanwhile, in 1-quart saucepan, mix ½ cup granulated sugar and the cornstarch. Gradually stir in ¾ cup water. Cook over medium heat, stirring constantly, until mixture thickens and boils. Boil and stir 1 minute. Remove from heat. Stir in remaining sauce ingredients. Serve warm or cool.

4 In chilled medium bowl, beat whipped cream ingredients on high speed until soft peaks form. Serve sauce and whipped cream with warm gingerbread.

1 Serving: Calories 540; Total Fat 23g (Saturated Fat 10g; Trans Fat 2.5g); Cholesterol 60mg; Sodium 390mg; Total Carbohydrate 77g (Dietary Fiber 1g); Protein 5g **Exchanges:** 1½ Starch, 3½ Other Carbohydrate, 4½ Fat **Carbohydrate Choices:** 5

SWEET TIP **Instead of making the whipped cream yourself, use purchased whipped cream topping from an aerosol can instead.**

Carrot Cake with Cream Cheese Frosting

Prep Time: 30 minutes ✳ Start to Finish: 2 hours 25 minutes ✳ **12 SERVINGS**

cake

1½	**cups granulated sugar**
1	**cup vegetable oil**
3	**eggs**
2	**cups all-purpose flour**
2	**teaspoons ground cinnamon**
1	**teaspoon baking soda**
1	**teaspoon baking powder**
1	**teaspoon vanilla**
½	**teaspoon salt**
3	**cups shredded carrots (5 medium)**
1	**cup coarsely chopped nuts**

frosting

1	**package (8 oz) cream cheese, softened**
¼	**cup butter, softened**
2	**to 3 teaspoons milk**
1	**teaspoon vanilla**
4	**cups (1 lb) powdered sugar**

1 Heat oven to 350°F. Grease bottom and sides of 13 × 9-inch pan with shortening or cooking spray; lightly flour.

2 In large bowl, beat granulated sugar, oil and eggs with electric mixer on low speed about 30 seconds or until blended. Add flour, cinnamon, baking soda, baking powder, 1 teaspoon vanilla and the salt; beat on low speed 1 minute. Stir in carrots and nuts. Pour batter into pan.

3 Bake 40 to 45 minutes or until toothpick inserted in center comes out clean. Cool completely, about 1 hour.

4 In medium bowl, beat cream cheese, butter, milk and 1 teaspoon vanilla with electric mixer on low speed until smooth. Gradually beat in powdered sugar, 1 cup at a time, on low speed until smooth and spreadable. Frost cake. Store covered in refrigerator.

1 Serving: Calories 710; Total Fat 36g (Saturated Fat 10g; Trans Fat 0g); Cholesterol 85mg; Sodium 370mg; Total Carbohydrate 87g (Dietary Fiber 2g); Protein 8g **Exchanges:** 1 Starch, 4 Other Carbohydrate, ½ Milk, ½ Vegetable, 6½ Fat **Carbohydrate Choices:** 6

SWEET TIP **Look for bags of shredded carrots in the produce aisle of your grocery store.**

Ginger-Carrot Cake

Prep Time: 20 minutes * Start to Finish: 1 hour 55 minutes * **9 SERVINGS**

cake

1	tablespoon all-purpose flour
¼	cup finely chopped crystallized ginger
1¼	cups all-purpose flour
¾	cup granulated sugar
¾	cup vegetable oil
2	teaspoons ground cinnamon
1	teaspoon baking soda
2	teaspoons vanilla
½	teaspoon salt
¼	teaspoon ground nutmeg
2	eggs
1½	cups grated or finely shredded carrots (about 3 medium)

frosting

1	package (3 oz) cream cheese, softened
¼	cup butter, softened
2	cups powdered sugar
1	teaspoon vanilla

1 Heat oven to 350°F. Grease bottom and sides of 8- or 9-inch square pan with shortening. Toss 1 tablespoon flour and the ginger to coat; set aside.

2 In large bowl, beat remaining cake ingredients except carrots with electric mixer on low speed 30 seconds. Beat on medium speed 3 minutes. Stir in carrots and ginger-flour mixture. Pour into pan.

3 Bake 30 to 35 minutes or until toothpick inserted in center comes out clean. Cool completely on cooling rack, about 1 hour.

4 In medium bowl, beat cream cheese and butter on medium speed until smooth. Gradually stir in powdered sugar and vanilla until smooth and spreadable. Spread over cake. Store covered in refrigerator.

1 Serving: Calories 530; Total Fat 28g (Saturated Fat 8g; Trans Fat 0g); Cholesterol 65mg; Sodium 370mg; Total Carbohydrate 64g (Dietary Fiber 1g); Protein 4g **Exchanges:** 1½ Starch, 3 Other Carbohydrate, 5½ Fat **Carbohydrate Choices:** 4

SWEET TIP **Crystallized ginger gives the unique flavor to this traditional carrot cake recipe. Try it sprinkled on top.**

Banana-Nut Cake with Peanut Butter Frosting

Prep Time: 25 minutes ∗ Start to Finish: 2 hours 25 minutes ∗ **24 SERVINGS**

cake

2⅓ cups all-purpose flour

1⅔ cups granulated sugar

1¼ cups mashed ripe bananas (2½ medium)

⅔ cup butter, softened

⅔ cup finely chopped nuts

⅔ cup buttermilk

1¼ teaspoons baking powder

1¼ teaspoons baking soda

¾ teaspoon salt

3 eggs

frosting

⅓ cup peanut butter

3 cups powdered sugar

1½ teaspoons vanilla

¼ to ⅓ cup milk

1 Heat oven to 350°F. Grease bottom and sides of 13 × 9-inch pan with shortening; lightly flour. In large bowl, beat cake ingredients with electric mixer on low speed 30 seconds, scraping bowl constantly. Beat on medium speed 3 minutes, scraping bowl occasionally. Pour into pan.

2 Bake 45 to 50 minutes, or until toothpick inserted in center comes out clean. Cool completely, about 1 hour.

3 In medium bowl, beat peanut butter and powdered sugar with spoon or electric mixer on low speed until blended. Add vanilla and ¼ cup milk; beat until smooth and spreadable. If necessary, beat in more milk, a few drops at a time. Frost cake.

1 Serving: Calories 280; Total Fat 10g (Saturated Fat 4g; Trans Fat 0g); Cholesterol 40mg; Sodium 230mg; Total Carbohydrate 43g (Dietary Fiber 1g); Protein 4g **Exchanges:** ½ Starch, 2½ Other Carbohydrate, 2 Fat **Carbohydrate Choices:** 3

SWEET TIP To make your own buttermilk, pour 2 teaspoons lemon juice or white vinegar into a liquid measuring cup and add enough milk to equal ⅔ cup. Let the mixture stand for 5 minutes before using.

Change the Pan Size

Follow the recipe as directed and pour batter into 2 (9-inch) round pans; bake 35 to 40 minutes. Cool 10 minutes; remove from pans to cooling rack. Cool completely, about 1 hour.

Sour Cream Spice Cake

Prep Time: 20 minutes * **Start to Finish:** 2 hours 5 minutes * **16 SERVINGS**

2¼ cups all-purpose flour

1½ cups packed brown sugar

2 teaspoons ground cinnamon

1¼ teaspoons baking soda

1 teaspoon baking powder

¾ teaspoon ground cloves

½ teaspoon salt

½ teaspoon ground nutmeg

1 cup raisins, chopped

1 cup sour cream

½ cup chopped walnuts

¼ cup butter, softened

¼ cup shortening

½ cup water

2 eggs

Browned Butter Frosting
(page 24), if desired

Additional walnuts,
if desired

1 Heat oven to 350°F. Grease bottom and sides of 13 × 9-inch pan with shortening; lightly flour.

2 In large bowl, beat all ingredients except frosting and additional walnuts with electric mixer on low speed 30 seconds, scraping bowl constantly. Beat on high speed 3 minutes, scraping bowl occasionally. Pour into pan.

3 Bake 40 to 45 minutes, or until toothpick inserted in center comes out clean. Cool completely, about 1 hour.

4 Frost cake. Sprinkle with additional walnuts.

1 Serving: Calories 290; Total Fat 12g (Saturated Fat 4.5g; Trans Fat 1g); Cholesterol 45mg; Sodium 240mg; Total Carbohydrate 42g (Dietary Fiber 1g); Protein 4g **Exchanges:** 1 Starch, 2 Other Carbohydrate, 2 Fat **Carbohydrate Choices:** 3

Change the Pan Size

Follow the recipe as directed and pour batter into 2 (8- or 9-inch) round pans; bake 30 to 35 minutes. Cool 10 minutes; remove from pans to cooling racks. Cool completely, about 1 hour.

Brown Sugar–Spice Cake with Caramelized Apples

Prep Time: 40 minutes * Start to Finish: 1 hour 40 minutes * **12 SERVINGS**

cake

- ½ **cup butter, softened**
- ½ **cup packed brown sugar**
- 2 **eggs**
- 1¼ **cups all-purpose flour**
- 1 **teaspoon baking powder**
- ½ **teaspoon baking soda**
- ½ **teaspoon ground ginger**
- ½ **teaspoon ground nutmeg**
- ¼ **teaspoon ground cloves**
- ¼ **teaspoon salt**
- ½ **cup sour cream**
- 1 **cup finely chopped peeled apple (1 medium)**

caramelized apples

- 6 **medium apples, peeled, sliced (about 8 cups)**
- 1 **cup packed brown sugar**

whipped cream

- 1 **cup whipping cream**

1 Heat oven to 350°F. Spray bottom only of 9-inch square pan with baking spray with flour.

2 In large bowl, beat butter, ½ cup brown sugar and the eggs with electric mixer on low speed until blended; beat on medium speed until well combined. On low speed, beat in flour, baking powder, baking soda, ginger, nutmeg, cloves, salt and sour cream until mixed; beat on medium speed 1 minute. Stir in chopped apple. Spoon batter evenly into pan.

3 Bake 35 to 40 minutes or until toothpick inserted in center comes out clean and top is golden brown. Cool 10 minutes. Run knife around pan to loosen cake. Remove cake to heatproof serving plate. Cool cake about 30 minutes.

4 Meanwhile, in 12-inch skillet, cook sliced apples and 1 cup brown sugar over medium-high heat 20 to 25 minutes, stirring occasionally, or until apples are tender and caramelized.

5 In chilled large deep bowl, beat whipping cream with electric mixer on low speed until cream begins to thicken. Gradually increase speed to high and beat just until soft peaks form. Spoon caramelized apples over cake. Top with dollops of whipped cream.

1 Serving: Calories 370; Total Fat 18g (Saturated Fat 11g; Trans Fat 0.5g); Cholesterol 90mg; Sodium 230mg; Total Carbohydrate 49g (Dietary Fiber 1g); Protein 3g **Exchanges:** ½ Starch, ½ Fruit, 2½ Other Carbohydrate, 3½ Fat **Carbohydrate Choices:** 3

SWEET TIP Chilling the bowl and beaters before whipping cream will make the cream whip faster. If you use the whisk attachment rather than regular beaters, the cream will thicken and form soft peaks more quickly. Don't overbeat, or the cream will curdle.

Chai Cake

Prep Time: 20 minutes * Start to Finish: 1 hour 55 minutes * **8 SERVINGS**

cake

- **2 tea bags flavored with orange rind and sweet spices**
- **⅔ cup boiling water**
- **1 cup all-purpose flour**
- **1½ teaspoons baking powder**
- **1 teaspoon ground cinnamon**
- **¼ teaspoon ground cardamom**
- **¼ teaspoon ground ginger**
- **¼ teaspoon ground cloves**
- **¼ teaspoon salt**
- **¾ cup granulated sugar**
- **½ cup butter, softened**
- **2 eggs**
- **1 teaspoon vanilla**

glaze

- **2 tablespoons butter**
- **1½ cups powdered sugar**
- **Reserved 2 tablespoons prepared tea**
- **1 teaspoon vanilla**
- **¼ teaspoon ground cinnamon**

  Additional ground cinnamon, if desired

1 Heat oven to 350°F. Line bottom and side of 8-inch round pan with cooking parchment paper. Grease paper with shortening; lightly flour.

2 Place tea bags in boiling water in measuring cup; let stand 5 minutes. Remove tea bags, squeezing liquid into measuring cup. Add enough water to tea to measure ⅔ cup. Measure ½ cup tea for cake; reserve 2 tablespoons tea for glaze.

3 In small bowl, mix flour, baking powder, 1 teaspoon cinnamon, the cardamom, ginger, cloves and salt; set aside. In large bowl, beat granulated sugar and ½ cup butter with electric mixer on medium speed, scraping bowl occasionally, until fluffy. Beat in eggs and vanilla until smooth and blended. Gradually beat in flour mixture alternately with ½ cup tea until smooth. Pour into pan.

4 Bake 28 to 33 minutes or until toothpick inserted in center comes out clean. Cool 10 minutes; remove from pan to cooling rack. Cool completely, about 1 hour.

5 In 1-quart saucepan, melt 2 tablespoons butter over medium heat. Stir in remaining glaze ingredients until smooth. Spread glaze over top of cake, allowing some to drizzle down side. Sprinkle with additional cinnamon.

1 Serving: Calories 380; Total Fat 16g (Saturated Fat 10g; Trans Fat 0.5g); Cholesterol 85mg; Sodium 310mg; Total Carbohydrate 54g (Dietary Fiber 0g); Protein 3g **Exchanges:** 1 Starch, 2½ Other Carbohydrate, 3 Fat **Carbohydrate Choices:** 3½

SWEET TIP *Chai* is the Hindi word for tea made with milk and spices such as cardamom, cinnamon, cloves, ginger, nutmeg and pepper.

Grasshopper Cake

Prep Time: 20 minutes * **Start to Finish:** 2 hours 5 minutes * **15 SERVINGS**

cake

2¼   cups all-purpose flour

1⅔   cups sugar

⅔   cup shortening

1   cup milk

¼   cup white crème de menthe

3½   teaspoons baking powder

1   teaspoon salt

1   teaspoon vanilla

5   egg whites

topping

1   jar (12 oz) fudge topping

3   tablespoons white crème de menthe or crème de menthe–flavored syrup

4   drops green food color

1   container (8 oz) frozen whipped topping, thawed

1   Heat oven to 350°F. Grease 13 x 9-inch pan with shortening; lightly flour.

2   In large bowl, beat flour, sugar, shortening, milk, ¼ cup crème de menthe, the baking powder, salt and vanilla with electric mixer on low speed 30 seconds, scraping bowl constantly. Beat on high speed 2 minutes, scraping bowl occasionally. Beat in egg whites on high speed 2 minutes, scraping bowl occasionally. Pour into pan.

3   Bake 40 to 45 minutes or until toothpick inserted in center comes out clean or until cake springs back when touched lightly in center. Cool completely, about 1 hour.

4   Spread fudge topping over cake. Carefully fold 3 tablespoons crème de menthe and the food color into whipped topping; spread over fudge topping. Store covered in refrigerator.

1 Serving: Calories 390; Total Fat 14g (Saturated Fat 6g; Trans Fat 0g); Cholesterol 0mg; Sodium 380mg; Total Carbohydrate 58g (Dietary Fiber 1g); Protein 5g **Exchanges:** 1½ Starch, 2½ Other Carbohydrate, 2½ Fat **Carbohydrate Choices:** 4

SWEET TIP **If crème de menthe is not available, use ¼ cup milk plus ½ teaspoon peppermint extract for the ¼ cup crème de menthe in the cake batter, and use 3 tablespoons milk plus ¼ teaspoon peppermint extract for the 3 tablespoons crème de menthe in the topping.**

Tres Leches Cake

Prep Time: 30 minutes * Start to Finish: 4 hours 15 minutes * **15 SERVINGS**

cake

2¼	cups all-purpose flour
1½	cups sugar
3½	teaspoons baking powder
½	teaspoon salt
½	cup butter, softened
1¼	cups milk
1	teaspoon vanilla
3	eggs

topping

2	cups whipping cream
1	cup whole milk
1	can (14 oz) sweetened condensed milk (not evaporated)
⅓	cup rum or 1 tablespoon rum extract plus enough water to measure ⅓ cup
2	tablespoons rum or 1 teaspoon rum extract
½	teaspoon vanilla
½	cup chopped pecans, toasted*

1 Heat oven to 350°F. Grease bottom only of 13 × 9-inch pan with shortening. In large bowl, beat all cake ingredients with electric mixer on low speed 30 seconds, scraping bowl constantly. Beat on high speed 3 minutes, scraping bowl occasionally. Pour into pan.

2 Bake 25 to 30 minutes or until toothpick inserted in center comes out clean or cake springs back when touched lightly in center. Let stand 5 minutes.

3 Pierce top of hot cake every ½ inch with long-tined fork, wiping fork occasionally to reduce sticking. In large bowl, stir 1 cup of the whipping cream, the whole milk, condensed milk and ⅓ cup rum until well mixed. Carefully pour milk mixture evenly over top of cake. Cover and refrigerate about 3 hours or until chilled and most of milk mixture has been absorbed into cake (when cutting cake to serve, you may notice some of the milk mixture on the bottom of the pan).

4 In chilled large deep bowl, beat remaining 1 cup whipping cream, 2 tablespoons rum and ½ teaspoon vanilla with electric mixer on low speed until mixture begins to thicken. Gradually increase speed to high and beat just until soft peaks form, lifting beaters occasionally to check thickness. Frost cake with whipped cream mixture. Sprinkle with pecans. Store covered in refrigerator.

To toast pecans or macadamia nuts, heat oven to 350°F. Spread nuts in ungreased shallow pan. Bake uncovered 6 to 10 minutes, stirring occasionally, until light brown.

**To toast coconut, heat oven to 350°F. Spread coconut in ungreased shallow pan. Bake uncovered 5 to 7 minutes, stirring occasionally, until golden brown.*

1 Serving: Calories 480; Total Fat 25g (Saturated Fat 14g; Trans Fat 1g); Cholesterol 110mg; Sodium 320mg; Total Carbohydrate 52g (Dietary Fiber 1g); Protein 7g **Carbohydrate Choices:** 3½

Tropical Tres Leches Cake: Make cake as directed through Step 3 except omit pecans. Sprinkle with 1 cup coconut, toasted**, and ½ cup chopped macadamia nuts, toasted*.

SWEET TIP In Spanish, *tres leches* means "three milks."

Margarita Cake

Prep Time: 20 minutes * Start to Finish: 3 hours * **15 SERVINGS**

crust

1½ **cups coarsely crushed pretzels**

½ **cup sugar**

½ **cup butter, melted**

cake

1 **box white cake mix with pudding**

¾ **cup bottled nonalcoholic margarita mix**

½ **cup water**

⅓ **cup vegetable oil**

1 **tablespoon grated lime peel**

3 **egg whites**

topping

1 **container (8 oz) frozen whipped topping, thawed**

Additional grated lime peel, if desired

1 Heat oven to 350°F (325°F for dark or nonstick pan). Grease bottom only and lightly flour 13 × 9-inch pan, or spray bottom with baking spray with flour. In medium bowl, mix crust ingredients. Sprinkle evenly on bottom of pan; press gently.

2 In large bowl, beat cake ingredients with electric mixer on low speed 30 seconds, then on medium speed 2 minutes, scraping bowl occasionally. Pour batter over crust.

3 Bake 34 to 39 minutes or until light golden brown and top springs back when touched lightly in center. Cool completely, about 2 hours. Frost with whipped topping; sprinkle with additional lime peel. Store loosely covered in refrigerator.

1 Serving: Calories 330; Total Fat 16g (Saturated Fat 8g; Trans Fat 0g); Cholesterol 15mg; Sodium 350mg; Total Carbohydrate 45g (Dietary Fiber 0g); Protein 3g **Exchanges:** 1 Starch, 2 Other Carbohydrate, 3 Fat **Carbohydrate Choices:** 3

SWEET TIPS You'll need about 3½ cups small pretzel twists to get the 1½ cups crushed pretzels.

Look for the bottled pale-green nonalcoholic margarita mix in the soft drink section of the supermarket. It is usually on the shelf with club soda, tonic water and other mixers.

Lemon Buttermilk Cake

Prep Time: 15 minutes ✳ **Start to Finish:** 1 hour 30 minutes ✳ **24 SERVINGS**

cake
- **1 box lemon cake mix with pudding**
- **1 cup buttermilk**
- **½ cup vegetable oil**
- **3 eggs**

frosting
- **⅓ cup shortening**
- **⅓ cup butter, softened**
- **1 teaspoon grated lemon peel**
- **2 tablespoons lemon juice**
- **3 cups powdered sugar**

1 Heat oven to 350°F (325°F for dark or nonstick pan). Spray bottom and sides of 15 × 10 × 1-inch pan with baking spray with flour.

2 In large bowl, beat cake ingredients with electric mixer on low speed 30 seconds, then on medium speed 2 minutes, scraping bowl occasionally. Pour into pan.

3 Bake 20 to 25 minutes (22 to 28 minutes for dark or nonstick pan) or until toothpick inserted in center comes out clean and cake springs back when lightly touched in center. Cool completely, about 1 hour.

4 In medium bowl, beat frosting ingredients on high speed until smooth and creamy; add more lemon juice if needed. Spread over cake. Store loosely covered.

1 Serving: Calories 230; Total Fat 11g (Saturated Fat 4g; Trans Fat 0.5g); Cholesterol 35mg; Sodium 170mg; Total Carbohydrate 31g (Dietary Fiber 0g); Protein 1g **Exchanges:** ½ Starch, 1½ Other Carbohydrate, 2 Fat **Carbohydrate Choices:** 2

SWEET TIP Take this great cake to a potluck, graduation party or picnic. For a large event, cut the cake into 48 small squares and serve in little paper baking cups.

Caramel Latte Cake

Prep Time: 30 minutes ✳ Start to Finish: 3 hours 15 minutes ✳ **16 SERVINGS**

cake
- 1 **box butter recipe yellow cake mix with pudding**
- 1 **cup warm water**
- 1 **tablespoon instant espresso coffee powder or granules**
- ⅓ **cup butter, melted**
- 3 **eggs**

filling
- 1 **can (13.4 oz) dulce de leche (caramelized sweetened condensed milk)**
- ½ **cup hot water**
- 3 **tablespoons instant espresso coffee powder or granules**
- 1 **tablespoon dark rum or 1 teaspoon rum extract plus 2 teaspoons water**

frosting and garnish
- 1 **cup whipping cream**
- ¼ **cup powdered sugar**
- 2 **oz semisweet baking chocolate, chopped, or 1 teaspoon unsweetened baking cocoa**

1 Heat oven to 350°F (325°F for dark or nonstick pan). Spray bottom only of 13 × 9-inch pan with baking spray with flour.

2 In large bowl, place cake mix. In 1-cup glass measuring cup, stir 1 cup warm water and 1 tablespoon espresso powder until it is dissolved. Add espresso mixture, butter and eggs to cake mix. Beat with electric mixer on low speed 30 seconds; scrape bowl. Beat on medium speed 2 minutes longer. Pour batter into pan.

3 Bake as directed on box for 13 × 9-inch pan. Cool in pan on cooling rack 15 minutes.

4 Meanwhile, spoon dulce de leche into medium microwavable bowl. In small bowl, mix ½ cup hot water, 3 tablespoons espresso powder and the rum; stir into dulce de leche until smooth. Microwave uncovered on High 2 to 3 minutes, stirring after about 1 minute with wire whisk, until pourable. Set aside while cake cools.

5 Poke cooled cake every ½ inch with handle end of wooden spoon. Pour dulce de leche mixture evenly over cake; spread mixture over top of cake with metal spatula to fill holes. Run knife around sides of pan to loosen cake. Cover; refrigerate 2 hours.

6 In medium bowl, beat whipping cream and powdered sugar on high speed until stiff. Spread whipped cream evenly over chilled cake. Sprinkle with chopped chocolate. Store covered in refrigerator.

1 Serving: Calories 310; Total Fat 14g (Saturated Fat 9g; Trans Fat 0g); Cholesterol 75mg; Sodium 260mg; Total Carbohydrate 41g (Dietary Fiber 1g); Protein 4g **Exchanges:** 1½ Starch, 1 Other Carbohydrate, 2½ Fat **Carbohydrate Choices:** 3

SWEET TIP **If garnishing with cocoa, place the cocoa in a tea strainer and lightly shake over the frosting to dust the top of the cake.**

Banana Split Cake

Prep Time: 25 minutes ✳ Start to Finish: 2 hours 15 minutes ✳ **12 SERVINGS**

cake

1 **box yellow cake mix with pudding**

1 **box (4-serving size) banana instant pudding and pie filling mix**

⅔ **cup buttermilk**

⅓ **cup vegetable oil**

1 **teaspoon vanilla**

4 **eggs**

2 **ripe bananas, mashed (about 1 cup)**

toppings

1½ **quarts (6 cups) vanilla ice cream**

1 **package (10 oz) frozen sweetened sliced strawberries, thawed**

¾ **cup hot fudge sauce**

¾ **cup frozen (thawed) whipped topping**

12 **maraschino cherries with stems**

1 Heat oven to 350°F (325°F for dark or nonstick pan). Spray bottom only of 13 × 9-inch pan with baking spray with flour. In large bowl, beat cake ingredients with electric mixer on low speed 30 seconds, then on medium speed 2 minutes. Pour into pan.

2 Bake 48 to 55 minutes or until deep golden brown and toothpick inserted in center comes out clean. Cool completely, about 1 hour. Cut cake in half lengthwise, then cut crosswise 11 times to make a total of 24 slices.

3 Place 2 cake slices in each parfait glass or banana split dish. Top each serving with 2 small scoops of ice cream. Spoon strawberries over one scoop. Drizzle hot fudge sauce over other scoop. Top each with whipped topping and cherry. Store cake covered.

1 Serving: Calories 520; Total Fat 19g (Saturated Fat 8g; Trans Fat 0g); Cholesterol 100mg; Sodium 530mg; Total Carbohydrate 79g (Dietary Fiber 2g); Protein 7g **Exchanges:** 2½ Starch, 3 Other Carbohydrate, 3½ Fat **Carbohydrate Choices:** 5

SWEET TIP If you don't have long banana split or parfait dishes, just cut the cake into squares and use round dessert bowls.

Blackberry Brunch Cake

Prep Time: 15 minutes ✳ Start to Finish: 1 hour ✳ **9 SERVINGS**

topping

- ⅓ **cup all-purpose flour**
- ⅓ **cup packed brown sugar**
- 2 **tablespoons butter, softened**
- ½ **teaspoon ground cinnamon**

cake

- 1 **cup Fiber One® original bran cereal**
- 1½ **cups all-purpose flour**
- 1½ **teaspoons baking powder**
- ½ **teaspoon baking soda**
- ½ **cup granulated sugar**
- ⅓ **cup butter, softened**
- 1 **teaspoon vanilla**
- 1 **teaspoon grated lemon peel**
- 1 **egg**
- ¾ **cup plain fat-free yogurt**
- 1 **cup fresh or frozen blackberries (do not thaw)**

1 Heat oven to 350°F. Grease bottom and sides of 9-inch square pan with shortening; lightly flour. In small bowl, mix topping ingredients; set aside.

2 Place cereal in resealable food-storage plastic bag; seal bag and crush with rolling pin or meat mallet (or crush in food processor). In medium bowl, stir together cereal, 1½ cups flour, baking powder and baking soda; set aside.

3 In large bowl, beat granulated sugar and butter with spoon until fluffy. Add vanilla, lemon peel and egg; beat until creamy. Stir in yogurt. Stir in flour mixture until blended. Gently stir in blackberries. Pour into pan; spread evenly. Sprinkle topping over batter.

4 Bake 40 to 45 minutes or until toothpick inserted in center comes out clean. Serve warm.

1 Serving: Calories 310; Total Fat 10g (Saturated Fat 6g; Trans Fat 0g); Cholesterol 45mg; Sodium 270mg; Total Carbohydrate 48g (Dietary Fiber 5g); Protein 5g **Exchanges:** 1½ Starch, 1½ Other Carbohydrate, 2 Fat **Carbohydrate Choices:** 3

SWEET TIP Change the flavor of this cake by using ground nutmeg or cardamom for the cinnamon in the topping. Blueberries make a great stand-in for the blackberries.

Raspberry Poke Cake

Prep Time: 15 minutes * Start to Finish: 3 hours 45 minutes * **12 SERVINGS**

1 box white cake mix with pudding

Water, vegetable oil and egg whites called for on cake mix box

1 box (4-serving size) raspberry-flavored gelatin

1 cup boiling water

½ cup cold water

1 container (8 oz) frozen whipped topping, thawed (3 cups)

Fresh raspberries, if desired

1 Heat oven to 350°F (325°F for dark or nonstick pan).

2 Make and bake cake as directed on box for 13 × 9-inch pan. Cool completely in pan, about 1 hour.

3 Pierce cooled cake all over with fork. In small bowl, stir gelatin and boiling water until smooth; stir in cold water. Pour over cake. Run knife around sides of pan to loosen cake. Refrigerate 2 hours. Frost with whipped topping; garnish with raspberries. Store covered in refrigerator.

1 Serving: Calories 290; Total Fat 12g (Saturated Fat 5g; Trans Fat 0g); Cholesterol 0mg; Sodium 320mg; Total Carbohydrate 41g (Dietary Fiber 0g); Protein 3g **Exchanges:** 1 Starch, 1½ Other Carbohydrate, 2½ Fat **Carbohydrate Choices:** 3

SWEET TIP Use any flavor of gelatin that you like for this recipe. Try strawberry gelatin and garnish the cake with strawberries, or experiment with strawberry-banana, strawberry-kiwi or sparkling berry gelatin.

Country Pear-Pecan Snack Cake

Prep Time: 20 minutes * Start to Finish: 1 hour 30 minutes * **9 SERVINGS**

streusel

⅓ **cup all-purpose flour**

⅓ **cup chopped pecans**

2 **tablespoons packed brown sugar**

2 **tablespoons butter, melted**

cake

1¾ **cups all-purpose flour**

½ **cup granulated sugar**

½ **cup packed brown sugar**

1 **teaspoon baking soda**

1 **teaspoon ground ginger**

½ **teaspoon salt**

⅔ **cup vegetable oil**

⅓ **cup buttermilk**

2 **eggs**

1½ **cups diced peeled pears (about 2 medium)**

1 Heat oven to 350°F (325°F for dark or nonstick pan). Spray bottom only of 8- or 9-inch square pan with cooking spray. In small bowl, mix all streusel ingredients; set aside.

2 In large bowl, mix 1¾ cups flour, the granulated sugar, ½ cup brown sugar, baking soda, ginger and salt with spoon. Add oil, buttermilk and eggs; mix with spoon until blended. Stir in pears. Spread batter in pan; sprinkle with streusel.

3 Bake 45 to 55 minutes or until deep golden brown and set on top. Cool 15 minutes. Serve warm or cool.

1 Serving: Calories 450; Total Fat 23g (Saturated Fat 5g; Trans Fat 0g); Cholesterol 50mg; Sodium 320mg; Total Carbohydrate 56g (Dietary Fiber 2g); Protein 5g **Exchanges:** 1½ Starch, 2 Other Carbohydrate, 4½ Fat **Carbohydrate Choices:** 4

SWEET TIPS Use any firm, ripe pear. Bartlett, Bosc or Anjou work well.

A dollop of whipped cream or a scoop of coffee ice cream is a delicious accompaniment to this cake.

Mango-Almond Coffee Cake

Prep Time: 20 minutes * Start to Finish: 1 hour 20 minutes * **9 SERVINGS**

streusel

- ⅓ **cup all-purpose flour**
- ⅓ **packed dark brown sugar**
- ⅓ **cup old-fashioned oats**
- ⅓ **cup chopped slivered almonds**
- 1 **teaspoon ground cinnamon**
- ¼ **cup cold butter, cut into small pieces**

cake

- 1 **cup all-purpose flour**
- ½ **cup granulated sugar**
- 1 **teaspoon baking powder**
- ½ **teaspoon salt**
- 1 **teaspoon ground cinnamon**
- ¼ **cup cold butter, cut into small pieces**
- ½ **cup milk**
- ½ **teaspoon almond extract**
- 1 **egg, slightly beaten**
- ¾ **cup chopped (¼- to ½-inch pieces) ripe mango (from 1 medium mango)**

1 Heat oven to 350°F. Grease bottom and sides of 8-inch square pan with shortening or spray with cooking spray. In small bowl, mix all streusel ingredients with pastry blender or fork until crumbly; set aside.

2 In large bowl, combine 1 cup flour, the granulated sugar, baking powder, salt and 1 teaspoon cinnamon; mix well. Cut in ¼ cup butter using pastry blender or fork until mixture is crumbly. Stir in milk, almond extract and egg until dry ingredients are moistened.

3 Spread half of the batter (about ¾ cup) in pan, forming thin layer. Top with half of the mango; sprinkle with half of the streusel. Drizzle remaining batter evenly over streusel. Carefully spread batter to completely cover streusel. Sprinkle with remaining mango and streusel.

4 Bake 40 to 45 minutes or until center is set when jiggled and toothpick inserted in moist spot near center comes out clean. Cool 15 minutes. Serve warm or cool.

1 Serving: Calories 300; Total Fat 13g (Saturated Fat 7g; Trans Fat 0g); Cholesterol 50mg; Sodium 290mg; Total Carbohydrate 39g (Dietary Fiber 2g); Protein 4g **Exchanges:** 1½ Starch, 1 Other Carbohydrate, 2½ Fat **Carbohydrate Choices:** 2½

SWEET TIP **Frozen mangoes (do not thaw) or refrigerated mango slices in light syrup can be substituted for the fresh ones. Drain refrigerated mangoes and pat dry with a paper towel. Be sure to chop any mango used to the size indicated in the recipe to avoid wet spots in the cake.**

Raspberry Crumb Cake

Prep Time: 20 minutes * Start to Finish: 1 hour 30 minutes * **9 SERVINGS**

cake
½ **box yellow cake mix with pudding (1⅔ cups)**
¼ **cup sour cream**
3 **tablespoons vegetable oil**
3 **tablespoons water**
1 **egg**
¾ **cup fresh raspberries**

topping
½ **cup sugar**
⅓ **cup sliced almonds**
3 **tablespoons all-purpose flour**
3 **tablespoons butter, softened**

garnish
Fresh raspberries, if desired
Fresh mint leaves, if desired

1 Heat oven to 350°F (325°F for dark or nonstick pan). Spray bottom and sides of 9-inch square pan with baking spray with flour.

2 In large bowl, beat cake mix, sour cream, oil, water and egg with electric mixer on low speed 30 seconds, then on medium speed 2 minutes, scraping bowl occasionally. Spread in pan. Place raspberries on top of batter.

3 In small bowl, stir topping ingredients with fork until well mixed. Sprinkle evenly over batter and raspberries.

4 Bake 30 to 40 minutes, or until toothpick inserted in center comes out clean. Cool at least 30 minutes before serving. Garnish with fresh raspberries and mint leaves.

1 Serving: Calories 270; Total Fat 13g (Saturated Fat 4.5g; Trans Fat 0g); Cholesterol 35mg; Sodium 210mg; Total Carbohydrate 35g (Dietary Fiber 1g); Protein 2g **Exchanges:** ½ Starch, 2 Other Carbohydrate, 2½ Fat **Carbohydrate Choices:** 2

SWEET TIP **You can use the remaining cake mix (about 1⅔ cups) to make about 12 cupcakes. Add 2 eggs, ½ cup water and 3 tablespoons vegetable oil to the cake mix. Mix and bake as directed on box.**

Change the Pan Size
Follow the recipe as directed and spread batter into 8-inch square pan; bake 35 to 45 minutes.

Almond Coffee Cake

Prep Time: 15 minutes * Start to Finish: 2 hours * **9 SERVINGS**

¾ **cup butter, softened**
1 **cup granulated sugar**
4 **oz almond paste (⅓ cup)**
½ **teaspoon almond extract**
2 **eggs**
1½ **cups all-purpose flour**
½ **teaspoon baking powder**
⅛ **teaspoon salt**
½ **cup sliced almonds**
   Powdered sugar, if desired
   Fresh berries, if desired

1 Heat oven to 350°F. Line 8-inch square pan with foil, leaving 1 inch of foil overhanging at 2 opposite sides of pan; spray foil with cooking spray.

2 In large bowl, beat butter, granulated sugar and almond paste with electric mixer on medium speed until light and fluffy. Beat in almond extract and eggs until well blended. On low speed, beat in flour, baking powder and salt just until blended. Spread batter in pan; sprinkle with almonds.

3 Bake 45 minutes or until toothpick inserted in center comes out clean. Cool completely in pan on cooling rack, about 1 hour. Use foil to lift cake out of pan; cut into squares. Sprinkle with powdered sugar. Garnish with berries.

1 Serving: Calories 410; Total Fat 22g (Saturated Fat 11g; Trans Fat 0.5g); Cholesterol 80mg; Sodium 210mg; Total Carbohydrate 47g (Dietary Fiber 2g); Protein 6g **Exchanges:** 2½ Starch, ½ Other Carbohydrate, 4 Fat **Carbohydrate Choices:** 3

SWEET TIP Look for almond paste in the bakery aisle at the grocery store. It's important to use fresh almond paste because if it is even slightly hardened, it will not mix well—check the date on the package.

Lemon Curd–Filled Butter Cake

Prep Time: 25 minutes * Start to Finish: 2 hours 40 minutes * **12 SERVINGS**

lemon curd

- ¼ cup granulated sugar
- 2 tablespoons cornstarch
- ¾ cup cold water
- 3 egg yolks
- 1 tablespoon grated lemon peel
- 3 tablespoons lemon juice

cake

- 1 cup butter, softened
- 1 cup granulated sugar
- 5 eggs
- 1¾ cups all-purpose flour
- 2 teaspoons grated lemon peel
- 1½ teaspoons baking powder
- 1 teaspoon vanilla
- ⅓ cup slivered almonds, toasted*
- ½ teaspoon powdered sugar, if desired

1 In 1-quart saucepan, mix ¼ cup granulated sugar and the cornstarch. Stir in water and egg yolks with wire whisk until well mixed and no lumps remain. Heat to boiling over medium heat, stirring constantly, until mixture begins to thicken. Cook and stir 1 minute; remove from heat. Stir in 1 tablespoon lemon peel and the lemon juice. Refrigerate uncovered 20 minutes, stirring once, until room temperature.

2 Heat oven to 350°F. Grease bottom and side of 9-inch springform pan with shortening; lightly flour. In large bowl, beat butter and 1 cup granulated sugar with electric mixer on medium speed about 1 minute or until smooth.

3 Beat in eggs, one at a time, until just blended, then continue beating on medium speed 2 minutes, scraping bowl once. On low speed, beat in flour, 2 teaspoons lemon peel, the baking powder and vanilla about 30 seconds or until just blended.

4 Spread half of cake batter (about 2 cups) in bottom of pan. Spoon lemon curd evenly onto batter, spreading to ½ inch of edge. Drop remaining batter by tablespoonfuls around edge of curd and pan; spread batter evenly and toward center to cover curd. Sprinkle almonds over top.

5 Bake 45 to 55 minutes or until center is set, cake is firm to the touch and top is golden brown. Cool in pan on cooling rack at least 1 hour (center will sink slightly). Run thin knife around side of cake; remove side of pan. Sprinkle with powdered sugar before serving. Store covered in refrigerator.

*To toast almonds, heat oven to 350°F. Spread almonds in ungreased shallow pan. Bake uncovered 6 to 10 minutes, stirring occasionally, until light brown.

1 Serving: Calories 360; Total Fat 20g (Saturated Fat 9g; Trans Fat 1g); Cholesterol 180mg; Sodium 190mg; Total Carbohydrate 37g (Dietary Fiber 0g); Protein 6g **Exchanges:** 1 Starch, 1½ Other Carbohydrate, 4 Fat **Carbohydrate Choices:** 2½

SWEET TIP **A classic lemon curd is the filling in this buttery-rich dense yellow cake. If you want to save time, use a jar of purchased lemon curd.**

Apple Dumpling Cake

Prep Time: 15 Minutes * Start to Finish: 1 Hour 30 Minutes * **15 SERVINGS**

⅔ cup packed brown sugar

½ cup butter, melted

8 small Gala apples, peeled, halved lengthwise

2½ cups all-purpose flour

2 teaspoons baking powder

1½ teaspoons apple pie spice

½ teaspoon salt

1 cup butter, softened

1½ cups granulated sugar

1 teaspoon vanilla

3 eggs

¾ cup milk

1 Heat oven to 350°F. Grease 13 x 9-inch pan with shortening or cooking spray. In small bowl, mix brown sugar and ½ cup melted butter until well mixed. Spread evenly in pan. Remove apple cores with melon baller. Place 15 apple halves, cut sides down, over sugar mixture in pan. Bake 15 minutes or until bubbling around edges.

2 In small bowl, mix flour, baking powder, apple pie spice and salt. In medium bowl, beat 1 cup butter and the granulated sugar with electric mixer on medium speed 3 minutes or until light and fluffy. Beat in vanilla. Add eggs, one at a time, beating until blended. On low speed, beat in flour mixture alternately with milk. Spoon mixture over hot apples in pan.

3 Bake 40 to 45 minutes or until apples are tender and toothpick inserted in center of cake comes out clean. Cool 5 minutes. Run knife around edge of pan to loosen cake. Place heatproof serving plate upside down on pan; turn plate and pan over. Leave pan over cake 1 minute so topping drizzles over cake. Remove pan; cool 10 minutes. Cut into squares around apples.

1 Serving: Calories 411; Total Fat 20g (Saturated Fat 12g, Trans Fat 0g); Cholesterol 0g; Sodium 285mg; Total Carbohydrate 56g (Dietary Fiber 2g); Protein 4g **Exchanges:** 1 Starch, ½ Fruit, 2 Other Carbohydrate, 4 Fat **Carbohydrate Choices:** 3½

chapter 3

Tube
and Loaf Cakes

Chocolate Cake à l'Orange

Prep Time: 40 minutes ✳ Start to Finish: 2 hours 35 minutes ✳ **12 SERVINGS**

cake

2	oz unsweetened baking chocolate
1	cup butter
1	cup granulated sugar
1	cup sour cream
2	tablespoons grated orange peel
2	teaspoons vanilla
3	eggs
1½	cups all-purpose flour
1	teaspoon baking powder
1	teaspoon baking soda
¼	teaspoon salt

glaze and garnish

1	oz unsweetened baking chocolate
2	tablespoons butter
⅓	cup powdered sugar
1	to 2 tablespoons orange juice
	Orange peel strips

1 Heat oven to 350°F. Grease 12-cup fluted tube cake pan with shortening; lightly flour. In small microwavable bowl, microwave 2 oz chocolate uncovered on High 1 minute. Stir; microwave in 30-second increments, stirring after each, until melted. Set aside to cool slightly.

2 In large bowl, beat 1 cup butter and the granulated sugar with electric mixer on medium speed until blended. Beat in melted chocolate. Add sour cream, orange peel, vanilla and eggs; beat until well blended. On low speed, beat in remaining cake ingredients. Spread batter in pan.

3 Bake 30 to 40 minutes or until toothpick inserted in center comes out clean. Cool 15 minutes. Remove from pan to cooling rack. Cool completely, about 1 hour.

4 In 1-quart saucepan, heat 1 oz chocolate and 2 tablespoons butter over low heat 2 to 3 minutes, stirring occasionally, until melted. Remove from heat. With wire whisk, beat in powdered sugar and 1 tablespoon of the orange juice. Beat in additional orange juice, 1 teaspoon at a time, until glaze is smooth and the consistency of thick syrup. Drizzle glaze over cake, allowing some to run down side. Garnish with orange peel strips.

1 Serving: Calories 400; Total Fat 26g (Saturated Fat 16g; Trans Fat 1g); Cholesterol 110mg; Sodium 340mg; Total Carbohydrate 36g (Dietary Fiber 2g); Protein 5g **Exchanges:** 1 Starch, 1½ Other Carbohydrate, ½ High-Fat Meat, 4 Fat **Carbohydrate Choices:** 2½

Chocolate-Pecan Bourbon Cake

Prep Time: 20 minutes * Start to Finish: 3 hours 40 minutes * **16 SERVINGS**

cake

2	cups all-purpose flour
2	cups granulated sugar
1	teaspoon baking soda
½	teaspoon baking powder
½	teaspoon salt
½	cup butter, softened
¾	cup buttermilk
½	cup water
¼	cup bourbon or water
1	teaspoon vanilla
2	eggs
4	oz unsweetened baking chocolate, melted, cooled
1	cup chopped pecans

glaze

1	oz unsweetened baking chocolate
1	teaspoon butter
1	cup powdered sugar
5	to 6 teaspoons boiling water
	Additional chopped pecans, if desired

1 Heat oven to 350°F. Grease bottom and side of 10-inch angel food (tube) cake pan or 12-cup fluted tube cake pan with shortening; lightly flour. In large bowl, beat all cake ingredients except 1 cup chopped pecans with electric mixer on low speed 30 seconds, scraping bowl constantly. Beat on high speed 3 minutes, scraping bowl occasionally. Stir in 1 cup pecans. Pour into pan.

2 Bake 60 to 65 minutes or until toothpick inserted in center comes out clean. Cool 10 minutes. Remove from pan to cooling rack. Cool completely, about 2 hours.

3 In 2-quart saucepan, melt 1 oz chocolate and 1 teaspoon butter over low heat, stirring occasionally. Stir in powdered sugar and boiling water until smooth and thin enough to drizzle. Drizzle glaze over cake. Sprinkle with additional pecans.

1 Serving: Calories 370; Total Fat 17g (Saturated Fat /g; Trans Fat 0g); Cholesterol 45mg; Sodium 230mg; Total Carbohydrate 49g (Dietary Fiber 2g); Protein 5g **Exchanges:** 1½ Starch, 1½ Other Carbohydrate, 3½ Fat **Carbohydrate Choices:** 3

SWEET TIP **Serve slices of this decadent cake with chocolate or vanilla ice cream.**

Cream Cheese–Filled Chocolate Cake

Prep Time: 35 minutes * Start to Finish: 4 hours * **16 SERVINGS**

½ **cup butter**

4 **oz unsweetened baking chocolate**

1 **cup water**

1¼ **cups white vanilla baking chips**

1 **package (3 oz) cream cheese, softened**

3 **eggs**

2 **cups sugar**

3 **cups all-purpose flour**

½ **teaspoon salt**

1½ **teaspoons baking powder**

½ **cup sour cream**

1 **teaspoon vanilla**

1 **bag (12 oz) miniature semisweet chocolate chips (2 cups)**

3 **tablespoons half-and-half**

1 Heat oven to 350°F. Grease 12-cup fluted tube cake pan with shortening (do not use cooking spray); coat lightly with flour. In small microwavable bowl, place butter, unsweetened chocolate and water. Microwave uncovered on High 1 minute; stir. Continue microwaving at 15-second intervals until butter is melted and chocolate is smooth.

2 In another small microwavable bowl, microwave 1 cup of the vanilla baking chips uncovered on High 1 minute; stir until chips are smooth. In small bowl, beat cream cheese and 1 egg with electric mixer on medium speed until smooth. Beat in melted vanilla chips on medium speed.

3 In large bowl, mix butter-chocolate mixture, remaining 2 eggs, sugar, flour, salt, baking powder, sour cream, vanilla and 1 cup of the semisweet chocolate chips on low speed just until mixed. Spoon 2 cups of the chocolate batter into cake pan. Drop cream cheese filling by teaspoonfuls onto batter in pan, being careful not to let filling touch side of pan. Spoon remaining chocolate batter on top.

4 Bake 1 hour to 1 hour 10 minutes or until toothpick inserted into chocolate cake comes out clean (white filling may cling). Cool in pan on cooling rack 15 minutes. Remove from pan to cooling rack. Cool completely, about 2 hours.

5 In small microwavable bowl, microwave remaining 1 cup semisweet chocolate chips uncovered on High 1 minute; stir until smooth. Stir in half-and-half until smooth. Spoon over cake, allowing some to drizzle down sides. In sealed small food-storage plastic bag, microwave remaining ¼ cup vanilla baking chips uncovered on High 30 seconds or until melted. Squeeze bag until chips are smooth. Cut small tip from one corner of bag; squeeze bag to drizzle melted chips over cake.

1 Serving: Calories 520; Total Fat 25g (Saturated Fat 14g; Trans Fat 0g); Cholesterol 65mg; Sodium 200mg; Total Carbohydrate 67g (Dietary Fiber 3g); Protein 7g **Exchanges:** 2 Starch, 2½ Other Carbohydrate, 5 Fat **Carbohydrate Choices:** 4½

SWEET TIP **Keep going with the black and white theme by serving slices of cake with warm hot fudge sauce and vanilla ice cream.**

Chocolate Stout Cake with Caramel Frosting

Prep Time: 40 minutes * Start to Finish: 3 hours 20 minutes * **12 SERVINGS**

cake

1	bottle (12 oz) stout or dark beer
4	oz unsweetened baking chocolate, chopped
2¼	cups all-purpose flour
2	cups granulated sugar
¾	cup sour cream
¼	cup butter, softened
1¼	teaspoons baking soda
½	teaspoon baking powder
1	teaspoon salt
1	teaspoon vanilla
2	eggs

frosting

¼	cup butter
½	cup packed brown sugar
3	tablespoons reserved beer
1	cup powdered sugar
¼	cup beer nuts, chopped

1 Heat oven to 350°F. Grease bottom and side of 10-inch angel food (tube) cake pan with shortening; lightly flour. Measure 3 tablespoons beer into small bowl; set aside. In 1-quart saucepan, heat remaining beer and chocolate over low heat, stirring occasionally, until chocolate is melted. Pour into large bowl; cool to lukewarm, 20 minutes.

2 Add remaining cake ingredients to beer mixture. Beat with electric mixer on low speed 30 seconds, scraping bowl occasionally. Beat on high speed 3 minutes, scraping bowl occasionally. Spread batter in pan.

3 Bake 1 hour to 1 hour 10 minutes or until toothpick inserted in center comes out clean. Cool 20 minutes; remove from pan to cooling rack. Cool completely, about 1 hour.

4 Meanwhile, in 2-quart saucepan over medium heat, melt ¼ cup butter. Stir in brown sugar. Heat to boiling, stirring constantly; reduce heat to low. Boil and stir 2 minutes. Stir in 2 tablespoons beer. Heat to boiling; remove from heat. Cool to lukewarm, about 20 minutes. Stir in powdered sugar. Add additional beer, 1 teaspoon at a time, until soft and spreadable. Spoon over top of cake, allowing some to run down side of cake. Sprinkle with beer nuts.

1 Serving: Calories 490; Total Fat 18g (Saturated Fat 10g; Trans Fat 0g); Cholesterol 60mg; Sodium 470mg; Total Carbohydrate 75g (Dietary Fiber 2g); Protein 5g **Exchanges:** 1½ Starch, 3½ Other Carbohydrate, 3½ Fat **Carbohydrate Choices:** 5

SWEET TIP For an added "hit" of chocolate, try one of the chocolate stout beers that are available in this recipe.

Fudge Marble Pound Cake

Prep Time: 20 minutes * Start to Finish: 2 hours 10 minutes * 12 SERVINGS

1 box yellow cake mix with pudding

1 box (4-serving size) vanilla instant pudding and pie filling mix

1 cup water

⅓ cup vegetable oil

1 teaspoon vanilla

4 eggs

¾ cup powdered sugar

¼ cup unsweetened baking cocoa

½ cup chocolate creamy ready-to-spread frosting

1 Heat oven to 325°F. Grease and flour 12-cup fluted tube cake pan, or spray with baking spray with flour. In large bowl, beat cake mix, pudding mix, water, oil, vanilla and eggs with electric mixer on low speed 30 seconds, then on medium speed 2 minutes, scraping bowl occasionally.

2 In medium bowl, mix powdered sugar and cocoa. Remove 1¼ cups batter; stir into cocoa mixture. Pour remaining batter into pan. Drop chocolate batter by generous tablespoonfuls randomly onto batter in pan. Cut through batter with knife for marbled effect.

3 Bake 40 to 46 minutes or until toothpick inserted in center comes out clean. Cool in pan 15 minutes; turn upside down onto heatproof serving plate. Remove pan. Cool completely, about 1 hour.

4 In microwavable bowl, microwave frosting uncovered on Medium 15 seconds. Spread over top of cake, allowing some to drizzle down side. Store loosely covered.

1 Serving: Calories 330; Total Fat 11g (Saturated Fat 3g; Trans Fat 0.5g); Cholesterol 70mg; Sodium 430mg; Total Carbohydrate 53g (Dietary Fiber 1g); Protein 3g Exchanges: 1 Starch, 2½ Other Carbohydrate, 2 Fat Carbohydrate Choices: 3½

SWEET TIP Enjoy a slice of this cake with a generous dollop of your favorite whipped topping.

Chocolate-Coconut Tunnel Cake

Prep Time: 30 minutes * **Start to Finish:** 2 hours 40 minutes * **16 SERVINGS**

filling

1 package (3 oz) cream cheese, softened
2 tablespoons sugar
1 pasteurized egg yolk*
⅓ cup semisweet chocolate chips
⅓ cup flaked coconut

cake

2⅔ cups all-purpose flour
¾ cup unsweetened baking cocoa
2 teaspoons baking soda
2 teaspoons baking powder
1½ teaspoons salt
⅔ cup buttermilk
⅔ cup cold brewed coffee
1 teaspoon vanilla
2 cups sugar
2 whole eggs
1 cup vegetable oil
½ cup chopped pecans

glazes

2 oz white chocolate baking bars or squares, chopped
4 tablespoons shortening
¼ cup semisweet chocolate chips

1 Heat oven to 350°F. Grease 12-cup fluted tube cake pan with shortening; lightly flour. In small bowl, beat cream cheese with electric mixer on medium speed until fluffy. Beat in 2 tablespoons sugar and the egg yolk until blended. Stir in ⅓ cup chocolate chips and the coconut; set aside.

2 In medium bowl, mix flour, cocoa, baking soda, baking powder and salt; set aside. In another bowl, mix buttermilk, coffee and vanilla; set aside. In large bowl, beat 2 cups sugar, the eggs and oil with electric mixer on medium speed 1 minute, scraping bowl occasionally. Alternately add flour mixture, about a third at a time, with buttermilk mixture, half at a time, beating until smooth. Stir in pecans.

3 Pour half of the batter into pan. Spoon cream cheese filling over batter. Top with remaining batter.

4 Bake 50 to 55 minutes or until toothpick inserted in center comes out clean. Cool 15 minutes; remove from pan to cooling rack. Cool completely, about 1 hour.

5 In 1-quart saucepan, melt white chocolate and 2 tablespoons of the shortening over low heat, stirring constantly, until smooth; remove from heat. In another 1-quart saucepan, repeat with ¼ cup chocolate chips and remaining 2 tablespoons shortening. Drizzle glazes over cake.

*Pasteurized eggs are uncooked eggs that have been heat-treated to kill bacteria that can cause food poisoning and gastrointestinal distress. They can be found in the dairy case at large supermarkets. Be sure to use a pasteurized egg yolk in the cream cheese filling.

1 Serving: Calories 470; Total Fat 27g (Saturated Fat 7g; Trans Fat 0.5g); Cholesterol 45mg; Sodium 480mg; Total Carbohydrate 53g (Dietary Fiber 3g); Protein 6g **Exchanges:** 2 Starch, 1½ Other Carbohydrate, 5 Fat **Carbohydrate Choices:** 3½

Cookies 'n' Cream Angel Cake

Prep Time: 15 minutes * Start to Finish: 3 hours 15 minutes * **12 SERVINGS**

 1   box white angel food
     cake mix
1¼   cups cold water
 3   reduced-fat chocolate
     sandwich cookies,
     finely crushed
 1   package fluffy white
     frosting mix
 ½   cup boiling water
 6   reduced-fat chocolate
     sandwich cookies,
     cut in half

1 Move oven rack to lowest position (remove other racks). Heat oven to 350°F.

2 In extra-large glass or metal bowl, beat cake mix and cold water with electric mixer on low speed 30 seconds. Beat on medium speed 1 minute. Carefully fold crushed cookies into batter. Pour into ungreased 10-inch angel food (tube) cake pan. (Do not use fluted tube cake pan or 9-inch angel food pan or batter will overflow.)

3 Bake 37 to 47 minutes or until top is dark golden brown and cracks feel very dry and are not sticky. Do not underbake. Immediately turn pan upside down onto heatproof bottle or funnel until cake is completely cool, about 2 hours.

4 Run knife around edge of cake; remove from pan. Place on serving plate.

5 In small glass or metal bowl, beat frosting mix and boiling water on low speed 30 seconds, scraping bowl constantly. Beat on high speed 5 to 7 minutes, scraping bowl occasionally, until stiff peaks form. Frost cake; garnish with sandwich cookie halves.

1 Serving: Calories 240; Total Fat 1g (Saturated Fat 0g; Trans Fat 0g); Cholesterol 0mg; Sodium 400mg; Total Carbohydrate 54g (Dietary Fiber 0g); Protein 3g **Exchanges:** 1 Starch, 2½ Other Carbohydrate **Carbohydrate Choices:** 3½

SWEET TIP **This cake is just as delicious without the frosting! Simply top each slice with a dollop of whipped topping and a sandwich cookie.**

White Chocolate–Raspberry Pecan Cake

Prep Time: 30 minutes * Start to Finish: 3 hours 50 minutes * **12 SERVINGS**

cake

- 8 **egg whites**
- ½ **teaspoon cream of tartar**
- 1½ **cups sugar**
- 2 **cups all-purpose flour or 2¼ cups cake flour**
- 1 **tablespoon baking powder**
- ½ **teaspoon salt**
- ½ **cup vegetable oil**
- ½ **cup cold water**
- 2 **tablespoons raspberry syrup (used for beverages)**
- 2 **teaspoons vanilla**
- 6 **egg yolks**
- 1 **package (6 oz) white baking bars (white chocolate), grated (1⅓ cups)**
- 1 **cup finely chopped pecans**

topping and garnish

- 1 **cup raspberry jam**
- 2 **oz white baking bars (white chocolate) (from 6-oz package)**
- 1 **tablespoon butter**
  Fresh raspberries, if desired

1 Heat oven to 325°F. In medium bowl, beat egg whites and cream of tartar with electric mixer on high speed until soft peaks form. Gradually beat in ½ cup of the sugar, 2 tablespoons at a time, until stiff peaks form; set aside.

2 In large bowl, mix flour, remaining 1 cup sugar, the baking powder and salt. Beat in oil, water, syrup, vanilla and egg yolks on medium speed, scraping bowl occasionally, until blended. Stir in grated white chocolate and chopped pecans. Gradually pour egg yolk mixture over beaten egg whites, folding with rubber spatula just until blended. Pour into ungreased 10-inch angel food (tube) cake pan.

3 Bake 1 hour 10 minutes to 1 hour 15 minutes or until top springs back when touched lightly. Immediately turn upside down onto heatproof bottle or funnel. Let hang about 2 hours or until cake is completely cool. Loosen side of cake with knife or long metal spatula; remove from pan.

4 In 1-quart saucepan, heat jam over medium heat, stirring constantly, until bubbly. Drizzle over cake. Cool completely. In 1-quart saucepan, heat 2 oz white chocolate and the butter over medium heat, stirring constantly, until smooth. Drizzle over jam. Garnish with raspberries.

1 Serving: Calories 560; Total Fat 25g (Saturated Fat 7g; Trans Fat 0g); Cholesterol 95mg; Sodium 300mg; Total Carbohydrate 75g (Dietary Fiber 2g); Protein 8g **Exchanges:** 1½ Starch, 3½ Other Carbohydrate, ½ Medium-Fat Meat, 4½ Fat **Carbohydrate Choices:** 5

Chocolate Angel Cake with Raspberry-Orange Sauce

Prep Time: 25 minutes ✳ Start to Finish: 3 hours 35 minutes ✳ **12 SERVINGS**

cake

2	**tablespoons unsweetened baking cocoa**
1	**box white angel food cake mix**
1¼	**cups cold water**

sauce and topping

1	**package (10 oz) frozen raspberries in light syrup, thawed**
¼	**cup sugar**
2	**tablespoons cornstarch**
2	**tablespoons orange juice**
3	**cups frozen (thawed) reduced-fat whipped topping**
	Fresh mint leaves, if desired

1 Move oven rack to lowest position (remove other racks). Heat oven to 350°F. In extra-large glass or metal bowl, stir cocoa into dry cake mix; add water. Beat with electric mixer on low speed 30 seconds. Beat on medium speed 1 minute. Pour into ungreased 10-inch angel food (tube) cake pan. (Do not use fluted tube cake pan or 9-inch angel food pan or batter will overflow.)

2 Bake 37 to 47 minutes or until top is dark golden brown and cracks feel very dry and not sticky. Do not underbake. Immediately turn pan upside down onto heatproof bottle or funnel. Let hang about 2 hours or until cake is completely cool. Run knife around edge of cake; remove from pan.

3 Drain raspberries, reserving liquid. Add enough water to raspberry liquid to measure ⅔ cup. In 1-quart saucepan, mix sugar and cornstarch; stir in liquid mixture. Heat over medium heat, stirring constantly, until mixture thickens and boils; boil and stir 1 minute. Stir in orange juice and raspberries. Cool completely.

4 Split cake horizontally to make 3 layers. (To split, mark side of cake with toothpicks and cut with long, thin serrated knife.) Spread 1 cup whipped topping and scant ½ cup sauce between each layer (sauce may not completely cover each layer). Spread remaining sauce over top of cake. Drop remaining whipped cream in dollops on top of sauce. Garnish with mint leaves, if desired. Store in refrigerator.

1 Serving: Calories 230; Total Fat 2.5g (Saturated Fat 2g; Trans Fat 0g); Cholesterol 0mg; Sodium 340mg; Total Carbohydrate 49g (Dietary Fiber 1g); Protein 4g **Exchanges:** 3½ Other Carbohydrate, ½ Medium-Fat Meat **Carbohydrate Choices:** 3

SWEET TIP **Although this simple raspberry sauce is just made for this cake, it makes a great topping for other desserts too.**

Mocha Angel Cake

Prep Time: 15 minutes * Start to Finish: 2 hours * **12 SERVINGS**

cake

1	**box white angel food cake mix**
1¼	**cups cold brewed coffee**
1	**tablespoon unsweetened baking cocoa**
	Chocolate candy sprinkles

topping

1	**envelope whipped topping mix (from 2.8-oz package)**
½	**cup cold fat-free (skim) milk**
1½	**teaspoons vanilla**
2	**tablespoons powdered sugar**
2	**teaspoons unsweetened baking cocoa**
	Additional chocolate candy sprinkles, if desired

1 Move oven rack to middle position (remove other racks). Heat oven to 350°F. In extra-large glass or metal bowl, beat cake mix, cold coffee and 1 tablespoon cocoa with electric mixer on low speed 30 seconds; beat on medium speed 1 minute. Pour into two ungreased 9 × 5-inch loaf pans. Sprinkle with candy sprinkles.

2 Bake 35 to 45 minutes or until top is dark golden brown and cracks feel very dry and not sticky. Do not underbake. Immediately place each loaf pan on its side on heatproof surface. Cool completely, about 1 hour. Run knife around sides of pans to loosen cakes; remove from pans.

3 Make topping mix as directed on package using milk and vanilla; add powdered sugar and 2 teaspoons cocoa for the last minute of beating.

4 Serve cake with topping. Sprinkle with additional candy sprinkles if desired. Store in refrigerator.

1 Serving: Calories 190; Total Fat 1.5g (Saturated Fat 1.5g; Trans Fat 0g); Cholesterol 0mg; Sodium 330mg; Total Carbohydrate 38g (Dietary Fiber 0g); Protein 4g **Exchanges:** 2½ Other Carbohydrate, ½ Lean Meat **Carbohydrate Choices:** 2½

SWEET TIP **Don't want to make the topping? Simply use frozen (thawed) whipped topping instead. It won't pack a chocolate punch, but the color will make an interesting contrast to the cake and candy sprinkles.**

Black Forest Chiffon Cake

Prep Time: 25 minutes * Start to Finish: 3 hours 15 minutes * **16 SERVINGS**

cake

- 1 jar (10 oz) maraschino cherries, drained, reserving juice
- 1⅔ cups all-purpose flour or 1¾ cups cake flour
- 3 teaspoons baking powder
- ½ teaspoon salt
- 1¾ cups sugar
- ½ cup unsweetened baking cocoa
- 1 teaspoon vanilla
- ½ teaspoon almond extract
- 7 egg yolks
- ½ cup vegetable oil
- ½ cup cold water
- ¼ cup cherry liqueur or amaretto
- ½ cup finely chopped toasted* slivered almonds
- 1 cup egg whites (about 8)
- ½ teaspoon cream of tartar

glaze, if desired

- Reserved cherry juice
- 2 teaspoons cornstarch
- 2 tablespoons light corn syrup
- 3 to 4 drops red food color, if desired

1 Move oven rack to lowest position. Heat oven to 325°F. Reserve 10 whole cherries; chop remaining cherries.

2 In medium bowl, mix flour, baking powder, salt, 1 cup of the sugar and the cocoa. Beat in vanilla, almond extract, egg yolks, oil, water and liqueur with electric mixer on low speed 30 seconds. Stir in chopped cherries and almonds.

3 In large bowl, beat egg whites and cream of tartar with electric mixer on medium speed until foamy. Gradually beat in remaining ¾ cup sugar until blended. Beat on high speed about 2 minutes or until stiff peaks form. Gradually pour egg yolk mixture over beaten egg whites, folding with rubber spatula just until blended. Pour into ungreased 10-inch angel food (tube) cake pan.

4 Bake 55 to 60 minutes or until top springs back when touched lightly. Immediately turn pan upside down onto heatproof bottle or funnel. Let hang about 2 hours or until completely cool.

5 Meanwhile, to make glaze, add enough water to reserved cherry juice to measure ⅓ cup. In 1-quart saucepan, mix cornstarch, cherry juice and corn syrup until cornstarch is dissolved. Heat to boiling over medium heat. Boil 2 to 3 minutes or until glossy and thickened; remove from heat. Stir in food color. Cool.

6 Loosen side of cake with knife or long metal spatula; remove from pan. Spread or drizzle glaze over top of cake. Garnish with whole cherries.

To toast almonds, heat oven to 350°F. Spread almonds in ungreased shallow pan. Bake uncovered 6 to 10 minutes, stirring occasionally, until light brown.

1 Serving: Calories 290; Total Fat 11g (Saturated Fat 2g; Trans Fat 0g); Cholesterol 80mg; Sodium 200mg; Total Carbohydrate 42g (Dietary Fiber 2g); Protein 5g **Exchanges:** ½ Starch, 2½ Other Carbohydrate, ½ Medium-Fat Meat, 1½ Fat **Carbohydrate Choices:** 3

Spiced Apple Cake with Maple Glaze

Prep Time: 30 minutes * **Start to Finish:** 2 hours 35 minutes * **16 SERVINGS**

cake

- 3 cups chopped peeled apples (3 medium)
- 3 cups all-purpose flour
- 1 teaspoon baking powder
- ½ teaspoon baking soda
- ½ teaspoon salt
- 2 teaspoons ground cinnamon
- ½ teaspoon ground nutmeg
- ¼ teaspoon ground cloves
- 2 cups packed brown sugar
- 1 cup vegetable oil
- 4 eggs
- 1 teaspoon vanilla

glaze

- 1½ cups powdered sugar
- 3 to 4 tablespoons whipping cream
- ¼ teaspoon maple flavor

1 Heat oven to 350°F. Generously grease 12-cup fluted tube cake pan with shortening; lightly flour.

2 In medium bowl, toss apples with 2 tablespoons of the flour. In another medium bowl, mix baking powder, baking soda, salt, cinnamon, nutmeg, cloves and remaining flour. In large bowl, beat brown sugar, oil, eggs and vanilla with electric mixer on medium speed until mixed. On low speed, beat in flour mixture just until blended. Stir in apples. Spoon batter into pan.

3 Bake 55 to 60 minutes or until toothpick inserted in center comes out clean. Cool 10 minutes; remove from pan to cooling rack. Cool completely, about 1 hour.

4 In medium bowl, mix all glaze ingredients until smooth. Drizzle glaze over cake.

1 Serving: Calories 400; Total Fat 16g (Saturated Fat 3g; Trans Fat 0g); Cholesterol 50mg; Sodium 170mg; Total Carbohydrate 60g (Dietary Fiber 1g); Protein 4g **Exchanges:** 1½ Starch, 2½ Other Carbohydrate, 3 Fat **Carbohydrate Choices:** 4

Streusel In-Between Pumpkin Cake

Prep Time: 20 minutes * Start to Finish: 3 hours 55 minutes * **16 SERVINGS**

streusel

- ½ **cup packed brown sugar**
- 2 **tablespoons all-purpose flour**
- 1 **teaspoon ground cinnamon**
- ¼ **teaspoon pumpkin pie spice**
- 1 **tablespoon butter, softened**

cake

- 3 **cups all-purpose flour**
- 2 **teaspoons baking soda**
- 1 **tablespoon ground cinnamon**
- 1 **teaspoon salt**
- 1 **cup butter, softened**
- 2 **cups granulated sugar**
- 4 **eggs**
- 1 **cup canned pumpkin (not pumpkin pie mix)**
- 1 **cup sour cream**
- 1 **teaspoon vanilla**
   Powdered sugar, if desired

1 Heat oven to 350°F. Grease 12-cup fluted tube cake pan with shortening; lightly flour. In small bowl, stir all streusel ingredients until crumbly; set aside.

2 In medium bowl, mix 3 cups flour, baking soda, 1 tablespoon cinnamon and the salt; set aside. In large bowl, beat 1 cup butter and the granulated sugar with electric mixer on medium speed, scraping bowl occasionally, until creamy. Add eggs, two at a time, beating well after each addition. Beat in pumpkin, sour cream and vanilla. Gradually beat in flour mixture on low speed until blended.

3 Spread half of the batter in pan. Sprinkle streusel over batter, making sure streusel does not touch side of pan. Top with remaining batter, making sure batter layer touches side of pan.

4 Bake 55 to 60 minutes or until toothpick inserted in cake comes out clean. Cool 30 minutes; remove from pan to cooling rack. Cool completely, about 2 hours. Sprinkle with powdered sugar.

1 Serving: Calories 380; Total Fat 17g (Saturated Fat 10g; Trans Fat 1g); Cholesterol 95mg; Sodium 420mg; Total Carbohydrate 53g (Dietary Fiber 2g); Protein 5g **Exchanges:** 1 Starch, 2½ Other Carbohydrate, 3½ Fat **Carbohydrate Choices:** 3½

SWEET TIP **Put the remaining pumpkin in a resealable food-storage plastic bag and freeze to use later in another recipe. Or, plan to make two cakes; one for your occasion and one to give away.**

Crunchy-Topped Peanut Butter Cake

Prep Time: 30 minutes * Start to Finish: 3 hours 35 minutes * **16 SERVINGS**

cake

1	**cup coarsely chopped honey-roasted peanuts**
2	**cups all-purpose flour**
1¼	**cups sugar**
2½	**teaspoons baking powder**
½	**teaspoon salt**
½	**cup butter, softened**
¾	**cup creamy peanut butter**
3	**eggs**
⅔	**cup milk**
1	**teaspoon vanilla**

glaze

½	**cup semisweet chocolate chips (3 oz)**
2	**tablespoons butter**
2	**tablespoons light corn syrup**
1	**to 2 teaspoons hot water**
3	**tablespoons creamy peanut butter**

1 Heat oven to 325°F. Grease 12-cup fluted tube cake pan with shortening; lightly flour. Sprinkle nuts evenly in bottom of pan. In medium bowl, mix flour, sugar, baking powder and salt; set aside. In large bowl, beat ½ cup butter and ¾ cup peanut butter with electric mixer on medium speed until smooth, scraping bowl occasionally. Beat in eggs. On low speed, beat in milk and vanilla. Beat in flour mixture just until blended, scraping bowl occasionally. Spread in pan.

2 Bake 55 to 65 minutes or until toothpick inserted in center comes out clean. Cool 10 minutes; remove from pan to cooling rack. Cool completely, about 2 hours.

3 In 1-quart saucepan, heat chocolate chips, 2 tablespoons butter and the corn syrup over low heat, stirring frequently, until chocolate chips are melted. Cool about 10 minutes. Stir in hot water, 1 teaspoon at a time, until glaze is smooth and has the consistency of thick syrup. Spoon over top of cake, allowing glaze to run down side.

4 In small microwavable bowl, microwave 3 tablespoons peanut butter on High 20 seconds or until it can be stirred smooth and is drizzling consistency. Drizzle over top of chocolate glaze.

1 Serving: Calories 390; Total Fat 22g (Saturated Fat 8g; Trans Fat 0g); Cholesterol 55mg; Sodium 330mg; Total Carbohydrate 39g (Dietary Fiber 2g); Protein 9g **Exchanges:** 2½ Other Carbohydrate, 1½ High-Fat Meat, 2 Fat **Carbohydrate Choices:** 2½

SWEET TIP Test the cake in the center, in a crack if there is one because the crust can clean off the toothpick as you remove it, making you think the cake is done when it might not be.

Caramel Snickerdoodle Cake

Prep Time: 20 minutes * Start to Finish: 2 hours 40 minutes * **16 SERVINGS**

1¾ cups plus 2 tablespoons sugar

2 teaspoons ground cinnamon

2½ cups all-purpose flour

2 teaspoons baking soda

1 teaspoon salt

1 can (5 oz) evaporated milk

1 cup sour cream

½ cup butter, melted

1 teaspoon vanilla

2 eggs, beaten

10 caramels, unwrapped

1 Heat oven to 350°F. Grease 12-cup fluted tube cake pan with shortening. In small bowl, mix 2 tablespoons of the sugar and 1 teaspoon of the cinnamon. Sprinkle mixture over inside of pan, turning to evenly coat. Shake out any excess.

2 In large bowl, mix remaining 1¾ cups sugar, remaining 1 teaspoon cinnamon, the flour, baking soda and salt. Reserve 1 tablespoon of the evaporated milk for the topping. Stir remaining evaporated milk, sour cream, butter, vanilla and eggs into dry ingredients until well blended. Pour into pan.

3 Bake 40 to 50 minutes or until toothpick inserted in center comes out clean. Let stand 30 minutes; remove from pan to cooling rack. Cool completely, about 1 hour.

4 In small microwavable bowl, microwave caramels with reserved evaporated milk uncovered on High 1 to 2 minutes, stirring every 30 seconds, until caramels are melted and mixture is smooth. Drizzle over cooled cake.

1 Serving: Calories 340; Total Fat 11g (Saturated Fat 6g; Trans Fat 0g); Cholesterol 50mg; Sodium 420mg; Total Carbohydrate 54g (Dietary Fiber 0g); Protein 4g **Exchanges:** 1½ Starch, 2 Other Carbohydrate, 2 Fat **Carbohydrate Choices:** 3½

Banana-Cinnamon Cake

Prep Time: 15 minutes * **Start to Finish:** 3 hours 20 minutes * **16 SERVINGS**

cake

- **1** **box yellow cake mix with pudding**
- **½** **cup water**
- **1** **cup mashed very ripe bananas (2 medium)**
- **½** **cup butter, softened**
- **2** **teaspoons ground cinnamon**
- **3** **eggs**
- **½** **cup chopped walnuts**

glaze

- **½** **cup cream cheese creamy ready-to-spread frosting**
- **2** **to 3 teaspoons milk**
- **¼** **teaspoon ground cinnamon**

1 Heat oven to 350°F (325°F for dark or nonstick pan). Grease and lightly flour 12-cup fluted tube cake pan, or spray with baking spray with flour.

2 In large bowl, beat cake mix, water, bananas, butter, 2 teaspoons cinnamon and the eggs with electric mixer on low speed 30 seconds, then on medium speed 2 minutes, scraping bowl occasionally. Stir in walnuts. Pour into pan.

3 Bake 45 to 55 minutes or until toothpick inserted in center comes out clean. Cool in pan 10 minutes. Turn pan upside down onto cooling rack or heatproof serving plate; remove pan. Cool completely, about 2 hours. In small bowl, stir glaze ingredients until thin enough to drizzle. Drizzle over cake. Store loosely covered.

1 Serving: Calories 240; Total Fat 11g (Saturated Fat 5g; Trans Fat 0.5g); Cholesterol 55mg; Sodium 260mg; Total Carbohydrate 32g (Dietary Fiber 1g); Protein 2g **Exchanges:** 1 Starch, 1 Other Carbohydrate, 2 Fat **Carbohydrate Choices:** 2

SWEET TIP **If you have extra bananas that are ripe, place them in the freezer, unpeeled. When you're ready for them, just thaw, cut off the top of the peel, then squeeze the banana straight into your mixing bowl.**

Buttermilk Banana Cake

Prep Time: 15 minutes * Start to Finish: 2 hours 30 minutes * **16 SERVINGS**

3½ cups all-purpose flour
or 4 cups cake flour

3 cups granulated sugar

1 cup shortening

1 cup buttermilk
(or 1 tablespoon white
vinegar plus enough milk
to measure 1 cup)

2 teaspoons vanilla

1½ teaspoons baking soda

1 teaspoon baking powder

1 teaspoon salt

4 eggs

2½ cups mashed ripe bananas
(5 medium)

1 cup chopped nuts,
if desired

Powdered sugar, if desired

1 Heat oven to 375°F. Grease 12-cup fluted tube cake pan with shortening; lightly flour.

2 In large bowl, beat all ingredients except bananas, nuts and powdered sugar with electric mixer on low speed, scraping bowl occasionally, until blended. Beat in bananas on medium speed 2 minutes. Stir in nuts. Pour into pan.

3 Bake 50 to 60 minutes or until toothpick inserted in center comes out clean. Cool 15 minutes; remove from pan to cooling rack. Cool completely, about 1 hour. Sprinkle with powdered sugar.

1 Serving: Calories 430; Total Fat 15g (Saturated Fat 4g; Trans Fat 0g); Cholesterol 50mg; Sodium 330mg; Total Carbohydrate 67g (Dietary Fiber 2g); Protein 5g **Exchanges:** 1½ Starch, 3 Other Carbohydrate, 3 Fat **Carbohydrate Choices:** 4½

Apple-Walnut Cake with Caramel Glaze

Prep Time: 25 minutes * Start to Finish: 2 hours 10 minutes * **16 SERVINGS**

cake

2	cups packed brown sugar
1½	cups vegetable oil
3	eggs
3	cups all-purpose flour
2	teaspoons baking soda
¼	teaspoon salt
1	teaspoon ground ginger
2	teaspoons ground cinnamon
¼	teaspoon ground cloves
1	cup chopped walnuts
2	large apples, peeled, shredded (about 2 cups)

glaze

1	cup powdered sugar
2	tablespoons butter, softened
3	tablespoons butterscotch-caramel topping
1	tablespoon milk
	Additional ground cinnamon, if desired

1 Heat oven to 350°F. Grease 12-cup fluted tube cake pan with shortening; lightly flour.

2 In large bowl, beat brown sugar, oil and eggs with electric mixer on medium speed until light and fluffy. Add remaining cake ingredients except walnuts and apples; beat on low speed until smooth. With spoon, gently stir in walnuts and apples. Spoon batter into pan.

3 Bake 1 hour to 1 hour 10 minutes or until toothpick inserted near center comes out clean. Cool 10 minutes. Place heatproof plate upside down over pan; turn plate and pan over. Remove pan. Cool 30 minutes.

4 Meanwhile, in medium bowl, beat all glaze ingredients except cinnamon until smooth. Pour glaze over top of cake, allowing some to run down side. Sprinkle with cinnamon.

1 Serving: Calories 500; Total Fat 28g (Saturated Fat 4.5g; Trans Fat 0g); Cholesterol 45mg; Sodium 240mg; Total Carbohydrate 58g (Dietary Fiber 2g); Protein 5g **Exchanges:** 1 Starch, 3 Other Carbohydrate, 5½ Fat **Carbohydrate Choices:** 4

SWEET TIP **It's okay to use any variety or color of apple for this cake.**

Apricot-Filled Pumpkin Cake with Browned Butter Frosting

Prep Time: 25 minutes * Start to Finish: 2 hours 55 minutes * 16 SERVINGS

filling
- ½ cup packed brown sugar
- 2 tablespoons all-purpose flour
- 3 tablespoons cold butter
- ½ cup finely chopped dried apricots (about 14)

cake
- 3 cups all-purpose flour
- 3 teaspoons baking powder
- 2 teaspoons ground cinnamon
- 1 teaspoon ground ginger
- ½ teaspoon salt
- 1 cup butter, softened
- 2 cups granulated sugar
- 5 eggs
- 1 cup canned pumpkin (not pumpkin pie mix)

frosting
- ⅓ cup butter (do not use margarine)
- 2 cups powdered sugar
- 3 to 4 tablespoons milk

garnish, if desired
- ¼ cup finely chopped dried apricots (about 7)

1 Heat oven to 325°F. Grease 12-cup fluted tube cake pan with shortening; lightly flour. (Do not use dark or nonstick pan.) In small bowl, mix filling ingredients except apricots with fork until fine crumbs form. Stir in ½ cup chopped apricots; set aside. In medium bowl, mix 3 cups flour, the baking powder, cinnamon, ginger and salt; set aside.

2 In large bowl, beat 1 cup butter and the granulated sugar with electric mixer on medium speed, scraping bowl occasionally, until creamy. Add eggs, one at a time, beating well after each addition. Beat in pumpkin. On low speed, gradually beat in flour mixture until blended.

3 Spread 3 cups of the batter in pan. With back of spoon, make ½-inch-deep tunnel in middle of batter. Spoon filling into tunnel, making sure filling does not touch side of pan. Top with remaining batter, making sure batter layer touches side of pan.

4 Bake 1 hour to 1 hour 15 minutes or until toothpick inserted in cake comes out clean and top is golden brown. Cool 15 minutes. Remove cake from pan to cooling rack. Cool completely, about 1 hour.

5 In 2-quart saucepan, heat ⅓ cup butter over medium heat, stirring constantly, until light golden brown; cool slightly. Stir in powdered sugar. Stir in 3 tablespoons of the milk until smooth. Add additional milk, 1 teaspoon at a time, until desired consistency. Spoon frosting over cake, allowing some to run down side. Garnish with ¼ cup chopped apricots.

1 Serving: Calories 470; Total Fat 20g (Saturated Fat 12g; Trans Fat 1g); Cholesterol 115mg; Sodium 310mg; Total Carbohydrate 69g (Dietary Fiber 2g); Protein 5g **Exchanges:** 1 Starch, 3½ Other Carbohydrate, 4 Fat **Carbohydrate Choices:** 4½

SWEET TIP To garnish cake, roll dried apricot halves between sheets of waxed paper to flatten slightly, then cut into desired shapes with small cookie cutters.

Triple-Ginger Pound Cake

Prep Time: 20 minutes * Start to Finish: 4 hours * **24 SERVINGS**

3 cups all-purpose flour
2 teaspoons ground ginger
1 teaspoon baking powder
¼ teaspoon salt
2½ cups sugar
1 cup butter, softened
1 tablespoon grated gingerroot
1 teaspoon vanilla
5 eggs
1 cup milk or evaporated milk
½ cup finely chopped crystallized ginger
Browned Butter Glaze (page 27)

1 Heat oven to 350°F. Generously grease bottom and sides of 10-inch angel food (tube) cake pan or 12-cup fluted tube cake pan with shortening; lightly flour.

2 In medium bowl, mix flour, ground ginger, baking powder and salt; set aside. In large bowl, beat sugar, butter, gingerroot, vanilla and eggs with electric mixer on low speed 30 seconds, scraping bowl constantly. Beat on high speed 5 minutes, scraping bowl occasionally. Beat flour mixture into sugar mixture alternately with milk on low speed, beating just until smooth after each addition. Fold in crystallized ginger. Pour into pan.

3 Bake 1 hour 10 minutes to 1 hour 20 minutes, or until toothpick inserted in center comes out clean. Cool 20 minutes; remove from pan to cooling rack. Cool completely, about 2 hours. Drizzle with glaze.

1 Serving: Calories 300; Total Fat 12g (Saturated Fat 7g; Trans Fat 0g); Cholesterol 70mg; Sodium 135mg; Total Carbohydrate 46g (Dietary Fiber 0g); Protein 3g **Exchanges:** 1 Starch, 2 Other Carbohydrate, 2½ Fat **Carbohydrate Choices:** 3

Change the Pan Size

Follow the recipe as directed and pour batter into 2 (9 x 5-inch) loaf pans; bake 55 to 60 minutes.

Spice Chiffon Cake

Prep Time: 25 minutes * Start to Finish: 3 hours 30 minutes * **16 SERVINGS**

cake

7	**egg whites**
½	**teaspoon cream of tartar**
2	**cups all-purpose flour**
1½	**cups granulated sugar**
2	**teaspoons baking powder**
1	**teaspoon salt**
1	**teaspoon ground cinnamon**
¼	**teaspoon ground nutmeg**
¼	**teaspoon ground allspice**
¼	**teaspoon ground cloves**
¾	**cup water**
½	**cup vegetable oil**
7	**egg yolks**

glaze

2	**cups powdered sugar**
⅓	**cup butter, melted**
1½	**teaspoons vanilla**
2	**to 4 tablespoons hot water**

1 Move oven rack to lowest position. Heat oven to 325°F. In large bowl, beat egg whites and cream of tartar with electric mixer on high speed until stiff peaks form.

2 In another large bowl, mix flour, granulated sugar, baking powder, salt, cinnamon, nutmeg, allspice and cloves. Add ¾ cup water, the oil and egg yolks; beat with electric mixer on low speed until smooth. Gradually pour egg yolk mixture over beaten egg whites, folding with rubber spatula just until blended. Pour into ungreased 10-inch angel food (tube) cake pan.

3 Bake 55 minutes. Increase oven temperature to 350°F. Bake about 10 minutes longer or until top springs back when touched lightly. Immediately turn pan upside down onto heatproof bottle or funnel. Let hang about 2 hours or until cake is completely cool. Run knife or long metal spatula around side of pan to loosen cake; remove from pan.

4 In medium bowl, mix powdered sugar, butter and vanilla. Stir in water, 1 tablespoon at a time, until smooth and consistency of thick syrup. Spread glaze over top of cake, allowing some to drizzle down side.

1 Serving: Calories 320; Total Fat 13g (Saturated Fat 4g; Trans Fat 0g); Cholesterol 90mg; Sodium 270mg; Total Carbohydrate 46g (Dietary Fiber 0g); Protein 4g **Exchanges:** 1½ Starch, 1½ Other Carbohydrate, 2½ Fat **Carbohydrate Choices:** 3

SWEET TIP **An easy substitution is to replace the cinnamon, nutmeg, allspice and cloves with 2 teaspoons of apple pie spice or pumpkin pie spice.**

Pumpkin Angel Food Cake with Ginger-Cream Filling

Prep Time: 10 minutes * Start to Finish: 3 hours * **12 SERVINGS**

cake

- 1 **box white angel food cake mix**
- 1 **tablespoon all-purpose flour**
- 1½ **teaspoons pumpkin pie spice**
- ¾ **cup canned pumpkin (not pumpkin pie mix)**
- 1 **cup cold water**

filling

- 2 **cups whipping cream**
- ¼ **cup powdered sugar**
- 2 **tablespoons finely chopped crystallized ginger**

  Additional pumpkin pie spice, if desired

1 Move oven rack to lowest position. Heat oven to 350°F. In extra-large glass or metal bowl, beat cake ingredients with electric mixer on low speed 30 seconds. Beat on medium speed 1 minute. Pour into ungreased 10-inch angel food (tube) cake pan.

2 Bake 37 to 47 minutes or until crust is dark golden brown and cracks are dry. Immediately turn pan upside down onto heatproof bottle or funnel. Let hang about 2 hours or until cake is completely cool. Loosen cake from side of pan with knife or long metal spatula. Turn cake upside down onto serving plate.

3 In chilled large bowl, beat whipping cream and powdered sugar with electric mixer on high speed until stiff. Fold in ginger. Cut cake horizontally in half to make 2 even layers. Spread half of the filling on bottom layer; replace top of cake. Spread remaining filling on top of cake. Sprinkle with additional pumpkin pie spice if desired.

1 Serving: Calories 280; Total Fat 12g (Saturated Fat 8g; Trans Fat 0g); Cholesterol 45mg; Sodium 330mg; Total Carbohydrate 38g (Dietary Fiber 0g); Protein 4g **Exchanges:** 1 Starch, 1½ Other Carbohydrate, 2½ Fat **Carbohydrate Choices:** 2½

SWEET TIP Look for the crystallized ginger in the produce or spice section of the grocery store. If you don't have it on hand and want a substitute, mix 1 teaspoon ground ginger with the powdered sugar when making the filling.

Orange Cream Angel Food Cake

Prep Time: 35 minutes * Start to Finish: 5 hours 25 minutes * **12 SERVINGS**

cake

- 1 **box white angel food cake mix**
- 1¼ **cups cold water**

filling and frosting

- 6 **egg yolks**
- 1 **cup sugar**
- 2 **teaspoons cornstarch**
- ⅔ **cup orange juice**
  Pinch salt
- ¾ **cup butter, cut into pieces**
- 1 **cup whipping cream**
- 1 **tablespoon grated orange peel**
  Orange peel twists, if desired

1 Move oven rack to lowest position (remove other racks). Heat oven to 350°F.

2 In extra-large glass or metal bowl, beat cake mix and cold water with electric mixer on low speed 30 seconds. Beat on medium speed 1 minute. Pour into ungreased 10-inch angel food (tube) cake pan. (Do not use fluted tube cake pan or 9-inch angel food pan or batter will overflow.)

3 Bake 37 to 47 minutes or until top is dark golden brown and cracks feel very dry and are not sticky. Do not underbake. Immediately turn pan upside down onto heatproof bottle or funnel. Let hang about 2 hours or until cake is completely cool.

4 Meanwhile, in 2-quart saucepan, beat egg yolks, sugar, cornstarch, orange juice and salt with wire whisk until blended. Add butter; cook 2 to 3 minutes over medium heat, stirring frequently, until boiling. Boil 3 to 5 minutes, stirring constantly, until thickened and mixture coats the back of a spoon. Immediately pour orange mixture (orange curd) through fine-mesh strainer into medium bowl. Cover with plastic wrap, pressing wrap directly onto surface of orange curd. Refrigerate about 1 hour or until completely chilled.

5 In medium bowl, beat whipping cream on high speed until stiff peaks form. Fold whipped cream and grated orange peel into orange curd.

6 Run knife around edge of cake; remove from pan. On serving plate, place cake with browned side down. Cut off top one-third of cake, using long, sharp knife; set aside. Scoop out 1-inch-wide and 1-inch-deep tunnel around cake. (Set aside scooped-out cake for another use.) Spoon 1⅓ cups orange cream into tunnel. Replace top of cake to seal filling. Frost top and side of cake with remaining orange cream. Refrigerate at least 2 hours before serving. Garnish with orange peel twists. Store covered in refrigerator.

SWEET TIP When frosting this cake, first seal in the crumbs by spreading a thin layer of orange cream around the side of the cake. Then frost the top and go back over the side for complete coverage.

1 Serving: Calories 420; Total Fat 21g (Saturated Fat 13g; Trans Fat 0.5g); Cholesterol 160mg; Sodium 410mg; Total Carbohydrate 51g (Dietary Fiber 0g); Protein 5g **Exchanges:** 3½ Other Carbohydrate, ½ High-Fat Meat, 3½ Fat **Carbohydrate Choices:** 3½

Strawberry Cream Angel Cake

Prep Time: 15 minutes * **Start to Finish:** 3 hours 30 minutes * **12 SERVINGS**

1 box white angel food cake mix
1¼ cups cold water
1½ cups whipping cream
¾ cup strawberry glaze (from 13.5-oz container)
1 quart fresh strawberries, finely chopped
2 tablespoons sugar

1 Move oven rack to lowest position (remove other racks). Heat oven to 350°F.

2 In extra-large glass or metal bowl, beat cake mix and cold water with electric mixer on low speed 30 seconds. Beat on medium speed 1 minute. Pour into ungreased 10-inch angel food (tube) cake pan. (Do not use fluted tube cake pan or 9-inch angel food pan or batter will overflow.)

3 Bake 37 to 47 minutes or until top is dark golden brown and cracks feel very dry and are not sticky. Do not underbake. Immediately turn pan upside down onto heatproof bottle or funnel until cake is completely cool, about 2 hours.

4 In chilled medium bowl, beat whipping cream on high speed until stiff peaks form. Fold in strawberry glaze. Run knife around side of pan to loosen cake; remove from pan. On serving plate, place cake, browned side down. Frost side and top of cake with strawberry cream. Refrigerate at least 30 minutes.

5 In medium bowl, mix strawberries and sugar; refrigerate until serving time. Slice cake; top each slice with about ¼ cup strawberry mixture. Store covered in refrigerator.

1 Serving: Calories 270; Total Fat 9g (Saturated Fat 6g; Trans Fat 0g); Cholesterol 35mg; Sodium 330mg; Total Carbohydrate 41g (Dietary Fiber 1g); Protein 4g **Exchanges:** 1½ Starch, 1½ Other Carbohydrate, 1½ Fat **Carbohydrate Choices:** 3

SWEET TIP **Look for the strawberry glaze in the produce section of your supermarket.**

Key Lime–Coconut Angel Cake

Prep Time: 25 minutes * Start to Finish: 3 hours * 12 SERVINGS

1 box white angel food cake mix

1¼ cups cold water

1 can (14 oz) sweetened condensed milk (not evaporated)

⅓ cup Key lime or regular lime juice

1 teaspoon grated lime peel

1 container (8 oz) frozen whipped topping, thawed

1 cup flaked coconut

1 Move oven rack to lowest position (remove other racks). Heat oven to 350°F.

2 In extra-large glass or metal bowl, beat cake mix and cold water with electric mixer on low speed 30 seconds; beat on medium speed 1 minute. Pour into ungreased 10-inch angel food (tube) cake pan. (Do not use fluted tube cake pan or 9-inch angel food pan or batter will overflow.)

3 Bake 37 to 47 minutes or until top is dark golden brown and cracks feel very dry and not sticky. Do not underbake. Immediately turn pan upside down onto heatproof bottle or funnel. Let hang about 2 hours or until completely cool.

4 In large bowl, beat condensed milk, lime juice and lime peel with wire whisk until smooth and thickened. Fold in whipped topping.

5 Run knife around side of pan to loosen cake; remove from pan. Cut cake horizontally to make 3 layers. Fill each layer with about 2 cups lime mixture. Frost side and top of cake with remaining lime mixture. Sprinkle with coconut. Store covered in refrigerator.

1 Serving: Calories 340; Total Fat 9g (Saturated Fat 7g; Trans Fat 0g); Cholesterol 10mg; Sodium 380mg; Total Carbohydrate 58g (Dietary Fiber 0g); Protein 6g **Exchanges:** 2 Starch, 2 Other Carbohydrate, 1½ Fat **Carbohydrate Choices:** 4

SWEET TIP **For a pretty finishing touch, garnish each piece of cake with a twisted lime slice.**

Fruit-Topped Lemon Pound Cake

Prep Time: 45 minutes * Start to Finish: 3 hours 45 minutes * **12 SERVINGS**

cake

1½	cups all-purpose flour
½	teaspoon baking powder
⅛	teaspoon salt
⅓	cup lemon curd (from 10-oz jar)
1	cup granulated sugar
¾	cup butter, softened
2	teaspoons grated lemon peel
½	teaspoon vanilla or almond extract
3	eggs
½	cup milk

fruit

4	cups sliced fresh strawberries (about 1½ lb)
3	nectarines, thinly sliced
¼	cup granulated sugar

topping

	Reserved lemon curd
2	cups whipping cream
¼	cup powdered sugar

1 Heat oven to 350°F. Generously grease bottom and sides of 9 x 5-inch loaf pan with shortening; lightly flour. In medium bowl, mix flour, baking powder and salt; set aside.

2 Spoon ⅓ cup lemon curd into small microwavable bowl. Microwave on High 10 to 15 seconds or just until softened. Measure 1 teaspoon into large bowl; reserve remaining lemon curd. In same large bowl, beat 1 cup granulated sugar, the butter, lemon peel, vanilla and eggs with electric mixer on low speed 30 seconds. Beat on high speed 5 minutes, scraping bowl occasionally. Beat flour mixture into sugar mixture alternately with milk on low speed, beating just until smooth after each addition. Pour into pan.

3 Bake 50 to 60 minutes, or until toothpick inserted in center crack comes out clean. Cool 20 minutes; remove from pan to cooling rack. Cool completely, about 2 hours.

4 Meanwhile, in large bowl, mix strawberries, nectarines and ¼ cup granulated sugar; set aside. Refrigerate, if desired.

5 In small microwavable bowl, microwave reserved lemon curd on High 10 to 15 seconds to soften; let cool 5 minutes. Place in large bowl. In chilled medium bowl, beat whipping cream and powdered sugar with electric mixer on high speed until stiff peaks form. Fold whipped cream mixture into lemon curd until thoroughly blended. Cover and refrigerate until serving.

6 Cut cake into 24 slices. For each serving, place 1 slice of cake on dessert plate; spoon about ¼ cup fruit and 2 heaping tablespoons topping over slice. Top with second slice of cake, ¼ cup fruit and 2 heaping tablespoons topping.

1 Serving: Calories 490; Total Fat 29g (Saturated Fat 17g; Trans Fat 1g); Cholesterol 140mg; Sodium 190mg; Total Carbohydrate 52g (Dietary Fiber 2g); Protein 5g **Exchanges:** 1½ Starch, ½ Fruit, 1½ Other Carbohydrate, 5½ Fat **Carbohydrate Choices:** 3½

SWEET TIP **Lemon curd adds an extra touch of lemon flavor to this pound cake. If you like a more tart flavor, add a little extra lemon curd when making the topping.**

Almond-Glazed Pound Cake

Prep Time: 15 minutes * Start to Finish: 2 hours 30 minutes * **12 SERVINGS**

cake
1¾   cups all-purpose flour
 1   cup granulated sugar
¼   cup shortening
¼   cup butter, softened
¾   cup milk
 2   teaspoons baking powder
 1   teaspoon vanilla
½   teaspoon salt
 2   eggs

glaze
½   cup powdered sugar
 1   to 1½ tablespoons milk
¼   teaspoon almond extract

1 Heat oven to 350°F. Grease bottom and sides of 9 × 5-inch loaf pan with shortening; lightly flour.

2 In large bowl, beat all cake ingredients with electric mixer on low speed 30 seconds, scraping bowl constantly. Beat on high speed 3 minutes, scraping bowl occasionally. Pour into pan.

3 Bake 60 to 65 minutes or until toothpick inserted in center comes out clean. Cool 10 minutes; remove from pan to cooling rack (place rack on waxed paper to catch drips from glaze). In small bowl, combine all glaze ingredients until smooth. Brush glaze over warm cake. Cool completely, about 1 hour.

1 Serving: Calories 250; Total Fat 9g (Saturated Fat 4g; Trans Fat 0g); Cholesterol 45mg; Sodium 230mg; Total Carbohydrate 37g (Dietary Fiber 0g); Protein 3g **Exchanges:** 1 Starch, 1½ Other Carbohydrate, 1½ Fat **Carbohydrate Choices:** 2½

Change the Pan Size
Follow the recipe as directed and pour batter into 2 (8 × 4-inch) loaf pans; bake 30 to 35 minutes.

Almond Pound Cake with Cherry-Berry Sauce

Prep Time: 30 minutes * Start to Finish: 3 hours 40 minutes * **16 SERVINGS**

cake

3	**cups all-purpose flour**
2	**teaspoons baking powder**
¾	**teaspoon salt**
¼	**teaspoon ground cinnamon**
1⅓	**cups granulated sugar**
½	**cup butter, softened**
½	**cup vegetable oil**
4	**eggs**
½	**cup milk**
1	**can (12.5 oz) almond pastry filling**

sauce

1½	**cups fresh cranberries**
1	**cup granulated sugar**
⅓	**cup dried cherries, halved**
¾	**cup orange juice**
2	**teaspoons cornstarch**

whipped cream

1	**cup whipping cream**
2	**tablespoons powdered sugar**
½	**teaspoon vanilla**

1 Heat oven to 350°F. Grease 12-cup fluted tube cake pan with shortening; lightly flour. In medium bowl, mix flour, baking powder, salt and cinnamon; set aside.

2 In large bowl, beat 1⅓ cups granulated sugar, the butter, oil and eggs with electric mixer on low speed 30 seconds, scraping bowl constantly. Beat on high speed 5 minutes, scraping bowl occasionally. Beat in flour mixture, milk and pastry filling on low speed until blended. Spread in pan.

3 Bake 55 to 65 minutes or until toothpick inserted in center comes out clean. Cool 20 minutes; remove from pan to cooling rack. Cool completely, about 2 hours.

4 In 2-quart saucepan, mix all sauce ingredients. Cook over medium-high heat, stirring occasionally, until cranberries pop and mixture boils and thickens slightly.

5 In chilled small bowl, beat all whipped cream ingredients with electric mixer on high speed until stiff peaks form. Serve slices of cake with sauce and whipped cream.

1 Serving: Calories 450; Total Fat 21g (Saturated Fat 9g; Trans Fat 0g); Cholesterol 85mg; Sodium 270mg; Total Carbohydrate 59g (Dietary Fiber 2g); Protein 5g **Exchanges:** 1½ Starch, 2½ Other Carbohydrate, 4 Fat **Carbohydrate Choices:** 4

SWEET TIP **To reheat the sauce, microwave uncovered on High 1 to 2 minutes, stirring once.**

Cherry-Almond Picnic Cake

Prep Time: 20 minutes * **Start to Finish:** 2 hours 15 minutes * **16 SERVINGS**

⅓ cup very finely chopped almonds

1 cup granulated sugar

½ cup butter, softened

½ cup milk

½ teaspoon almond extract

1 container (15 oz) ricotta cheese

2 eggs

2½ cups all-purpose flour

1 cup dried cherries or prunes, chopped

1 cup chopped almonds, toasted* if desired

3 teaspoons baking powder

½ teaspoon salt

Powdered sugar, if desired

1 Heat oven to 350°F. Grease 12-cup fluted tube cake pan or 10-inch angel food (tube) cake pan with shortening. Coat pan with ⅓ cup very finely chopped almonds. In large bowl, beat granulated sugar, butter, milk, almond extract, ricotta cheese and eggs on low speed until blended. Beat on medium speed 2 minutes, scraping bowl occasionally. Beat in remaining ingredients except powdered sugar (batter will be very thick). Spread in pan.

2 Bake 55 to 65 minutes or until toothpick inserted near center comes out clean. Cool 20 minutes. Remove from pan to cooling rack. Cool 30 minutes. Sprinkle with powdered sugar. Serve warm or cool.

To toast almonds, heat oven to 350°F. Spread almonds in ungreased shallow pan. Bake uncovered 6 to 10 minutes, stirring occasionally, until light brown.

1 Serving: Calories 330; Total Fat 16g (Saturated Fat 7g; Trans Fat 0g); Cholesterol 55mg; Sodium 250mg; Total Carbohydrate 39g (Dietary Fiber 2g); Protein 8g **Exchanges:** 2 Other Carbohydrate, 1 Milk, 1½ Fat **Carbohydrate Choices:** 2½

Key Lime–Coconut Cream Cake

Prep Time: 30 minutes * Start to Finish: 2 hours 40 minutes * **16 SERVINGS**

cake

- 1 **cup graham cracker crumbs**
- ⅓ **cup packed brown sugar**
- 3 **tablespoons butter, melted**
- 3 **cups all-purpose flour**
- 2½ **teaspoons baking powder**
- ½ **teaspoon salt**
- ¾ **cup butter, softened**
- 1½ **cups granulated sugar**
- 4 **eggs**
- ¾ **cup whipping cream**
- 4 **teaspoons grated lime peel**
- ¼ **cup Key lime juice**
- 1 **cup flaked coconut**

glaze

- 1 **cup powdered sugar**
- ½ **teaspoon grated lime peel**
- 4 **to 5 teaspoons Key lime juice**
- 2 **tablespoons flaked coconut, toasted***

1 Heat oven to 350°F. Grease 12-cup fluted tube cake pan with shortening; lightly flour. In small bowl, mix cracker crumbs, brown sugar and 3 tablespoons butter. In medium bowl, mix flour, baking powder and salt; set aside.

2 In large bowl, beat ¾ cup butter and granulated sugar with electric mixer on medium speed 2 minutes. Add eggs, one at a time, beating after each addition. On low speed, alternately beat in flour mixture and whipping cream. Add 4 teaspoons lime peel and ¼ cup lime juice; beat just until blended. Stir in 1 cup coconut. Sprinkle half of crumb mixture in bottom of pan. Spoon half of batter over mixture in pan; spread evenly. Sprinkle with remaining crumb mixture; top with remaining batter.

3 Bake 45 to 55 minutes or until toothpick comes out clean. Cool 15 minutes. Remove cake from pan to cooling rack. Cool completely, about 1 hour.

4 In small bowl, stir powdered sugar, ½ teaspoon lime peel and 4 to 5 teaspoons lime juice. Spoon glaze over top of cake. Sprinkle with 2 tablespoons coconut. Use serrated knife to cut cake.

To toast coconut, heat oven to 350°F. Spread coconut in ungreased shallow pan. Bake uncovered 5 to 7 minutes, stirring occasionally, until golden brown.

1 Serving: Calories 410; Total Fat 18g (Saturated Fat 11g; Trans Fat 0.5g); Cholesterol 95mg; Sodium 300mg; Total Carbohydrate 57g (Dietary Fiber 1g); Protein 5g **Exchanges:** 1 Starch, 3 Other Carbohydrate, 3½ Fat **Carbohydrate Choices:** 4

SWEET TIP Freshly squeezed lime juice can be used in place of the Key lime juice. One lime yields about 5 teaspoons juice and 3 teaspoons grated peel.

Lemon-Zucchini Pound Cake

Prep Time: 30 minutes * Start to Finish: 2 hours 30 minutes * 16 SERVINGS

cake

- **3 cups all-purpose flour**
- **1 teaspoon baking powder**
- **¼ teaspoon baking soda**
- **¼ teaspoon salt**
- **1 cup butter, softened**
- **2 cups powdered sugar**
- **4 eggs**
- **⅔ cup milk**
- **2 teaspoons grated lemon peel**
- **2 tablespoons lemon juice**
- **1 cup shredded zucchini (about 1 medium), squeezed to drain**

glaze

- **1 cup powdered sugar**
- **1 tablespoon butter, softened**
- **1 tablespoon half-and-half**
- **1 teaspoon grated lemon peel**
- **2 tablespoons lemon juice**

1 Heat oven to 350°F. Grease 12-cup fluted tube cake pan with shortening; lightly flour.

2 In medium bowl, mix flour, baking powder, baking soda and salt. In large bowl, beat 1 cup butter with electric mixer on medium speed about 2 minutes or until creamy. Beat in 2 cups powdered sugar. Add eggs, one at a time, beating well after each addition. Add flour mixture alternately with milk, beating well on low speed. Stir in 2 teaspoons lemon peel, 2 tablespoons lemon juice and the zucchini. Spoon batter into pan.

3 Bake 50 to 60 minutes or until toothpick inserted in center comes out clean. Cool 15 minutes; remove from pan to cooling rack. Cool completely, about 1 hour.

4 Meanwhile, in 1-quart saucepan, heat all glaze ingredients just to boiling over medium heat, stirring constantly; remove from heat. Let stand 30 minutes. Drizzle over cake.

1 Serving: Calories 310; Total Fat 14g (Saturated Fat 7g; Trans Fat 0.5g); Cholesterol 85mg; Sodium 190mg; Total Carbohydrate 42g (Dietary Fiber 0g); Protein 5g **Exchanges:** 2 Starch, 1 Other Carbohydrate, 2 Fat **Carbohydrate Choices:** 3

SWEET TIP **If you prefer an orange glaze, substitute orange juice for the lemon juice and orange peel for the lemon peel.**

Butter-Rum Pound Cake

Prep Time: 20 minutes * **Start to Finish:** 2 hours 55 minutes * **16 SERVINGS**

cake

- **1 box butter recipe yellow cake mix with pudding**
- **1 box (4-serving size) vanilla instant pudding and pie filling mix**
- **¾ cup water**
- **⅓ cup sour cream**
- **¼ cup butter, softened**
- **¼ cup dark rum**
- **1 teaspoon grated orange peel**
- **4 eggs**

frosting

- **½ cup vanilla creamy ready-to-spread frosting**
- **2 teaspoons dark rum**
- **¼ cup chopped pecans**

1 Heat oven to 325°F. Grease and flour 12-cup fluted tube cake pan or 10-inch angel food (tube) cake pan, or spray with baking spray with flour. In large bowl, beat cake mix, dry pudding mix, water, sour cream, butter, ¼ cup rum, the orange peel and eggs with electric mixer on low speed 30 seconds, then on medium speed 2 minutes. Spread in pan.

2 Bake 45 to 55 minutes or until toothpick inserted in center comes out clean. Cool 15 minutes; remove from pan. Cool completely, about 1½ hours.

3 In small microwavable bowl, microwave frosting uncovered on Medium (50%) 15 seconds. Stir in 2 teaspoons rum. Spread over top of cake, allowing some to drizzle down side. Sprinkle with pecans. Store loosely covered.

1 Serving: Calories 230; Total Fat 9g (Saturated Fat 4g; Trans Fat 0.5g); Cholesterol 65mg; Sodium 340mg; Total Carbohydrate 35g (Dietary Fiber 0g); Protein 2g **Exchanges:** 1 Starch, 1½ Other Carbohydrate, 1½ Fat **Carbohydrate Choices:** 2

SWEET TIP To substitute for the rum, you can use water for the ¼ cup rum in the cake. For the frosting, use ½ teaspoon rum extract instead of the 2 teaspoons rum.

Apricot Brandy Pound Cake

Prep Time: 15 minutes * Start to Finish: 3 hours 5 minutes * **16 SERVINGS**

3 cups all-purpose flour

3 cups granulated sugar

1½ cups butter, softened

½ cup sour cream

½ cup apricot brandy or apricot nectar

1 teaspoon almond extract

½ teaspoon salt

½ teaspoon baking powder

6 eggs

1 tablespoon powdered sugar, if desired

1 Heat oven to 325°F. Grease 12-cup fluted tube cake pan or 10-inch angel food (tube) cake pan with shortening; lightly flour.

2 In large bowl, beat all ingredients except powdered sugar with electric mixer on low speed 30 seconds, scraping bowl constantly. Beat on medium speed 2 minutes, scraping bowl occasionally. Pour into pan.

3 Bake 1 hour 25 minutes to 1 hour 30 minutes or until toothpick inserted in center comes out clean. Cool 20 minutes; remove from pan to cooling rack. Cool completely, about 1 hour. Sprinkle with powdered sugar.

1 Serving: Calories 450; Total Fat 21g (Saturated Fat 12g; Trans Fat 0.5g); Cholesterol 120mg; Sodium 270mg; Total Carbohydrate 58g (Dietary Fiber 0g); Protein 5g **Exchanges:** 1½ Starch, 2½ Other Carbohydrate, 4 Fat **Carbohydrate Choices:** 4

SWEET TIP **Freeze this unfrosted pound cake, tightly wrapped, for up to 3 months. Sprinkle with the powdered sugar after thawing.**

Espresso Cake with Mocha Streusel Ribbon

Prep Time: 25 minutes * Start to Finish: 4 hours * **16 SERVINGS**

streusel

- 2 **tablespoons all-purpose flour**
- 2 **tablespoons packed brown sugar**
- 1 **tablespoon instant espresso coffee powder or granules**
- 1 **tablespoon cold butter, cut into 6 pieces**
- ½ **cup miniature semisweet chocolate chips**
- ¼ **cup chopped pecans**

cake

- 3 **cups all-purpose flour**
- 1 **teaspoon baking powder**
- ¼ **teaspoon salt**
- 1 **cup milk**
- ¼ **cup instant espresso coffee powder or granules**
- 2½ **cups granulated sugar**
- 1 **cup butter, softened**
- 1 **teaspoon vanilla**
- 5 **eggs**

glaze

- 3 **tablespoons whipping cream**
- ⅔ **cup miniature semisweet chocolate chips**
- 2 **teaspoons instant espresso coffee powder or granules**

1 Heat oven to 325°F. Grease 12-cup fluted tube cake pan with shortening (do not use cooking spray); lightly flour. In small bowl, mix 2 tablespoons flour, brown sugar and 1 tablespoon espresso powder. Using pastry blender or fork, cut in 1 tablespoon butter pieces until crumbly. Stir in ½ cup chocolate chips and pecans; set aside.

2 In medium bowl, mix 3 cups flour, baking powder and salt; set aside. In 1-cup glass measuring cup, combine milk and ¼ cup espresso powder; set aside.

3 In large bowl, beat granulated sugar, 1 cup butter, the vanilla and eggs with electric mixer on low speed 30 seconds. Beat on high speed 5 minutes, scraping bowl occasionally. Beat flour mixture into sugar mixture alternately with milk mixture on low speed, beating just until smooth after each addition. Spread 3 cups batter into pan. Sprinkle streusel mixture over batter. Carefully spread remaining batter over streusel.

4 Bake 1 hour 30 minutes to 1 hour 40 minutes or until toothpick inserted in center comes out clean and crack at the center top of cake no longer looks moist. Cool 20 minutes; remove from pan to cooling rack. Cool completely, about 2 hours.

5 In small microwavable bowl, combine glaze ingredients. Microwave on High 30 seconds; stir until smooth. Spoon over cake, allowing some to drip down side of cake.

1 Serving: Calories 450; Total Fat 20g (Saturated Fat 11g; Trans Fat 0.5g); Cholesterol 95mg; Sodium 210mg; Total Carbohydrate 61g (Dietary Fiber 2g); Protein 6g **Exchanges:** 2 Starch, 2 Other Carbohydrate, 4 Fat **Carbohydrate Choices:** 4

SWEET TIP Espresso coffee powder is richer and darker than regular instant coffee and gives this cake an intense coffee flavor.

Brown Sugar Cake

Prep Time: 20 minutes * Start to Finish: 3 hours 40 minutes * **16 SERVINGS**

cake

2¼	cups all-purpose flour
½	teaspoon baking powder
½	teaspoon salt
1½	cups packed light brown sugar
¾	cup granulated sugar
1	cup butter, softened
4	eggs
2	teaspoons vanilla
¾	cup milk

sauce

1	cup butter
½	cup packed light brown sugar
2	tablespoons milk
1	tablespoon light corn syrup
1	teaspoon vanilla

1 Heat oven to 350°F. Grease 12-cup fluted tube cake pan with shortening; lightly flour. In medium bowl, mix flour, baking powder and salt; set aside.

2 In large bowl, beat 1½ cups brown sugar, the granulated sugar and butter with electric mixer on low speed 30 seconds, scraping bowl constantly. Beat on medium speed about 5 minutes, until light and fluffy. Add eggs, one at a time, beating well after each. Add 2 teaspoons vanilla. On low speed, alternately beat in flour mixture and ¾ cup milk. Pour into pan. Bake 55 to 65 minutes or until toothpick comes out clean. Cool 10 minutes. Remove cake from pan to cooling rack. Cool completely, about 2 hours.

3 Meanwhile, in 2-quart saucepan, heat all sauce ingredients except vanilla to boiling over medium heat, stirring constantly. Boil and stir 2 minutes. Cool to room temperature. Stir in 1 teaspoon vanilla. Serve warm sauce with cake.

1 Serving: Calories 450; Total Fat 25g (Saturated Fat 15g; Trans Fat 1g); Cholesterol 115mg; Sodium 280mg; Total Carbohydrate 52g (Dietary Fiber 0g); Protein 4g **Exchanges:** 1 Starch, 2½ Other Carbohydrate, 5 Fat **Carbohydrate Choices:** 3½

SWEET TIP **Resist the temptation to use margarine instead of butter in this recipe. Butter will give you far better flavor.**

Cranberry-Filled Sour Cream Coffee Cake with Orange Glaze

Prep Time: 25 minutes * Start to Finish: 2 hours 10 minutes * **16 SERVINGS**

filling

- **2 cups fresh cranberries**
- **½ cup sugar**
- **1 tablespoon grated orange peel**

coffee cake

- **3 cups all-purpose flour**
- **1½ teaspoons baking powder**
- **1½ teaspoons baking soda**
- **¾ teaspoon salt**
- **1½ cups granulated sugar**
- **¾ cup butter, softened**
- **1½ teaspoons vanilla**
- **3 eggs**
- **1½ cups sour cream**

glaze

- **¾ cup powdered sugar**
- **2 to 3 teaspoons orange juice**

1 Heat oven to 350°F. Grease or spray with cooking spray 12-cup fluted tube cake pan. In food processor, place filling ingredients. Cover; process until finely chopped. Set aside.

2 In large bowl, stir flour, baking powder, baking soda and salt until well mixed; set aside.

3 In another large bowl, beat granulated sugar, butter, vanilla and eggs with electric mixer on medium speed 2 minutes, scraping bowl occasionally. Beat about one-quarter of the flour mixture and sour cream at a time alternately into sugar mixture on low speed until blended.

4 Spread half of the batter (about 3 cups) in pan; spoon cranberry filling over batter (do not let filling touch side of pan). Top with remaining batter; spread evenly.

5 Bake 55 to 65 minutes or until toothpick inserted near center comes out clean. Cool 10 minutes in pan on cooling rack. Remove from pan to cooling rack. Cool 20 minutes. In small bowl, mix glaze ingredients until thin enough to drizzle. Drizzle over coffee cake. Serve warm or cool.

1 Serving: Calories 350; Total Fat 14g (Saturated Fat 8g; Trans Fat 0g); Cholesterol 75mg; Sodium 360mg; Total Carbohydrate 51g (Dietary Fiber 1g); Protein 4g **Exchanges:** 1 Starch, 2½ Other Carbohydrate, 2½ Fat **Carbohydrate Choices:** 3½

Candy Cane Cake

Prep Time: 20 minutes ✳ **Start to Finish:** 2 hours 40 minutes ✳ **12 SERVINGS**

cake

1 **box white cake mix with pudding**

Water, vegetable oil and egg whites called for on cake mix box

½ **teaspoon red food color**

½ **teaspoon peppermint extract**

icing

1 **cup powdered sugar**

1 **tablespoon milk or water**

½ **teaspoon vanilla, if desired**

decoration

Crushed candy canes or crushed hard peppermint candies, if desired

1 Heat oven to 350°F (325°F for dark or nonstick pan). Generously grease and flour 12-cup fluted tube cake pan. Make cake batter as directed on box. Pour about 2 cups batter into pan. In small bowl, pour about ¾ cup batter; stir in food color and peppermint extract. Carefully pour pink batter over white batter in pan. Carefully pour remaining white batter over pink batter.

2 Bake and cool cake as directed on box.

3 In small bowl, mix icing ingredients. If necessary, stir in additional milk, 1 teaspoon at a time, until smooth and spreadable. Spread over cake. Sprinkle crushed candy on top. Store loosely covered.

1 Serving: Calories 240; Total Fat 8g (Saturated Fat 2g; Trans Fat 0g); Cholesterol 0mg; Sodium 280mg; Total Carbohydrate 41g (Dietary Fiber 0g); Protein 2g **Exchanges:** 1 Starch, 1½ Other Carbohydrate, 1½ Fat **Carbohydrate Choices:** 3

SWEET TIP **Fluted tube cake pans can be a challenge to grease. Try this: Place a dab of shortening on the outside of a small food-storage plastic bag. Slip the bag on your hand and rub shortening on the inside of the pan. Repeat with more shortening until every nook and cranny is greased. Give the inside of the pan a good sprinkling with flour, shake excess from pan, and your baked cake will slip right out!**

Jeweled Fruitcake

Prep Time: 15 minutes * Start to Finish: 1 day 2 hours * **32 SERVINGS**

2 cups pitted dates (12 oz)

2 cups dried apricots (12 oz)

1½ cups nuts (8 oz)

1 cup red and green maraschino cherries (12 oz), drained

1 cup red and green candied pineapple (7 oz), chopped

¾ cup all-purpose flour

¾ cup sugar

½ teaspoon baking powder

½ teaspoon salt

1½ teaspoons vanilla

3 eggs

Light corn syrup, if desired

1 Heat oven to 300°F. Line 9 × 5- or 8 × 4-inch loaf pan with foil; grease foil with shortening.

2 In large bowl, stir all ingredients except corn syrup until well mixed. Spread in pan.

3 Bake about 1 hour 45 minutes or until toothpick inserted in center comes out clean. If necessary, cover with foil during last 30 minutes of baking to prevent excessive browning.

4 Remove fruitcake from pan (with foil) to cooling rack. For a glossy top, immediately brush with corn syrup. Allow loaf to cool completely and become firm before cutting, about 24 hours. Wrap tightly and store in refrigerator no longer than 2 months.

1 Serving: Calories 200; Total Fat 6g (Saturated Fat 0.5g; Trans Fat 0g); Cholesterol 20mg; Sodium 70mg; Total Carbohydrate 36g (Dietary Fiber 3g); Protein 2g **Exchanges:** 1 Starch, 1 Fruit, 1 Fat **Carbohydrate Choices:** 2½

SWEET TIP **Dried cherries or cranberries can be substituted for the candied pineapple.**

Change the Pan Size

Generously grease bottoms and sides of 8 miniature loaf pans (4½ × 2½ × 1½ inches), with shortening, or line with foil and grease with shortening. Divide batter evenly among pans (about 1 cup each). Bake 55 to 60 minutes or until toothpick inserted in center comes out clean. Remove from pans to cooling rack. Allow loaves to cool completely and become firm before cutting, about 24 hours. Makes 8 mini loaves.

Holiday Chiffon Fruit Cake

Prep Time: 25 minutes * Start to Finish: 3 hours 25 minutes * **16 SERVINGS**

cake

- **7** egg whites
- **½** teaspoon cream of tartar
- **2** tablespoons all-purpose flour or cake flour
- **½** cup red or green candied cherries (or combination)
- **¼** cup finely chopped pecans
- **2** cups all-purpose flour or 2¼ cups cake flour
- **1½** cups granulated sugar
- **3** teaspoons baking powder
- **1** teaspoon salt
- **¾** cup cold water
- **½** cup vegetable oil
- **5** egg yolks
- **2** teaspoons vanilla

frosting

- **1** package (8 oz) cream cheese, softened
- **¼** cup butter, softened
- **1** to 2 tablespoons milk
- **½** teaspoon vanilla
- **3** cups powdered sugar
- Additional chopped pecans, if desired

1 Heat oven to 325°F. In large bowl, beat egg whites and cream of tartar with electric mixer on high speed until stiff peaks form; set aside. In small bowl, mix 2 tablespoons flour and the cherries; snip with kitchen shears into small pieces. Stir in ¼ cup pecans; set aside.

2 In medium bowl, mix 2 cups flour, the granulated sugar, baking powder and salt. Beat in water, oil, egg yolks and vanilla vigorously with spoon until smooth and blended. Gradually pour egg yolk mixture over beaten egg whites, folding with rubber spatula just until blended. Pour half the batter into ungreased 10-inch angel food (tube) cake pan. Spoon cherry mixture over batter to within ½ inch of edge. Top with remaining batter.

3 Bake 50 minutes. Increase oven temperature to 350°F. Bake about 10 minutes longer or until top springs back when touched lightly. Immediately turn upside down onto heatproof bottle or funnel. Let hang about 2 hours or until cake is completely cool. Loosen side of cake with knife or long metal spatula; remove from pan.

4 In medium bowl, beat cream cheese, butter, milk and vanilla on low speed until smooth. Gradually beat in powdered sugar until smooth. Spread frosting on side and top of cake. Sprinkle with additional pecans. Store covered in refrigerator.

1 Serving: Calories 420; Total Fat 17g (Saturated Fat 6g; Trans Fat 0g); Cholesterol 80mg; Sodium 340mg; Total Carbohydrate 60g (Dietary Fiber 0g); Protein 5g **Exchanges:** ½ Starch, 3½ Other Carbohydrate, ½ Medium-Fat Meat, 3 Fat **Carbohydrate Choices:** 4

chapter 4

Fancy
Layer Cakes

Cherry-Chocolate Cake

Prep Time: 25 minutes * Start to Finish: 2 hours 5 minutes * **16 SERVINGS**

cake

4	oz unsweetened baking chocolate
¾	cup cold brewed coffee or water
2¼	cups packed brown sugar
½	cup butter, softened
2	eggs
1	teaspoon vanilla
2¼	cups all-purpose flour or 2½ cups cake flour
1	teaspoon baking powder
¾	teaspoon baking soda
½	teaspoon salt
¾	cup buttermilk

frosting

⅔	cup shortening
⅓	cup butter, softened
¼	cup evaporated milk
¼	teaspoon salt
3	envelopes (1 oz each) premelted unsweetened baking chocolate
6	cups powdered sugar
3	to 4 tablespoons milk

filling

	Reserved 1½ cups frosting
3	tablespoons finely chopped maraschino cherries
1	tablespoon maraschino cherry juice
	Long-stemmed cherries, if desired

1 Heat oven to 350°F. Grease bottoms and sides of 3 (8-inch) round pans with shortening; lightly flour. Heat 4 oz chocolate and the coffee until chocolate is melted; cool. In large bowl, beat brown sugar and ½ cup butter with electric mixer on high speed until fluffy. Add eggs, one at a time, beating well after each addition. Beat in vanilla.

2 In medium bowl, mix flour, baking powder, baking soda and salt. Beat in flour mixture alternately with chocolate mixture and buttermilk, beating after each addition until smooth. Pour into pans.

3 Bake 30 to 35 minutes or until cake springs back when touched lightly or toothpick inserted in center comes out clean. Cool 10 minutes. Remove from pans to cooling rack. Cool completely, about 1 hour.

4 Meanwhile, to make frosting, beat shortening and ⅓ cup butter with electric mixer on high speed until fluffy; beat in evaporated milk, salt and chocolate. Gradually beat in powdered sugar and milk, beating until spreadable. Reserve 1½ cups.

5 To make filling, beat reserved frosting, chopped cherries and cherry juice until blended. Spread half of the filling on cake layer; top with second layer and spread with remaining filling. Top with third layer. Frost side and top of cake. Garnish with long-stemmed cherries.

1 Serving: Calories 630; Total Fat 26g (Saturated Fat 13g; Trans Fat 0g); Cholesterol 50mg; Sodium 320mg; Total Carbohydrate 95g (Dietary Fiber 2g); Protein 5g **Exchanges:** 1½ Starch, 5 Other Carbohydrate, 5 Fat **Carbohydrate Choices:** 6

Chocolate-Toffee Rum Cake

Prep Time: 35 minutes * Start to Finish: 2 hours 40 minutes * **16 SERVINGS**

mousse

- **2 cups whipping cream**
- **1 envelope unflavored gelatin**
- **6 oz semisweet baking chocolate, melted and cooled**
- **¼ cup rum (or 1 teaspoon rum extract and enough water to measure ¼ cup)**
- **2 teaspoons vanilla**

cake

- **2 cups all-purpose flour or 2¼ cups cake flour**
- **¾ cup unsweetened baking cocoa**
- **2 teaspoons baking soda**
- **½ teaspoon baking powder**
- **½ teaspoon salt**
- **1 cup butter, softened**
- **2 cups sugar**
- **2 teaspoons vanilla**
- **2 eggs**
- **1 cup buttermilk**
- **¾ cup sour cream**
- **⅔ cup English toffee sundae syrup**

ganache

- **12 oz unsweetened baking chocolate, grated**
- **1 cup whipping cream**
- **1 tablespoon butter**
- **Chocolate curls, if desired**

1 To make mousse, in small bowl, mix ⅓ cup of the whipping cream and the gelatin; let stand 5 minutes. In medium bowl, mix melted semisweet chocolate and 1 cup of the whipping cream until blended. Stir in gelatin mixture, rum and 2 teaspoons vanilla. In chilled medium bowl, beat remaining ⅔ cup whipping cream on medium speed until soft peaks form; gently stir into chocolate mixture until blended. Refrigerate about 2 hours or until thickened.

2 Heat oven to 350°F. Grease bottoms and sides of 2 (9-inch) round pans with shortening; lightly flour. In medium bowl, mix flour, cocoa, baking soda, baking powder and salt; set aside. In large bowl, beat 1 cup butter, sugar and 2 teaspoons vanilla with electric mixer on medium speed, scraping bowl occasionally, until fluffy. Beat in eggs, one at a time, until blended. Beat in flour mixture alternately with buttermilk and sour cream, beating after each addition until smooth. Pour into pans.

3 Bake 35 to 38 minutes or until toothpick inserted in center comes out clean. Cool 10 minutes; remove from pans to cooling rack. Cool completely, about 1 hour.

4 Cut each cake horizontally to make 2 layers. (Mark side of cake with toothpicks and cut with long, thin serrated knife.) Place 1 layer, cut side up, on serving plate. Spread with about 3 tablespoons of the syrup. Spread one third of the mousse over syrup to within ¼ inch of edge. Repeat with remaining layers, except do not spread syrup or mousse on top layer.

5 To make ganache, place unsweetened chocolate in medium bowl; set aside. In 3-quart saucepan, heat whipping cream and butter to boiling over medium-high heat, stirring constantly. Pour over chocolate; let stand 5 minutes. Stir until smooth. Spread on top and side of cake. Garnish with chocolate curls. Store in refrigerator.

1 Serving: Calories 730; Total Fat 49g (Saturated Fat 30g; Trans Fat 1g); Cholesterol 125mg; Sodium 410mg; Total Carbohydrate 60g (Dietary Fiber 7g); Protein 9g **Carbohydrate Choices:** 4

German Chocolate Crazy Cake

Prep Time: 40 minutes * **Start to Finish:** 2 hours 50 minutes * **16 SERVINGS**

cake

1 box German chocolate
  cake mix with pudding

  Water, vegetable oil and
  eggs called for on cake
  mix box

filling and topping

1½ **cups sugar**

¾ **cup butter**

1 **can (12 oz) evaporated milk**

4 **egg yolks**

1 **package (7 oz) flaked
  coconut (2⅔ cups)**

2 **cups chopped pecans**

3 **teaspoons vanilla**

½ **cup chocolate creamy
  ready-to-spread frosting
  (from 1-lb container)**

1 Heat oven to 350°F. Grease bottoms only of 2 (9-inch) round cake pans with shortening. Make and bake cake mix as directed on box for 9-inch round pans, using water, oil and eggs. Cool 10 minutes. Remove from pans to cooling racks. Cool completely, about 1 hour.

2 Meanwhile, in 3-quart heavy saucepan, mix sugar, butter, milk and egg yolks. Heat to simmering over medium heat, stirring frequently. Cook 9 to 10 minutes, stirring occasionally, until thickened. Remove from heat. Stir in coconut, pecans and vanilla. Cool completely, about 1 hour.

3 Cut each cake layer horizontally into 2 layers. (Mark side of cake with toothpicks and cut with long, thin serrated knife.) On serving plate, place 1 layer, cut side up. Spread with about 1⅓ cups filling. Repeat with second and third layers and 2⅔ cups filling.

4 With serrated knife, cut remaining cake layer into 1½-inch-wide strips. Cut strips into irregular pieces. Place cake pieces randomly over filling to cover top of cake, pressing gently into cake and fitting snugly together. Refrigerate cake several hours before serving, if desired.

5 In small microwavable bowl, microwave frosting 10 seconds on High or until thin enough to drizzle. Drizzle over top of cake. Store covered in refrigerator.

1 Serving: Calories 470; Total Fat 34g (Saturated Fat 13g; Trans Fat 1g); Cholesterol 105mg; Sodium 190mg; Total Carbohydrate 34g (Dietary Fiber 2g); Protein 5g **Exchanges:** ½ Starch, 2 Other Carbohydrate, ½ Lean Meat, 6½ Fat **Carbohydrate Choices:** 2

Chocolate-Hazelnut Truffle Torte

Prep Time: 25 minutes * Start to Finish: 2 hours * **12 SERVINGS**

cake

- **1 cup semisweet chocolate chips (6 oz)**
- **½ cup butter, cut into pieces**
- **½ cup all-purpose flour**
- **4 eggs, separated**
- **½ cup sugar**
- **⅔ cup hazelnuts (filberts), toasted*, finely chopped**

filling and frosting

- **2 cups semisweet chocolate chips (12 oz)**
- **¼ cup butter, cut into pieces**
- **½ cup whipping cream or hazelnut-flavored liquid nondairy creamer**

Whole or chopped hazelnuts, if desired

1 Heat oven to 325°F. Grease bottoms and sides of 2 (9-inch) round pans with shortening. Line pan bottoms with waxed paper or cooking parchment paper.

2 In 2-quart saucepan, melt 1 cup chocolate chips and ½ cup butter over medium heat, stirring constantly; cool 5 minutes. Stir in flour until smooth. Stir in egg yolks until well blended.

3 In large bowl, beat egg whites with electric mixer on high speed until foamy. Beat in sugar, 1 tablespoon at a time, until soft peaks form. Fold chocolate mixture into egg whites. Fold in ⅔ cup hazelnuts. Spread in pans.

4 Bake 25 minutes or until tops of cakes appear dry and toothpick inserted in center comes out clean. Cool 5 minutes. Run knife around side of each cake to loosen; remove from pans to cooling racks. Remove waxed paper. Cool completely, about 1 hour.

5 Meanwhile, in 2-quart saucepan, melt 2 cups chocolate chips and ¼ cup butter over low heat, stirring constantly; remove from heat. Stir in whipping cream. Refrigerate 30 to 40 minutes, stirring frequently, just until thick enough to mound and hold its shape when dropped from a spoon. (If filling becomes too thick, microwave on High 10 to 15 seconds to soften.)

6 Spread ⅔ cup of the filling on bottom cake layer. Top with other layer. Frost top of cake with remaining filling. Garnish with hazelnuts.

* To toast hazelnuts (filberts), heat oven to 350°F. Spread hazelnuts in ungreased shallow pan. Bake uncovered 6 to 10 minutes, stirring occasionally, until light brown.

1 Serving: Calories 490; Total Fat 34g (Saturated Fat 18g; Trans Fat 0.5g); Cholesterol 115mg; Sodium 110mg; Total Carbohydrate 41g (Dietary Fiber 3g); Protein 5g **Exchanges:** 1½ Starch, 1 Other Carbohydrate, 6½ Fat **Carbohydrate Choices:** 3

SWEET TIP **With rubber spatula, fold chocolate mixture into egg whites just until well blended. Overmixing will reduce egg white volume, so fold gently.**

Chocolate Malt Ice-Cream Cake

Prep Time: 30 minutes * Start to Finish: 7 hours 5 minutes * **16 SERVINGS**

1½ cups all-purpose flour

1 cup sugar

¼ cup unsweetened baking cocoa

1 teaspoon baking soda

½ teaspoon salt

⅓ cup vegetable oil

1 teaspoon white vinegar

1 teaspoon vanilla

1 cup water

1 cup chocolate fudge topping

1½ quarts (6 cups) vanilla ice cream, slightly softened

2 cups malted milk ball candies, coarsely chopped

1 cup whipping cream

¼ cup chocolate fudge topping

Additional malted milk ball candies, if desired

1 Heat oven to 350°F. Grease bottom and side of 9- or 10-inch springform pan with shortening; lightly flour. In large bowl, mix flour, sugar, cocoa, baking soda and salt. Add oil, vinegar, vanilla and water. Stir vigorously about 1 minute or until well blended. Immediately pour into pan.

2 Bake 30 to 35 minutes or until toothpick inserted in center comes out clean. Cool completely, about 1 hour.

3 Spread 1 cup fudge topping over cake; freeze about 1 hour or until topping is firm. In large bowl, mix ice cream and coarsely chopped candies; spread over cake. Freeze about 4 hours or until ice cream is firm.

4 In chilled medium bowl, beat whipping cream with electric mixer on high speed until stiff peaks form. Remove side of pan; place cake on serving plate. Top with whipped cream. Melt ¼ cup fudge topping; drizzle over whipped cream. Garnish with additional candies.

1 Serving: Calories 380; Total Fat 20g (Saturated Fat 11g; Trans Fat 0g); Cholesterol 45mg; Sodium 310mg; Total Carbohydrate 45g (Dietary Fiber 2g); Protein 5g **Exchanges:** ½ Starch, 2 Other Carbohydrate, ½ Milk, 3 Fat **Carbohydrate Choices:** 3

Chocolate Tiramisu Cake

Prep Time: 25 minutes * Start to Finish: 2 hours * **8 SERVINGS**

cake
1 box German chocolate cake mix with pudding

Water, vegetable oil and eggs called for on cake mix box

soaking syrup
¼ cup granulated sugar

1 teaspoon instant coffee granules or crystals

¼ cup water

¼ cup coffee-flavored liqueur

filling
1 cup whipping cream

1 container (8 oz) mascarpone cheese or 1 package (8 oz) cream cheese, softened

2 tablespoons powdered sugar

2 teaspoons vanilla

garnish
Unsweetened baking cocoa

1 Heat oven to 350°F. Grease bottoms and sides of 2 (9-inch) round pans with shortening or cooking spray. Make and bake cake as directed on box. Cool 10 minutes. Remove from pans to cooling racks. Cool completely, about 1 hour.

2 In 1-quart saucepan, mix granulated sugar, coffee granules and water. Heat to boiling over medium heat. Boil and stir 1 minute. Remove from heat. Stir in liqueur. Cool completely. Brush flat side of each cake layer with soaking syrup until absorbed. Place cakes in freezer for 5 minutes.

3 In chilled small bowl, beat whipping cream with electric mixer on high speed until stiff peaks form. In another small bowl, beat mascarpone cheese, powdered sugar and vanilla with electric mixer on low speed until blended. Fold whipped cream into mascarpone mixture until smooth. Place 1 cake layer, bottom side up, on serving plate. Spread with half of the mascarpone mixture. Top with second cake layer, bottom side up. Spread with remaining mascarpone mixture. Store in refrigerator. Sprinkle with cocoa before serving.

1 Serving: Calories 640; Total Fat 38g (Saturated Fat 16g; Trans Fat 1g); Cholesterol 135mg; Sodium 540mg; Total Carbohydrate 67g (Dietary Fiber 2g); Protein 7g **Exchanges:** 1½ Starch, 3 Other Carbohydrate, 7½ Fat **Carbohydrate Choices:** 4½

SWEET TIP **If you'd prefer not to use coffee liqueur in the soaking syrup, increase the water to ½ cup and increase the instant coffee granules to 2½ teaspoons.**

Chocolate and Orange Marble Cake

Prep Time: 25 minutes ✴ **Start to Finish:** 2 hours 10 minutes ✴ **12 SERVINGS**

cake

2¾	cups all-purpose flour or 3 cups cake flour
1	teaspoon baking soda
½	teaspoon baking powder
½	teaspoon salt
¾	cup butter, softened
2	cups granulated sugar
4	egg whites
1¾	cups buttermilk
2	envelopes (1 oz each) premelted unsweetened baking chocolate
⅛	teaspoon ground cinnamon, if desired
½	teaspoon orange extract

frosting

½	cup butter, softened
6	cups powdered sugar
¼	cup whipping cream
1	tablespoon grated orange peel
⅓	cup orange juice

topping

Chocolate topping, if desired

Candied orange slices, if desired

1 Heat oven to 350°F. Grease bottoms and sides of 2 (9-inch) round pans with shortening; lightly flour. In medium bowl, mix flour, baking soda, baking powder and salt; set aside. In large bowl, beat ¾ cup butter and the sugar with electric mixer on medium speed until fluffy. Beat in egg whites until light and creamy. Gradually beat in flour mixture alternately with buttermilk until blended.

2 Spoon 2 cups of the batter into small bowl; stir in chocolate and cinnamon. Stir orange extract into remaining batter. Divide orange batter evenly between pans. Drop chocolate batter by spoonfuls randomly onto orange batter. Cut through batters with knife for marbled design.

3 Bake 30 to 35 minutes or until toothpick inserted in center comes out clean. Cool 10 minutes; remove from pans to cooling rack. Cool completely, about 1 hour.

4 To make frosting, in medium bowl, beat ½ cup butter until creamy. Beat in remaining frosting ingredients on high speed until smooth. Fill layers and frost side and top of cake with frosting. Drizzle with chocolate topping. Garnish with candied orange slices. Store covered in refrigerator.

1 Serving: Calories 730; Total Fat 25g (Saturated Fat 15g; Trans Fat 1g); Cholesterol 60mg; Sodium 450mg; Total Carbohydrate 120g (Dietary Fiber 1g); Protein 6g **Exchanges:** 2 Starch, 6 Other Carbohydrate, 5 Fat **Carbohydrate Choices:** 8

Red Velvet Cake

Prep Time: 15 minutes * **Start to Finish:** 2 hours * **12 SERVINGS**

cake

2½	**cups all-purpose flour**
1½	**cups sugar**
2	**tablespoons unsweetened baking cocoa**
1	**tablespoon baking powder**
1	**teaspoon salt**
1½	**cups vegetable oil**
1	**cup buttermilk**
1	**teaspoon vanilla**
1	**bottle (1 oz) red food color**
2	**eggs**

frosting

½	**cup all-purpose flour**
1½	**cups milk**
1½	**cups sugar**
1½	**cups butter, softened**
1	**tablespoon vanilla**

1 Heat oven to 350°F. Grease bottoms and sides of 3 (8- or 9-inch) round pans with shortening; lightly flour.

2 In large bowl, beat all cake ingredients with electric mixer on low speed 30 seconds, scraping bowl constantly. Beat 2 minutes on medium speed, scraping bowl occasionally. Pour into pans.

3 Bake 25 to 35 minutes or until toothpick inserted in center comes out clean. Cool 10 minutes; remove from pans to cooling rack. Cool completely, about 1 hour.

4 In medium saucepan, mix ½ cup flour and 1½ cups milk with wire whisk until smooth. Cook over medium heat until mixture is very thick, stirring constantly. Remove from heat; cool 10 minutes. In large bowl, beat 1½ cups sugar and the butter with electric mixer on medium speed until light and fluffy. Gradually add flour mixture by tablespoonfuls; beat on high speed until smooth. Beat in 1 tablespoon vanilla. Fill and frost cake, using 1 cup frosting between layers. Store covered in refrigerator.

1 Serving: Calories 800; Total Fat 52g (Saturated Fat 20g; Trans Fat 1g); Cholesterol 100mg; Sodium 510mg; Total Carbohydrate 76g (Dietary Fiber 1g); Protein 5g **Exchanges:** 1½ Starch, 3½ Other Carbohydrate, 10½ Fat **Carbohydrate Choices:** 5

Change the Pan Size

Place a paper baking cup in each of 24 regular-size muffin cups. Heat oven and make cake batter as directed in recipe. Spoon batter evenly into muffin cups, filling each about two-thirds full. Bake 20 to 22 minutes or until toothpick inserted in center comes out clean. Remove cupcakes from pan to cooling rack. Cool completely, about 30 minutes. Frost with frosting.

Deep Dark Mocha Torte

Prep Time: 40 minutes * Start to Finish: 2 hours 15 minutes * **12 SERVINGS**

torte
- **1 box chocolate fudge cake mix with pudding**
- **Water, vegetable oil and eggs called for on cake mix box**
- **⅓ cup granulated sugar**
- **⅓ cup rum or water**
- **1¼ teaspoons instant espresso coffee powder or granules**

filling
- **2 packages (8 oz each) cream cheese, softened**
- **1 cup powdered sugar**
- **1 teaspoon vanilla**
- **2 to 3 teaspoons milk**

ganache
- **1½ cups semisweet chocolate chips**
- **6 tablespoons butter (do not use margarine)**
- **⅓ cup whipping cream**

1 Heat oven to 350°F (325°F for dark or nonstick pans). Grease and lightly flour bottoms and sides of 2 (8- or 9-inch) round pans, or spray with baking spray with flour. Make and cool cakes as directed on box. Refrigerate layers about 45 minutes for easier handling.

2 Meanwhile, in 1-quart saucepan, stir granulated sugar, rum and coffee powder until coffee is dissolved. Heat to boiling, stirring occasionally; remove from heat. Cool completely.

3 In medium bowl, beat filling ingredients with electric mixer on low speed just until blended, adding enough milk for spreading consistency; set aside.

4 In 1-quart saucepan, heat ganache ingredients over low heat, stirring frequently, until chips are melted and mixture is smooth. Refrigerate about 30 minutes, stirring occasionally, until slightly thickened.

5 Cut each cake layer horizontally to make 2 layers. (Mark side of cake with toothpicks and cut with long, thin serrated knife.) Brush about 1 tablespoon of the rum mixture over cut side of each layer; let stand 1 minute to soak into cake. Fill each layer with about ⅔ cup filling. Spread ganache over side and top of torte. Store loosely covered in refrigerator.

1 Serving: Calories 600; Total Fat 39g (Saturated Fat 19g; Trans Fat 1g); Cholesterol 120mg; Sodium 500mg; Total Carbohydrate 54g (Dietary Fiber 2g); Protein 6g **Exchanges:** 2 Starch, 1½ Other Carbohydrate, 7½ Fat **Carbohydrate Choices:** 3½

SWEET TIP **If ganache becomes too thick to spread, let it stand at room temperature a few minutes and stir to soften before spreading on torte.**

Mocha Mousse Cake

Prep Time: 20 minutes * Start to Finish: 3 hours 45 minutes * **12 SERVINGS**

cake

1	box chocolate fudge cake mix with pudding
1¼	cups water
⅓	cup vegetable oil
2	tablespoons coffee-flavored liqueur or cold brewed coffee
4	eggs

mousse

¾	cup whipping cream
2	tablespoons granulated sugar
⅓	cup coffee-flavored liqueur or cold brewed coffee
1	cup semisweet chocolate chips (6 oz)
2	teaspoons vanilla

topping

1	cup whipping cream
¾	cup powdered sugar
¼	cup unsweetened Dutch-processed baking cocoa
½	teaspoon vanilla

1 Heat oven to 350°F (325°F for dark or nonstick pans). Grease bottoms and sides of 2 (8-inch) round pans with shortening; lightly flour. In large bowl, beat cake mix, water, oil, 2 tablespoons liqueur and the eggs with electric mixer on low speed 30 seconds, then on medium speed 2 minutes, scraping bowl occasionally. Pour into pans.

2 Bake 34 to 40 minutes, or until toothpick inserted in center comes out clean. Cool 10 minutes. Run knife around sides of pans to loosen cakes; remove from pans to cooling rack. Cool completely, about 1 hour. Refrigerate layers 45 minutes for easier handling.

3 Meanwhile, to make mousse, in 2-quart saucepan, mix ¼ cup of the whipping cream, the granulated sugar and ⅓ cup liqueur. Cook over medium heat, stirring constantly, until sugar is dissolved and mixture simmers; remove from heat. Stir in chocolate chips with wire whisk until chips are melted. Stir in 2 teaspoons vanilla. Pour into large bowl; cool to room temperature, about 10 minutes.

4 In chilled medium bowl, beat remaining ½ cup whipping cream on high speed just until soft peaks form. Fold whipped cream into chocolate mixture. Cover and refrigerate 30 minutes.

5 In another chilled medium bowl, beat topping ingredients on high speed until soft peaks form.

6 Trim off rounded top of 1 cake layer. Cut each cake layer horizontally to make 2 layers. (Mark side of cake with toothpicks and cut with long, thin serrated knife.) Place 1 layer, cut side up, on serving plate; spread with one-third of the mousse. Repeat with second and third layers. Top with fourth layer, cut side down. Spread topping over side and top of cake. Cover; refrigerate at least 1 hour before serving. Store covered in refrigerator.

1 Serving: Calories 470; Total Fat 26g (Saturated Fat 13g; Trans Fat 0g); Cholesterol 120mg; Sodium 350mg; Total Carbohydrate 51g (Dietary Fiber 2g); Protein 5g **Exchanges:** 1½ Starch, 2 Other Carbohydrate, 5 Fat **Carbohydrate Choices:** 3½

Change the Pan Size

Follow the recipe as directed and pour batter into 2 (9-inch) round pans; bake 31 to 37 minutes.

SWEET TIP **In a hurry? You can use 1 container of chocolate whipped ready-to-spread frosting instead of the whipped cream topping.**

Peanut Butter Silk Cake

Prep Time: 20 minutes * Start to Finish: 2 hours 10 minutes * **12 SERVINGS**

cake

- 1 **box yellow cake mix with pudding**
- 1 **cup water**
- ½ **cup creamy peanut butter**
- ⅓ **cup vegetable oil**
- 3 **eggs**

filling and frosting

- ¼ **cup butter**
- ¼ **cup packed brown sugar**
- 1 **cup whipping cream**
- ½ **cup creamy peanut butter**
- 1 **container chocolate creamy ready-to-spread frosting**
- 1 **cup chopped peanuts, if desired**

1 Heat oven to 350°F (or 325°F for dark or nonstick pans). Generously grease or spray bottoms only of 2 (8-inch) round pans with cooking spray.

2 In large bowl, beat cake mix, water, ½ cup peanut butter, the oil and eggs with electric mixer on low speed 30 seconds, then on medium speed 2 minutes, scraping bowl occasionally. Pour into pans.

3 Bake 34 to 38 minutes, or until toothpick inserted in center comes out clean. Cool 10 minutes. Run knife around sides of pans to loosen cakes; remove from pans to cooling rack. Cool completely, about 1 hour. Place cake layers in refrigerator until ready to use.

4 In 2-quart saucepan, melt butter over medium heat; stir in brown sugar. Heat to boiling; boil and stir 1 minute. Remove from heat. Refrigerate 10 minutes.

5 In chilled medium bowl, beat whipping cream on high speed until soft peaks form; set aside. In another medium bowl, beat ½ cup peanut butter and the brown sugar mixture on medium speed until smooth and creamy. Add whipped cream to peanut butter mixture; beat on medium speed until mixture is smooth and creamy.

6 Split each cake layer horizontally to make 2 layers. Fill each layer with about ⅔ cup peanut butter mixture to within ½ inch of edge. Frost side and top of cake with chocolate frosting. Press peanuts onto frosting on side of cake. Store covered in refrigerator.

1 Serving: Calories 610; Total Fat 36g (Saturated Fat 13g; Trans Fat 2.5g); Cholesterol 90mg; Sodium 510mg; Total Carbohydrate 62g (Dietary Fiber 1g); Protein 8g **Exchanges:** 2½ Starch, 1½ Other Carbohydrate, 7 Fat **Carbohydrate Choices:** 4

SWEET TIP **For a fun garnish, top this cake with coarsely cut-up chocolate-covered peanut butter cups. Or dot the top with mini cups that have been cut in half crosswise.**

Change the Pan Size

Follow the recipe as directed and pour batter into 2 (9-inch) round pans; bake 30 to 35 minutes.

Apricots and Cream Cheese Cake

Prep Time: 50 minutes * Start to Finish: 2 hours 20 minutes * **16 SERVINGS**

cake

1	**can (15.5 oz) apricot halves in heavy syrup, well drained**
1	**cup butter, softened**
1¾	**cups granulated sugar**
4	**eggs**
1	**teaspoon vanilla**
2¾	**cups all-purpose flour**
3	**teaspoons baking powder**
½	**teaspoon baking soda**
½	**teaspoon salt**
1	**can (5.5 oz) apricot nectar (about ⅔ cup)**

frosting

4	**oz (half of 8-oz package) cream cheese, softened**
1	**cup butter, softened**
5	**cups powdered sugar**
2	**teaspoons vanilla**
¼	**cup reserved apricot puree**

garnish

5	**soft dried apricots**
¼	**teaspoon granulated sugar**
2	**lemon leaves or rose leaves**

SWEET TIPS An easy way to fill the decorating bag is to fit the bag with the tip, then place the bag, tip side down, in a tall glass. Fold the top edge of the bag down over the outside of the glass and spoon in the frosting.

Do you have only 2 cake pans? Refrigerate the batter for the third layer while you bake the first 2 layers. When the first two cakes are done, wash the pan, prepare the pan as directed, and bake the third layer.

1 Heat oven to 350°F. Grease bottoms and sides of 3 (8- or 9-inch) round pans with shortening. Line pan bottoms with waxed paper or cooking parchment paper; grease again and lightly flour. In food processor bowl with metal blade, process canned apricots 30 seconds or until smooth, scraping bowl after 15 seconds; set aside.

2 In large bowl, beat 1 cup butter and 1¾ cups granulated sugar with electric mixer on medium speed until light and fluffy. Add eggs, one at a time, beating well after each addition. Beat in 1 teaspoon vanilla. Add flour, baking powder, baking soda and salt; beat on low speed until mixed. Measure ¼ cup apricot puree; set aside. Add remaining apricot puree and apricot nectar to batter; beat on low speed until mixed. Beat on medium speed 2 minutes. Spread about 2 cups batter in each pan.

3 Bake 25 to 30 minutes or until toothpick inserted in center comes out clean. Cool in pans 10 minutes; remove from pans to cooling racks. Cool completely, about 40 minutes.

4 In large bowl, beat cream cheese and 1 cup butter with electric mixer on medium speed until creamy. Add powdered sugar, 2 teaspoons vanilla and reserved puree. Beat on low speed until mixed. Beat on medium speed until creamy. Spoon about 1½ cups frosting into decorating bag fitted with medium star tip. Place one cake layer on cake plate, top side down. Spread about ¾ cup frosting over top. With decorating bag, pipe a wavy ring of frosting around outside top edge of cake, extending slightly over edge. Top with second layer, top side down. Repeat frosting and piping. Top with third layer, top side up. Frost top with remaining frosting; pipe edge. (Side of cake is not frosted.)

5 For garnish, separate 2 dried apricots into 4 halves. With rolling pin, roll each apricot half between 2 pieces of plastic wrap to 1½-inch diameter. Set aside. Roll remaining 3 apricots between plastic wrap to about 2-inch diameters. To form rose, roll one of the apricot halves into a tight roll (center of rose). Place remaining 3 apricot halves around roll to form petals, pinching at bottom to secure. Place larger apricot circles around smaller ones, pinching together at bottom to complete rose. Sprinkle lightly with ¼ teaspoon sugar. Place in center of cake. Place lemon leaves next to rose. Store in refrigerator.

1 Serving: Calories 600; Total Fat 27g (Saturated Fat 16g; Trans Fat 1g); Cholesterol 115mg; Sodium 450mg; Total Carbohydrate 83g (Dietary Fiber 1g); Protein 4g **Exchanges:** 1 Starch, 4½ Other Carbohydrate, 5½ Fat **Carbohydrate Choices:** 5½

Date-Nut Spice Cake

Prep Time: 30 minutes * **Start to Finish:** 2 hours * **16 SERVINGS**

cake

2	cups all-purpose flour or 2¼ cups cake flour
1	cup granulated sugar
¾	cup packed brown sugar
¾	cup shortening
1	cup buttermilk
1	teaspoon baking powder
1	teaspoon salt
1	teaspoon ground cinnamon
¾	teaspoon baking soda
½ to 1	teaspoon ground cloves
3	eggs

filling

½	cup orange juice
1	package (8 oz) pitted dates, cut up
1	teaspoon grated orange peel, if desired
¼	cup coarsely chopped walnuts

frosting

¾	cup granulated sugar
¾	cup packed brown sugar
⅓	cup cold water
¼	teaspoon cream of tartar
	Pinch of salt
2	egg whites
1	teaspoon vanilla

1 Heat oven to 350°F. Grease and flour bottoms and sides of 3 (8- or 9-inch) round pans. In large bowl, beat all cake ingredients with electric mixer on low speed 30 seconds. Beat on high speed 3 minutes, scraping bowl occasionally. Pour into pans.

2 Bake 20 to 25 minutes or until toothpick inserted in center comes out clean. Cool 10 minutes; remove from pans to cooling rack. Cool completely, about 1 hour.

3 Meanwhile, to make filling, in 2-quart saucepan over medium heat, heat orange juice and dates 2 to 3 minutes, stirring frequently, until dates are almost tender and mixture thickens. Stir in orange peel. Cool; stir in walnuts.

4 To make frosting, in heavy 3-quart saucepan (do not use nonstick saucepan), beat all ingredients except vanilla with electric mixer on high speed 1 minute, scraping pan constantly. Place over low heat. Beat on high speed about 10 minutes or until stiff peaks form; remove from heat. Add vanilla. Beat on high speed 2 minutes or until fluffy.

5 Spread date filling between cake layers. Frost side and top of cake with frosting. Store cake loosely covered.

1 Serving: Calories 400; Total Fat 12g (Saturated Fat 3g; Trans Fat 0g); Cholesterol 35mg; Sodium 280mg; Total Carbohydrate 67g (Dietary Fiber 2g); Protein 4g **Exchanges:** 1 Starch, ½ Fruit, 3 Other Carbohydrate, 2½ Fat **Carbohydrate Choices:** 4½

SWEET TIP Chopped dried apricots can be used in place of the dates.

Harvest Cake

Prep Time: 25 minutes * Start to Finish: 2 hours 10 minutes * **16 SERVINGS**

cake

1¾	cups all-purpose flour or 2 cups cake flour
1	cup granulated sugar
¾	cup packed brown sugar
2	teaspoons baking powder
1	teaspoon ground cinnamon
¾	teaspoon salt
½	teaspoon baking soda
½	teaspoon ground ginger
½	teaspoon ground nutmeg
1	cup mashed canned yams (vacuum-packed)
1	teaspoon vanilla
¾	cup chopped walnuts
½	cup sweetened dried cranberries
¾	cup butter, softened
½	cup buttermilk
2	eggs

frosting

3	tablespoons butter
½	cup packed brown sugar
3	tablespoons milk
3	cups powdered sugar
½	cup butter, softened
1½	teaspoons vanilla
2	tablespoons milk

1 Heat oven to 350°F. Grease and flour bottoms and sides of 2 (8-inch) round pans. In large bowl, beat all cake ingredients with electric mixer on low speed 30 seconds, scraping bowl occasionally. Beat on high speed 3 minutes, scraping bowl occasionally. Pour into pans.

2 Bake 33 to 38 minutes or until toothpick inserted in center comes out clean. Cool 10 minutes; remove from pans to cooling rack. Cool completely, about 1 hour.

3 Meanwhile, in 1-quart saucepan, heat 3 tablespoons butter and ½ cup brown sugar to boiling over medium heat, stirring frequently. Stir in 3 tablespoons milk; boil 3 minutes, stirring constantly. Remove from heat; cool to room temperature. In large bowl, beat powdered sugar, ½ cup butter and the vanilla with electric mixer on medium speed until smooth. Beat in brown sugar mixture and 2 tablespoons milk until smooth and spreadable. Fill layers and frost top and side of cake with frosting.

1 Serving: Calories 490; Total Fat 21g (Saturated Fat 11g; Trans Fat 0.5g); Cholesterol 70mg; Sodium 390mg; Total Carbohydrate 71g (Dietary Fiber 1g); Protein 4g **Exchanges:** 4½ Other Carbohydrate, ½ Lean Meat, 4 Fat **Carbohydrate Choices:** 5

SWEET TIP Dried cherries can be used in place of the cranberries, and pecans will be as delicious instead of the walnuts.

Carrot-Cranberry Cake

Prep Time: 20 minutes * Start to Finish: 2 hours 5 minutes * **12 SERVINGS**

cake

1¾	cups all-purpose flour or 2 cups cake flour
2	teaspoons baking soda
2	teaspoons baking powder
2	teaspoons ground cinnamon
½	teaspoon salt
½	teaspoon ground allspice
1½	cups granulated sugar
1	cup mayonnaise or sour cream
3	eggs
1	tablespoon ginger-flavored brandy or water
2	cups shredded carrots (about 4 medium)
1	can (8 oz) crushed pineapple in juice, undrained
½	cup chopped pecans or walnuts
½	cup sweetened dried cranberries

frosting

2	packages (3 oz each) cream cheese, softened
3	tablespoons butter, softened
½	teaspoon ginger-flavored brandy or vanilla
⅛	teaspoon salt, if desired
2½	to 3 cups powdered sugar
	Sugared cranberries, if desired
	Sugared orange peel, if desired

1 Heat oven to 350°F. Grease bottoms and sides of 3 (8-inch) round pans with shortening; lightly flour. In medium bowl, mix flour, baking soda, baking powder, cinnamon, ½ teaspoon salt and allspice; set aside. In large bowl, beat sugar, mayonnaise and eggs with electric mixer on medium speed until blended, scraping bowl occasionally. Beat in 1 tablespoon brandy. Gradually beat in flour mixture until batter is smooth. Stir in carrots, pineapple, pecans and cranberries. Pour into pans.

2 Bake 30 to 35 minutes or until toothpick inserted in center comes out clean. Cool 10 minutes; remove from pans to cooling rack. Cool completely, about 1 hour.

3 Meanwhile, in medium bowl, beat cream cheese, butter, ½ teaspoon brandy and ⅛ teaspoon salt on medium speed until smooth. Gradually beat in powdered sugar on low speed until smooth and spreadable. Fill layers and frost side and top of cake with frosting. Garnish with cranberries and orange peel. Store covered in refrigerator.

1 Serving: Calories 570; Total Fat 27g (Saturated Fat 7g; Trans Fat 0g); Cholesterol 75mg; Sodium 590mg; Total Carbohydrate 75g (Dietary Fiber 2g); Protein 5g **Exchanges:** ½ Starch, 4 Other Carbohydrate, ½ Milk, 4½ Fat **Carbohydrate Choices:** 5

SWEET TIP Regular brandy can be substituted for the ginger-flavored brandy in the cake and frosting; add ⅛ teaspoon ground ginger with the cake's dry ingredients.

Banana-Ginger-Macadamia Cake

Prep Time: 25 minutes * Start to Finish: 2 hours * **12 SERVINGS**

cake

2	cups all-purpose flour
1½	teaspoons baking powder
1	teaspoon baking soda
2	teaspoons ground ginger
1	teaspoon ground nutmeg
¼	teaspoon salt
1½	cups granulated sugar
½	cup butter, softened
2	eggs
1¼	cups mashed ripe bananas (2 to 3 medium)
¾	cup buttermilk
½	cup finely chopped macadamia nuts (not toasted)

frosting

4	oz (half of 8-oz package) cream cheese, softened
½	cup butter, softened (do not use margarine)
4	cups powdered sugar
1	teaspoon vanilla

garnish

¼	cup coarsely chopped toasted* macadamia nuts

1 Heat oven to 350°F. Grease bottoms only of 2 (9-inch) round pans with shortening or cooking spray. Line bottoms with cooking parchment paper; grease and flour paper and sides of pans. In medium bowl, mix flour, baking powder, baking soda, ginger, nutmeg and salt.

2 In large bowl, beat granulated sugar and ½ cup butter with electric mixer on medium speed 3 to 4 minutes or until fluffy. On low speed, beat in eggs, one at a time, beating well after each addition. Beat in bananas. (Mixture will look curdled.) Alternately beat in flour mixture and buttermilk, beginning and ending with flour mixture. Stir in ½ cup nuts. Spread batter evenly in pans.

3 Bake 30 to 35 minutes or until dark golden brown and cakes begin to pull away from sides of pans. Cool 5 minutes; remove from pans to cooling racks. Cool completely, about 1 hour.

4 In large bowl, beat frosting ingredients with electric mixer on medium speed until smooth.

5 On serving plate, place 1 cake layer, rounded side down. Spread with half of frosting. Place remaining cake layer, rounded side up, on frosting, pressing gently to secure (frosting should show around edge). Spread frosting on top of cake, leaving side unfrosted. Sprinkle ¼ cup nuts around top edge of cake.

To toast macadamia nuts, heat oven to 350°F. Spread nuts in ungreased shallow pan. Bake uncovered 6 to 10 minutes, stirring occasionally, until light brown.

1 Serving: Calories 600; Total Fat 25g (Saturated Fat 13g; Trans Fat 0.5g); Cholesterol 85mg; Sodium 380mg; Total Carbohydrate 89g (Dietary Fiber 2g); Protein 5g **Exchanges:** 1 Starch, 5 Other Carbohydrate, 5 Fat **Carbohydrate Choices:** 6

SWEET TIP **Put overripe bananas, unpeeled, in the freezer for later use. When you're ready to use them, just thaw, cut off one end and squeeze the banana into a measuring cup. The banana will be very mushy and not look great, but it'll work just fine in your recipe.**

Butter Brickle Cake

Prep Time: 15 minutes ✻ Start to Finish: 2 hours 15 minutes ✻ **16 SERVINGS**

1 **box yellow cake mix with pudding**
1 **package (4-serving size) butterscotch instant pudding and pie filling mix**
1 **cup water**
½ **cup butter, melted**
4 **eggs**
2 **packages (8 oz each) toffee bits, about 2 cups**
1 **tablespoon all-purpose flour**
1½ **cups whipping cream**
2 **tablespoons packed brown sugar**

1 Heat oven to 350°F (325°F for dark or nonstick pans). Generously grease bottom and sides of 2 (9-inch) round pans or spray with baking spray with flour. (Do not use 8-inch rounds because batter will overflow.)

2 In large bowl, beat cake mix, dry pudding mix, water, butter and eggs with electric mixer on low speed 30 seconds; beat on medium speed 2 minutes. In small bowl, toss ½ cup of the toffee bits with flour; stir into cake batter (batter will be thick). Spoon batter evenly into pans.

3 Bake 30 to 35 minutes or until toothpick inserted in center comes out clean. Cool 10 minutes. Run knife around sides of pans to loosen cakes; remove from pans to cooling racks. Cool completely, about 1 hour.

4 In chilled large bowl, beat whipping cream and brown sugar with electric mixer on high speed until soft peaks form. Spread about ½ cup whipped cream mixture over 1 cake layer to within about ¼ inch of edge; sprinkle with ½ cup of the toffee bits. Top with second layer. Frost side and top of cake with remaining whipped cream mixture. Press remaining 1 cup toffee bits into side of cake. Store covered in refrigerator.

1 Serving: Calories 610; Total Fat 35g (Saturated Fat 20g, Trans Fat 1.5g); Cholesterol 155mg; Sodium 660mg; Total Carbohydrate 70g (Dietary Fiber 0g); Protein 4g **Exchanges:** 1 Starch, 3½ Other Carbohydrate, 7 Fat **Carbohydrate Choices:** 4½

SWEET TIP The flavor of this easy cake is amazing! For the best results and flavor, use toffee bits that are very fresh—check the date on the package for freshness.

Spice Cake with Dulce de Leche Frosting

Prep Time: 1 hour 10 minutes * Start to Finish: 2 hours * 16 SERVINGS

cake

1½ cups butter, softened
1½ cups packed brown sugar
 1 cup granulated sugar
 ½ cup milk
 1 teaspoon vanilla
 5 eggs
 3 cups all-purpose flour
 1 teaspoon baking powder
 2 teaspoons ground cinnamon
 ½ teaspoon salt
 ¼ teaspoon ground nutmeg
 ¼ teaspoon ground ginger
 ⅛ teaspoon ground cloves

caramel acorns

16 vanilla caramels, unwrapped
 3 tablespoons plus 16 miniature semisweet chocolate chips
 ¾ teaspoon shortening
 1 teaspoon turbinado sugar (raw sugar) or coarse sugar

frosting

 ½ cup butter, softened
 1 can (13.4 oz) dulce de leche (caramelized sweetened condensed milk)
 1 teaspoon vanilla
 4 cups powdered sugar
 ¼ cup whipping cream
 ⅛ teaspoon salt
   Cinnamon sticks, if desired

1 Heat oven to 325°F. Grease bottoms and sides of 3 (8-inch) round pans with shortening; lightly flour. In large bowl, beat 1½ cups butter, 1½ cups brown sugar and 1 cup granulated sugar with electric mixer on medium speed until well blended, scraping bowl frequently. Add milk, 1 teaspoon vanilla and eggs. Beat on medium speed 3 minutes, scraping bowl occasionally. Beat in remaining cake ingredients until mixture is smooth and well blended. (Batter will be thick.) Spread about 2½ cups batter in each pan.

2 Bake 25 to 30 minutes or until toothpick inserted in center comes out clean. Cool 10 minutes. Run sharp knife around edges of pans; remove from pans to cooling racks. Cool completely, about 40 minutes.

3 Meanwhile, place 16 caramels on microwavable plate. Microwave on High 15 seconds or until softened. Roll each into ball; pinch one side of ball to form acorn shape. Line cookie sheet with waxed paper. In microwavable custard cup, heat 3 tablespoons chocolate chips and shortening on High 45 seconds or until melted; stir until smooth. Dip tops of acorns into chocolate; press one chocolate chip onto top of each acorn for stem. Sprinkle with turbinado sugar. Place on cookie sheet. Let stand until chocolate sets, about 15 minutes.

4 In large bowl, beat ½ cup butter with electric mixer on medium speed 30 seconds. Beat in dulce de leche and 1 teaspoon vanilla, scraping bowl frequently. On low speed, beat in powdered sugar, 1 cup at a time. Add whipping cream and ⅛ teaspoon salt; beat until smooth and spreading consistency.

5 Using serrated knife, cut rounded top off each cake layer to make a level surface. Spread about ¾ cup frosting between cake layers. Frost top and side with remaining frosting. Place acorns on top of cake. Break cinnamon sticks as desired to resemble twigs; place with acorns on cake.

1 Serving: Calories 720; Total Fat 30g (Saturated Fat 18g; Trans Fat 1g); Cholesterol 135mg; Sodium 410mg; Total Carbohydrate 104g (Dietary Fiber 1g); Protein 7g **Exchanges:** 2 Starch, 5 Other Carbohydrate, 6 Fat **Carbohydrate Choices:** 7

SWEET TIP **If you have only 2 cake pans, refrigerate the batter for the third pan. Once the first 2 pans have baked, cooled 10 minutes and the cakes have been removed, wash the pan, grease and flour it, then bake the third layer.**

Coconut Cake

Prep Time: 50 minutes ✳ Start to Finish: 2 hours ✳ **16 SERVINGS**

cake

2¾	cups all-purpose flour
2	teaspoons baking powder
1	teaspoon salt
1	cup butter, softened
2	cups sugar
4	whole eggs
1½	teaspoons vanilla
1½	teaspoons almond extract
1	cup milk

frosting

1½	cups sugar
½	cup water
4	egg whites
½	teaspoon cream of tartar
⅛	teaspoon salt
6	large marshmallows, cut into small pieces

filling

2	tablespoons sugar
¼	cup reduced-fat (lite) coconut milk (not cream of coconut)
2	to 3 cups flaked coconut

1 Heat oven to 350°F. Grease bottoms and sides of 3 (9-inch) round pans with shortening; lightly flour. In medium bowl, mix flour, baking powder and 1 teaspoon salt; set aside.

2 In large bowl, beat butter with electric mixer on medium speed 30 seconds. Gradually add 2 cups sugar, ¼ cup at a time, beating well after each addition. Beat 2 minutes longer. Add whole eggs, one at a time, beating well after each addition. Beat in vanilla and almond extract. On low speed, alternately add flour mixture and milk, beating just until blended. Divide batter evenly among pans.

3 Bake 18 to 20 minutes or until toothpick inserted in center comes out clean. Cool 10 minutes; remove from pans to cooling racks. Cool completely, about 1 hour.

4 In heavy 2-quart saucepan, mix 1½ cups sugar and the water. Cook over medium heat, stirring constantly, until mixture is clear. Cook, without stirring, to 240°F on candy thermometer, about 10 minutes. Meanwhile, in large bowl, beat egg whites with electric mixer on low speed until foamy. Add cream of tartar and ⅛ teaspoon salt; beat on medium speed until soft peaks form. Increase speed to high; pour hot syrup into egg white mixture. Add marshmallows, a few pieces at a time, beating until stiff peaks form and frosting is thick enough to spread.

5 In small microwavable bowl, microwave 2 tablespoons sugar and the coconut milk on High 1 minute; stir until sugar dissolves. Brush half of the coconut milk mixture over 1 cake layer to within ½ inch of edge. Frost with 1 cup of the frosting; sprinkle with ½ cup of the coconut. Top with second cake layer; brush with remaining coconut milk mixture. Frost with 1 cup frosting; sprinkle with ½ cup coconut. Top with remaining cake layer. Spread remaining frosting on top and side of cake; sprinkle with remaining coconut.

1 Serving: Calories 460; Total Fat 17g (Saturated Fat 11g; Trans Fat 0g); Cholesterol 80mg; Sodium 400mg; Total Carbohydrate 70g (Dietary Fiber 1g); Protein 5g **Exchanges:** ½ Starch, 4 Other Carbohydrate, ½ Lean Meat, 3 Fat **Carbohydrate Choices:** 4½

Strawberry-Lime Daiquiri Poke Cake

Prep Time: 35 minutes * Start to Finish: 2 hours 15 minutes * **12 SERVINGS**

1 box white cake mix
with pudding

Water, vegetable oil and
egg whites called for on
cake mix box

2 tablespoons grated lime
peel

1 cup water

⅔ cup light rum

⅓ cup lime juice (from 2 limes)

2 boxes (4-serving size each)
strawberry- or strawberry
Daiquiri–flavored gelatin

2½ cups vanilla whipped
ready-to-spread frosting
(from two 1-lb containers)

Fresh strawberries and lime
slices, if desired

1 Make and bake cake mix as directed on box for 2 (8-inch) round pans, adding grated lime peel to batter. Remove from pan to cooling rack; cool completely, about 1 hour. Wash and dry cake pans.

2 Return cooled cake layers to clean 8-inch round pans. With thin stirring straw, toothpick or skewer, pierce cakes at ½-inch intervals.

3 In 1-quart saucepan, heat 1 cup water to boiling. Remove from heat; stir in rum, lime juice and gelatin. Stir until completely dissolved. Spoon half of gelatin mixture over each cake. Refrigerate 1 to 3 hours to allow gelatin to set in cakes.

4 To remove cakes from pans, dip pans in warm water 10 seconds. Unmold 1 cake onto serving platter; spread about 1 cup frosting on top of cake. Unmold second cake; carefully place on first cake on platter.

5 Frost side and top of cake with remaining frosting. Refrigerate 1 hour before serving. Garnish with strawberries and lime. Loosely cover and refrigerate any remaining cake.

1 Serving: Calories 470 (Calories from Fat 140); Total Fat 16g (Saturated Fat 4.5g, Trans Fat 2.5g); Cholesterol 0mg; Sodium 390mg; Total Carbohydrate 69g (Dietary Fiber 0g, Sugars 52g); Protein 3g **Carbohydrate Choices:** 4½

SWEET TIP **Light rum works best in this recipe to give a light flavor, but you could use dark or spiced rum in a pinch.**

Raspberry-Laced Vanilla Cake

Prep Time: 25 minutes * Start to Finish: 2 hours 5 minutes * **16 SERVINGS**

cake

2⅔ cups all-purpose flour
3 teaspoons baking powder
½ teaspoon salt
¼ teaspoon baking soda
1½ cups butter, softened
1¼ cups granulated sugar
⅔ cup milk
1½ teaspoons vanilla
4 eggs

filling and frosting

1 cup butter, softened
3 cups powdered sugar
½ cup raspberry-flavored liqueur or raspberry syrup for pancakes
½ teaspoon vanilla
1 cup seedless raspberry jam
Fresh raspberries, if desired

1 Heat oven to 350°F. Grease bottoms and sides of 3 (9-inch) round pans with shortening; lightly flour.

2 In small bowl, mix flour, baking powder, salt and baking soda; set aside. In large bowl, beat 1½ cups butter and the granulated sugar with electric mixer on high speed, scraping bowl occasionally, until fluffy. On medium speed, beat in flour mixture, milk, 1½ teaspoons vanilla and the eggs until blended. Beat 2 minutes longer. Pour into pans.

3 Bake 25 to 30 minutes or until toothpick inserted in center comes out clean. Cool 10 minutes; remove cakes from pans to cooling racks. Cool completely, about 1 hour.

4 In medium bowl, beat 1 cup butter and the powdered sugar on medium speed until smooth. Gradually beat in liqueur and ½ teaspoon vanilla until smooth and spreadable.

5 Cut each cake horizontally to make 2 layers. (Mark side of cake with toothpicks and cut with long, thin serrated knife.) Place 1 layer, cut side up, on serving plate; spread with ⅓ cup jam to within ¼ inch of edge. Top with another layer, cut side down; spread with ⅓ cup frosting. Repeat with remaining layers.

6 Frost side and top of cake with remaining frosting. Garnish with raspberries. Store loosely covered.

1 Serving: Calories 590; Total Fat 31g (Saturated Fat 19g; Trans Fat 1g); Cholesterol 130mg; Sodium 420mg; Total Carbohydrate 71g (Dietary Fiber 0g); Protein 4g **Exchanges:** 1 Starch, 4 Other Carbohydrate, 6 Fat **Carbohydrate Choices:** 5

SWEET TIP If you only have 2 round pans, cover and refrigerate one-third of the batter while the other two layers bake. Remove the baked cakes from the pans and wash the pan before you bake the last layer.

Vanilla Cake with Fondant Ribbons

Prep Time: 2 hours 10 minutes ∗ Start to Finish: 3 hours ∗ **16 SERVINGS**

cake

2	**cups all-purpose flour**
1¾	**cups granulated sugar**
½	**cup butter, softened**
1	**teaspoon baking powder**
¾	**teaspoon baking soda**
1	**teaspoon salt**
1	**cup buttermilk**
2	**teaspoons vanilla**
3	**eggs**

frosting and fondant

⅔	**cup butter, softened**
1	**bar (4 oz) white chocolate baking bar, melted and cooled**
3	**to 4 tablespoons milk**
2	**teaspoons vanilla**
6	**cups powdered sugar**
	Fondant (page 176)
	Purple or lavender paste food color

1 Heat oven to 350°F. Grease bottoms and sides of 3 (8- or 9-inch) round pans with shortening. Line pan bottoms with waxed paper or cooking parchment paper; grease again and lightly flour. In large bowl, beat all cake ingredients with electric mixer on low speed 30 seconds. Beat on high speed 3 minutes. Spread 1½ cups batter in each pan.

2 Bake 20 to 25 minutes or until toothpick inserted in center comes out clean. Cool 10 minutes; remove from pans to cooling racks. Remove waxed paper. Cool completely, about 40 minutes.

3 In large bowl, beat ⅔ cup butter and melted white chocolate with electric mixer on low speed until creamy. Beat in 2 tablespoons of the milk and 2 teaspoons vanilla. Gradually beat in powdered sugar on low speed until blended. Add additional milk, 1 tablespoon at a time, until frosting is smooth and spreadable. Place 1 cake layer on cake plate, top side up. Spread ¾ cup frosting over top. Top with another layer, top side down; spread with ¾ cup frosting. Top with remaining layer, top side up. Frost side and top of cake with remaining frosting; set aside.

4 Make fondant as directed in recipe. Shape fondant into brick; cut in half. Wrap half tightly in plastic wrap; set aside. Grease rolling pin with some of the shortening in fondant recipe. Add food color to half of fondant until desired color for the darkest of the ribbons (there will be 6 ribbons, 2 of each color: 1 dark pair, 1 medium pair, 1 light pair). Roll with hands into 15-inch log. Roll with greased rolling pin into 26 × 2½-inch strip. Cut two ¾-inch-wide strips the length of the fondant. With small brush or finger, lightly brush water around bottom inch of cake. Fold one strip back onto itself and transfer to cake. Gently press ribbon to bottom edge of cake, pleating slightly. With knife, trim off any excess to create small seam. Repeat with second ribbon, slightly overlapping first ribbon and beginning and ending at same spot as first ribbon so all seams align.

5 To remaining dark purple trimmings, knead in enough of the reserved white fondant to make about 1 cup medium-colored fondant. Roll, cut and attach 2 more ribbons as directed without pleating. Repeat for last and lightest color of ribbons. With remaining fondant trimmings, cut small purple circles with appetizer cutter or sharp knife. Garnish top of cake with fondant circles.

1 Serving: Calories 820; Total Fat 24g (Saturated Fat 12g, Trans Fat 0.5g); Cholesterol 70mg; Sodium 410mg; Total Carbohydrate 146g (Dietary Fiber 0g); Protein 4g **Exchanges:** 1½ Starch, 8 Other Carbohydrate, 4½ Fat **Carbohydrate Choices:** 10

Fondant

Prep Time: 30 minutes * Start to Finish: 30 minutes *
2½ POUNDS (COVERS 13 × 9-INCH CAKE OR 8- OR 9-INCH
2-LAYER CAKE); 16 SERVINGS

6¾ cups miniature marshmallows (from 1-lb bag)
3 to 5 tablespoons water
6 cups powdered sugar
1½ teaspoons vanilla
½ cup shortening
    Paste food color, if desired

1 In large microwavable bowl, place marshmallows and 3 tablespoons of the water. Microwave uncovered on High 90 seconds, stirring every 30 seconds until mixture is smooth. Fold in 1½ cups of the powdered sugar. Stir in vanilla.

2 Generously grease hands and counter with some of the shortening. Place marshmallow mixture on counter. Sprinkle 1 cup of the powdered sugar over marshmallow mixture; knead as you would dough. Continue to gradually add remaining 3½ cups powdered sugar, greasing hands and counter often to prevent sticking. (If fondant begins to tear, it is too dry.) Add remaining water, ½ teaspoon at a time, and knead until fondant forms a smooth, elastic ball that will stretch without tearing, about 8 minutes. Shape fondant into a brick shape; wrap in a double thickness of plastic wrap, squeezing out any air.

3 Roll or shape fondant on surface sprinkled with powdered sugar, and as directed in recipe. Add food color as desired. When not working with fondant, keep it covered with plastic wrap to prevent it from drying out.

1 Serving: Calories 310; Total Fat 6g (Saturated Fat 1.5g; Trans Fat 0g); Cholesterol 0mg; Sodium 20mg; Total Carbohydrate 62g (Dietary Fiber 0g); Protein 0g **Exchanges:** ½ Starch, 3½ Other Carbohydrate, 1 Fat **Carbohydrate Choices:** 4

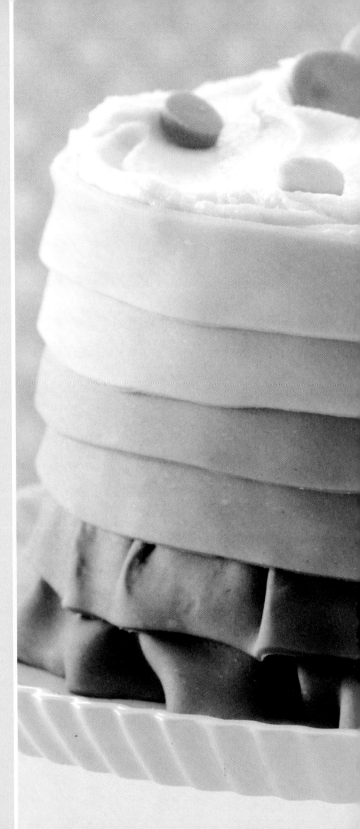

Citrus Cake with Lemon Whipped Cream Frosting

Prep Time: 30 minutes * Start to Finish: 2 hours 10 minutes * **12 SERVINGS**

cake

- **1 box lemon cake mix with pudding**
- **½ cup water**
- **½ cup orange juice**
- **½ cup vegetable oil**
- **3 eggs**

filling and frosting

- **2 cups whipping cream**
- **¼ cup powdered sugar**
- **1 can (15.75 oz) lemon pie filling**
- **2 teaspoons grated orange peel**
- **Strips of lemon and orange peel**

1 Heat oven to 350°F for shiny metal pans (325°F for dark or nonstick pans). Grease bottoms and sides of 2 (8- or 9-inch) round pans with shortening or cooking spray; lightly flour (or spray with cooking spray or baking spray with flour).

2 In large bowl, beat cake ingredients with electric mixer on low speed 30 seconds, then on medium speed 2 minutes, scraping bowl occasionally. Pour into pans.

3 Bake and cool as directed on box.

4 In chilled medium bowl, beat whipping cream and powdered sugar with electric mixer on high speed until stiff peaks form. Fold in ½ cup of the pie filling and the grated orange peel.

5 Place 1 cake layer, rounded side down, on serving plate. Spread remaining pie filling over layer to within ¼ inch of edge. Top with second layer, rounded side up. Spread whipped cream mixture over side and top of cake. Garnish top of cake with strips of lemon and orange peel. Store covered in refrigerator.

1 Serving: Calories 430; Total Fat 27g (Saturated Fat 12g; Trans Fat 0.5g); Cholesterol 110mg; Sodium 410mg; Total Carbohydrate 43g (Dietary Fiber 0g); Protein 4g **Exchanges:** 1 Starch, 2 Other Carbohydrate, 5½ Fat **Carbohydrate Choices:** 3

SWEET TIP **Instead of using pie filling, try lemon, lime or orange curd. Look for 10-ounce jars of curds near the jams and jellies at your supermarket.**

Heavenly Almond-Apricot Layer Cake

Prep Time: 50 minutes * Start to Finish: 2 hours 35 minutes * **16 SERVINGS**

cake

- **2 cups all-purpose flour**
- **¾ cup almond flour**
- **2 teaspoons baking powder**
- **½ teaspoon salt**
- **1½ cups granulated sugar**
- **¾ cup butter, softened**
- **1 cup milk**
- **3 eggs**
- **¼ teaspoon almond extract**

frosting and filling

- **6 cups powdered sugar**
- **⅔ cup butter, softened**
- **¼ cup plus 2 to 3 tablespoons milk**
- **1 teaspoon vanilla**
- **½ teaspoon almond extract**
- **1 jar (12 oz) apricot preserves (1 cup)**

garnish

- **¾ cup toasted* sliced almonds**

1 Heat oven to 350°F. Grease bottoms and sides of 2 (8-inch) round pans with shortening; lightly flour. In large bowl, combine all cake ingredients. Beat with electric mixer on low speed until blended. Beat on medium speed 2 minutes. Spread batter in pans.

2 Bake 35 to 40 minutes, or until cake springs back when touched lightly in center. Cool 10 minutes; remove from pans to cooling racks. Cool completely, about 1 hour. Wrap each cake layer in plastic wrap; freeze 15 minutes or refrigerate 30 minutes. With long, sharp serrated knife, cut each cake layer horizontally into 2 layers.

3 Meanwhile, in large bowl, beat powdered sugar, ⅔ cup butter and ¼ cup milk with electric mixer on low speed until blended. Beat in vanilla, almond extract and enough additional milk to make frosting smooth and spreadable.

4 In small bowl, stir preserves until softened. Cut up any large pieces of fruit. On serving plate, place 1 cake layer, cut side up. Frost with ¾ cup frosting; spread ⅓ cup preserves to within ¼ inch of edge. Repeat with second and third cake layers, frosting and preserves. Top with remaining cake layer, cut side down; frost top and side with remaining frosting. Press sliced almonds generously onto side of cake.

*To toast almonds, heat oven to 350°F. Spread almonds in ungreased shallow pan. Bake uncovered 6 to 10 minutes, stirring occasionally, until light brown.

1 Serving: Calories 570; Total Fat 22g (Saturated Fat 11g; Trans Fat 0.5g); Cholesterol 80mg; Sodium 310mg; Total Carbohydrate 86g (Dietary Fiber 1g); Protein 4g **Exchanges:** 1½ Starch, 4 Other Carbohydrate, 4½ Fat **Carbohydrate Choices:** 6

Change the Pan Size

Follow the recipe as directed and pour batter into 2 (9-inch) round pans; bake 25 to 30 minutes.

Tangerine Ombre Cake

Prep Time: 1 hour * Start to Finish: 2 hours 10 minutes * **16 SERVINGS**

cake

- **1** box white cake mix with pudding
- **1¼** cups tangerine or orange juice
- **1** box (4-serving size) orange-flavored gelatin
- **⅓** cup vegetable oil
- **4** eggs
  Orange gel food color

frosting

- **2** cups butter, softened
- **12** cups powdered sugar
- **¾** cup fresh tangerine or orange juice
- **1** tablespoon vanilla

1 Heat oven to 350°F. Grease or spray bottoms and sides of 4 (8-inch) round pans with cooking spray; place 8-inch round piece cooking parchment paper in bottom of each pan. Grease or spray parchment paper. In large bowl, beat all cake ingredients except food color on low speed 30 seconds, then on high speed about 2 minutes or until smooth. Spoon and spread 1½ cups of the batter into 1 pan. Divide remaining batter evenly among 3 small bowls (about 1½ cups each). Add different amounts of food color to each to make different shades of the same color. Stir each until color is well blended.

2 Pour 1 bowl of batter into each of 3 remaining pans. Baking 2 pans at a time, bake 22 to 26 minutes (refrigerate remaining pans until baking). Cool 5 minutes. Remove from pans to cooling rack; remove parchment paper. Cool completely, about 30 minutes.

3 In large bowl, beat butter and powdered sugar with spoon or electric mixer on low speed until blended. Stir in ¾ cup tangerine juice and the vanilla. If frosting is too thick, beat in more juice, a few drops at a time. If too thin, beat in a small amount of powdered sugar.

4 To assemble, place deepest color cake layer on cake plate. Spread with ½ cup frosting. Stack layers from darkest to lightest, spreading ½ cup frosting between layers. Thinly spread top and side of cake with 1½ cups frosting to seal in crumbs. Divide remaining frosting among 4 small bowls. Add different amounts of food color to each to make different shades of the same color to match cake layers.

5 To frost, place each color in individual resealable food-storage plastic bag. Cut ½ inch off 1 corner of each bag, and pipe each frosting on corresponding color cake layer. Pipe a dot of frosting and use back of table spoon to spread frosting horizontally around cake, with deepest color at bottom and working up to lighter colors; repeat around cake, slightly overlapping dots of frosting. To frost top, use remaining frosting as desired. Store cake loosely covered in refrigerator.

1 Serving: Calories 770 (Calories from Fat 270); Total Fat 30g (Saturated Fat 16g, Trans Fat 1g); Cholesterol 110mg; Sodium 450mg; Total Carbohydrate 121g (Dietary Fiber 0g, Sugars 106g); Protein 3g **Exchanges:** 1 Starch, 7 Other Carbohydrate, 6 Fat **Carbohydrate Choices:** 8

SWEET TIP **If you don't have enough pans, store batter covered in the refrigerator while baking other layers. Cool pans completely before baking the next layers.**

Pink Champagne Layer Cake

Prep Time: 30 minutes * Start to Finish: 2 hours 15 minutes * **12 SERVINGS**

cake

1	**box white cake mix with pudding**
1¼	**cups champagne, room temperature**
⅓	**cup vegetable oil**
3	**egg whites**
4	**or 5 drops red food color**

frosting

½	**cup butter, softened**
4	**cups powdered sugar**
¼	**cup champagne, room temperature**
1	**teaspoon vanilla**
4	**to 5 drops red food color**

garnishes, if desired

Pink decorator sugar crystals

Edible pink pearls and/or edible pink glitter

1 Heat oven to 350°F (325°F for dark or nonstick pans). Spray bottoms and sides of 2 (8- or 9-inch) round pans with baking spray with flour.

2 In large bowl, stir cake mix and 1¼ cups champagne. Add oil, egg whites and food color; beat with electric mixer on medium speed 2 minutes. Pour into pans.

3 Bake as directed on box. Cool 10 minutes. Remove cakes from pans to cooling racks. Cool completely, about 1 hour.

4 In medium bowl, beat frosting ingredients with electric mixer on medium speed until smooth. On serving plate, place 1 cake layer, rounded side down. Frost top of cake layer. Top with second layer, rounded side up. Frost side and top of cake. Sprinkle with garnishes. Store loosely covered.

1 Serving: Calories 460; Total Fat 15g (Saturated Fat 7g; Trans Fat 0g); Cholesterol 20mg; Sodium 340mg; Total Carbohydrate 72g (Dietary Fiber 0g); Protein 2g **Exchanges:** ½ Starch, 4½ Other Carbohydrate, 3 Fat **Carbohydrate Choices:** 5

SWEET TIPS Champagne is a sparkling wine, and while many expensive champagnes are available, this is one time you can use less expensive champagne.

Sprinkle garnishes on cake just before serving to maximize sparkle and keep them from absorbing moisture and melting into frosting.

Peaches and Buttercream Cake

Prep Time: 50 minutes * Start to Finish: 2 hours * **16 SERVINGS**

cake

2¾	**cups all-purpose flour**
1	**teaspoon baking powder**
1	**teaspoon baking soda**
½	**teaspoon salt**
2½	**cups peach slices (canned or frozen and thawed, drained, or fresh)**
⅔	**cup peach nectar or juice**
2	**teaspoons vanilla**
1	**teaspoon grated orange peel**
1	**cup butter, softened**
¾	**cup granulated sugar**
3	**eggs**

filling and frosting

3	**cups butter, softened**
12	**cups powdered sugar**
6	**tablespoons reserved peach puree**
1½	**teaspoons vanilla**
1	**or 2 drops pink gel food color**
1	**or 2 drops orange gel food color**

SWEET TIPS The first layer of frosting for this cake is called a crumb coat. It coats and sets the crumbs so they don't combine with the outer frosting, making for a much prettier cake.

Got leftover pureed peaches? Add them to a smoothie for a delicious flavor twist.

1 Heat oven to 350°F. Grease bottoms and sides of 3 (8- or 9-inch) round pans with shortening; lightly flour. In medium bowl, mix flour, baking powder, baking soda and salt; set aside. Place peach slices in blender container. Cover; blend about 30 seconds or until smooth. Pour 1 cup pureed peaches into small bowl; stir in peach nectar, 2 teaspoons vanilla and orange peel. Reserve remaining puree for frosting.

2 In large bowl, beat 1 cup butter with electric mixer on medium speed 30 seconds. Gradually add granulated sugar, about ¼ cup at a time, beating well after each addition. Beat 2 minutes longer. Add eggs, one at a time, beating well after each addition. On low speed, alternately add flour mixture, about one-third at a time, and peach mixture, about half at a time, beating just until blended. Pour 2 cups batter into each pan.

3 Bake 25 to 30 minutes or until toothpick inserted in center comes out clean. Cool 10 minutes; remove from pans to cooling racks. Cool completely, about 40 minutes.

4 For filling, in large bowl, beat 1 cup of the butter with electric mixer on medium speed until creamy. Beat in 4 cups of the powdered sugar on low speed, 1 cup at a time, until smooth. Beat in 2 tablespoons reserved peach puree and ½ teaspoon vanilla. Place 1 cake layer on cake plate, top side up. Spread ⅔ cup frosting over top. Top with second layer, top side down; spread with ⅔ cup filling. Top with remaining layer, top side up. Thinly frost side and top of cake with remaining filling; set aside.

5 In large bowl, beat remaining 2 cups butter with electric mixer on medium speed until creamy. Beat in remaining 8 cups powdered sugar on low, about 1 cup at a time, until creamy. Beat in 4 tablespoons peach puree, 1 teaspoon vanilla and food color until desired peach color.

6 Fill decorating bag fitted with large open star tip (½-inch opening). Starting about 1½ inches from bottom edge of cake, make center of rosette flower by squeezing frosting in a tight circle. Continue making concentric circles around center, to make flower about 3 inches in diameter. Make flowers to cover side of cake, staggering up and down around cake. Make flowers on top of cake and fill in open spaces with wavy lines.

1 Serving: Calories 940; Total Fat 47g (Saturated Fat 29g, Trans Fat 2g); Cholesterol 155mg; Sodium 610mg; Total Carbohydrate 122g (Dietary Fiber 1g); Protein 4g **Exchanges:** 1 Starch, 7 Other Carbohydrate, 9½ Fat **Carbohydrate Choices:** 8

Lemon Buttercream Cake with Blueberries

Prep Time: 40 minutes * Start to Finish: 4 hours 40 minutes * **12 SERVINGS**

2¾ cups all-purpose flour

2½ teaspoons baking powder

1 teaspoon salt

1½ cups granulated sugar

¾ cup butter, softened

3 eggs

1¼ cups milk

1 cup powdered sugar

⅓ cup lemon juice

1½ cups butter, softened

4 cups powdered sugar

3 tablespoons milk

2 tablespoons lemon juice

3 cups fresh blueberries

3 teaspoons grated lemon peel

1 Heat oven to 350°F. Grease and flour bottoms and sides of 2 (8- or 9-inch) round pans. In bowl, mix flour, baking powder and salt. In large bowl, beat granulated sugar and ¾ cup butter with electric mixer on medium speed until fluffy. Add eggs, one at a time, beating well. On low speed, alternately beat in flour mixture and milk until blended. Pour into pans.

2 Bake 25 to 35 minutes or until toothpick comes out clean. Cool 10 minutes. With fork, poke tops every 1 inch. Mix 1 cup powdered sugar and ⅓ cup lemon juice until smooth. Spoon over cakes. Let stand 10 minutes. Remove from pans; place top side up on cooling racks. Cool completely, about 1 hour.

3 In large bowl, beat 1½ cups butter, 4 cups powdered sugar, 3 tablespoons milk and 2 tablespoons lemon juice on low speed until blended. Beat 3 minutes on medium speed until fluffy.

4 On plate, place 1 cake layer, rounded side up. Spread with ½ cup frosting. Top with 1½ cups berries. Spoon ¾ cup frosting over berries; carefully spread to cover. Place remaining layer, top side up, over berries. Frost top and side. Arrange remaining berries on cake. Sprinkle with lemon peel. Refrigerate 2 hours. Before serving, let cake stand at room temperature 15 minutes. Store in refrigerator.

1 Serving: Calories 770; Total Fat 37g (Saturated Fat 23g; Trans Fat 1.5g); Cholesterol 145mg; Sodium 570mg; Total Carbohydrate 104g (Dietary Fiber 2g); Protein 6g **Exchanges:** 2 Starch, 5 Other Carbohydrate, 7 Fat **Carbohydrate Choices:** 7

SWEET TIP **One medium lemon yields about 3 tablespoons juice and 2 to 3 teaspoons grated lemon peel.**

Italian Cream Cake

Prep Time: 45 minutes * Start to Finish: 2 hours * **16 SERVINGS**

cake

- ½ cup butter, softened
- 2 cups granulated sugar
- 5 eggs
- 2 cups all-purpose flour
- 1 teaspoon baking soda
- 1 cup buttermilk
- ½ cup vegetable oil
- 1 teaspoon vanilla
- 1 cup flaked coconut

frosting and garnish

- 12 oz cream cheese, softened
- ¼ cup butter, softened
- 1 teaspoon vanilla
- 5 cups powdered sugar
- 1 to 2 tablespoons milk
- ½ cup chopped pecans
- 16 pecan halves

1 Heat oven to 350°F. Grease bottoms and sides of 3 (8- or 9-inch) round pans with shortening. Line pan bottoms with waxed paper or cooking parchment paper; grease again and lightly flour. In large bowl, combine ½ cup butter and granulated sugar; beat with electric mixer on low speed until creamy.

2 Add eggs; beat on medium speed until creamy. Add flour and baking soda; mix on low speed until mixed. Beat on medium speed until smooth. Add buttermilk, oil and 1 teaspoon vanilla; beat on low speed until mixed. Beat on medium speed 2 minutes or until smooth and creamy. Fold in coconut. Spoon one-third of batter (about 2 cups) into each pan.

3 Bake 20 to 25 minutes, or until toothpick inserted in center comes out clean. Cool in pans 10 minutes; remove from pans to cooling racks. Remove waxed paper. Cool completely, about 45 minutes.

4 In large bowl, combine cream cheese, ¼ cup butter, 1 teaspoon vanilla, powdered sugar and 1 tablespoon of the milk. Beat with electric mixer on low speed until blended. Gradually beat in enough remaining milk to make frosting smooth and spreadable.

5 Place 1 cake layer on cake plate, top side up. Spread with ⅔ cup frosting. Top with another layer, top side down; spread with ⅔ cup frosting. Top with remaining layer, top side up. Spread side and top of cake with remaining frosting. Press chopped pecans into side of cake. Top cake with pecan halves. Store in refrigerator.

1 Serving: Calories 630; Total Fat 31g (Saturated Fat 13g; Trans Fat 0.5g); Cholesterol 105mg; Sodium 270mg; Total Carbohydrate 80g (Dietary Fiber 1g); Protein 6g **Exchanges:** 2 Starch, 3½ Other Carbohydrate, 6 Fat **Carbohydrate Choices:** 5

SWEET TIP Do you have only 2 cake pans? Refrigerate the batter for the third pan. Once the first 2 pans have baked, cooled 10 minutes and the cakes have been removed, wash the pan. Prepare the pan as directed; bake the third layer.

Lemon Velvet Cream Cake

Prep Time: 20 minutes * **Start to Finish:** 3 hours 50 minutes * **12 SERVINGS**

1 **box lemon cake mix with pudding**

Water, vegetable oil and eggs called for on cake mix box

1 **package (3 oz) cream cheese, softened**

1 **tablespoon milk**

1 **tablespoon grated lemon peel**

2 **cups whipping cream**

⅔ **cup powdered sugar**

Lemon twist, if desired

1 Heat oven to 350°F (325°F for dark or nonstick pans). Grease bottoms only of 2 (8- or 9-inch) round pans with shortening (do not use cooking spray).

2 Make, bake and cool cake as directed on box. Refrigerate layers 45 minutes for easier handling.

3 Meanwhile, in large bowl, beat cream cheese, milk and 1 tablespoon lemon peel with electric mixer on low speed until smooth. Beat in whipping cream and powdered sugar. Beat on high speed, scraping bowl occasionally, until stiff peaks form.

4 Slice each cake layer in half horizontally to make a total of 4 layers. (Mark side of cake with toothpicks and cut with long, thin serrated knife.) Fill each layer with ½ cup whipped cream mixture. Frost side and top of cake with remaining whipped cream mixture. Garnish with lemon twist. Store covered in refrigerator.

1 Serving: Calories 430; Total Fat 29g (Saturated Fat 13g; Trans Fat 0.5g); Cholesterol 115mg; Sodium 320mg; Total Carbohydrate 38g (Dietary Fiber 0g); Protein 3g **Exchanges:** 1 Starch, 1½ Other Carbohydrate, 5½ Fat **Carbohydrate Choices:** 2½

SWEET TIP **For a quick frosting, stir 2 teaspoons grated lemon peel into each of 2 containers of whipped cream whipped ready-to-spread frosting.**

Lemon Meringue Cake

Prep Time: 30 minutes * Start to Finish: 2 hours 10 minutes * **8 SERVINGS**

1½ **cups cake flour**
¾ **cup sugar**
1½ **teaspoons baking powder**
½ **teaspoon salt**
¾ **cup shortening**
⅔ **cup milk**
1½ **teaspoons vanilla**
4 **eggs, separated**
1 **cup sugar**
1 **package (4-serving size) lemon pudding and pie filling mix (not instant)**

1 Heat oven to 325°F. Grease sides of 2 (9- or 8-inch) round pans. Line bottoms of pans with cooking parchment paper.

2 In medium bowl, beat flour, ¾ cup sugar, the baking powder, salt, shortening, milk, vanilla and egg yolks with electric mixer on low speed 30 seconds, scraping bowl constantly. Beat on high speed 2 minutes, scraping bowl occasionally. (Batter will be stiff.) Spread evenly in pans.

3 In small bowl, beat egg whites with electric mixer on medium speed until foamy. Beat in 1 cup sugar, 1 tablespoon at a time, on high speed until stiff peaks form. Spread half of mixture over batter in each pan. Bake 30 to 35 minutes or until meringue looks set and dry. Cool 10 minutes. Loosen meringues from edges of pans with knife point if necessary. Carefully remove from pans and peel off paper. Cool completely, meringue sides up on cooling racks, about 1 hour.

4 Prepare pudding mix as directed on package for pudding. Refrigerate about 1½ hours or until chilled. Spread 1¼ cups pudding over meringue on 1 cake layer. Place remaining layer on top, meringue side up. Top with remaining pudding. Serve within 30 minutes.

1 Serving: Calories 530; Total Fat 23g (Saturated Fat 6g; Trans Fat 0g); Cholesterol 95mg; Sodium 350mg; Total Carbohydrate 76g (Dietary Fiber 0g); Protein 6g **Exchanges:** 1 Starch, 4 Other Carbohydrate, ½ Medium-Fat Meat, 4 Fat **Carbohydrate Choices:** 5

SWEET TIP **To substitute for cake flour, use 1½ cups minus 3 tablespoons all-purpose flour.**

Red, White and Blue Layered Flag Cake

Prep Time: 1 hour * Start to Finish: 2 hours 30 minutes * **18 SERVINGS**

red cake layers

- 1 **box white cake mix with pudding**
- 1 **pint (2 cups) strawberries, stems removed, pureed in blender or food processor to about 1¼ cups**
- ⅓ **cup vegetable oil**
- 3 **egg whites**
- 1 **teaspoon red gel paste food color**

blue cake layer

- ½ **box white cake mix with pudding (about 1⅔ cups dry mix)**
- ½ **cup blueberries, pureed in blender or food processor**
- 3 **tablespoons vegetable oil**
- 2 **whole eggs**
- ½ **teaspoon blue gel paste food color**

white cake layer

- ½ **box white cake mix with pudding (about 1⅔ cups dry mix)**
- ½ **cup water**
- 2 **tablespoons vegetable oil**
- 2 **egg whites**

frosting and sprinkles

- 3 **containers fluffy white whipped ready-to-spread frosting**
  Red, white and blue sprinkles, as desired

SWEET TIP Don't have a 4-inch round biscuit cutter? Cut out a 4-inch circle of cooking parchment paper, and use it as a pattern.

1 For all cake layers, heat oven to 350°F. Grease or spray with cooking spray bottoms and sides of 4 (8-inch) round pans; place 8-inch round piece of cooking parchment paper in bottom of each pan. Grease or spray parchment paper.

2 To make red cake layers, in large bowl, beat red cake ingredients with electric mixer on low speed 30 seconds, then on high speed about 2 minutes or until smooth. Spread evenly in two of the pans. Bake 29 to 34 minutes or until top springs back when lightly touched. Cool 10 minutes; run knife around sides of pans to loosen cakes. Gently remove from pans to cooling rack; remove parchment paper. Cool completely, about 30 minutes. Flatten cake layers by trimming off rounded tops. Cut layers in half horizontally to make 4 thin red layers. In 1 layer, cut small round out of center, using 4-inch biscuit cutter. Wrap and freeze 1 thin layer and the layer that was cut out of; save for another use.

3 To make blue and white cake layers, in medium bowl, for each color, beat blue or white cake ingredients with electric mixer on low speed 30 seconds, then on high speed about 2 minutes or until smooth. Spread each color cake in one pan. Bake 29 to 34 minutes or until top springs back when lightly touched. Cool 10 minutes; run knife around side of pan to loosen cake. Gently remove from pans to cooling racks; remove parchment paper. Cool completely, about 30 minutes. Flatten each cake layer by trimming off rounded top. Do not cut blue cake in half horizontally. Cut small round out of center, using 4-inch round biscuit cutter. Wrap and freeze 4-inch round; save for another use. Cut white cake in half horizontally to make 2 thin white layers. In 1 layer, cut small round out of center, using 4-inch biscuit cutter. Wrap and freeze the layer that was cut out of; save for another use.

4 Place 1 red cake layer on cake plate; spread ⅓ cup frosting on top. Top with 1 white cake layer; spread ⅓ cup frosting on top. Top with second red layer; spread ⅓ cup frosting on top. Gently top with blue layer. Carefully spread thin layer of frosting on cut edge inside of blue layer. Gently insert white 4-inch cake round; top with frosting and then red 4-inch cake round; press slightly. Frost side and top of cake using remaining frosting. Top with sprinkles. Store loosely covered in refrigerator.

1 Serving: Calories 590 (Calories from Fat 230); Total Fat 25g (Saturated Fat 7g, Trans Fat 4g); Cholesterol 25mg; Sodium 470mg; Total Carbohydrate 87g (Dietary Fiber 1g, Sugars 62g); Protein 4g **Exchanges:** 1 Starch, 5 Other Carbohydrate, 5 Fat **Carbohydrate Choices:** 6

Green Tea with Lemon Cake

Prep Time: 45 minutes * Start to Finish: 2 hours 20 minutes * **12 SERVINGS**

cake

- **1 tablespoon finely ground green tea powder**
- **¾ cup milk**
- **2¼ cups all-purpose flour**
- **1⅓ cups granulated sugar**
- **2½ teaspoons baking powder**
- **1 teaspoon salt**
- **⅔ cup butter, softened**
- **1 teaspoon vanilla**
- **5 egg whites**

frosting

- **2½ cups butter, softened**
- **4 teaspoons grated lemon peel**
- **2 to 3 tablespoons lemon juice**
- **6 cups powdered sugar**

garnish

- **Lemon peel**

1 Heat oven to 350°F. Grease bottoms and sides of 2 (9-inch) round pans with shortening; lightly flour. In 1-cup microwavable measuring cup, stir tea powder into milk. Microwave 30 to 45 seconds on High or until warm. Stir until tea is dissolved; cool 10 minutes.

2 In large bowl, beat tea mixture and all remaining cake ingredients except egg whites with electric mixer on low speed 30 seconds. Beat on high speed 2 minutes, scraping bowl occasionally. Beat in egg whites on high speed 2 minutes, scraping bowl occasionally. Pour into pans.

3 Bake 30 to 35 minutes, or until toothpick inserted in center comes out clean. Cool 10 minutes; remove from pans to cooling racks. Cool completely, about 1 hour.

4 Meanwhile, in medium bowl, beat 2½ cups butter, 4 teaspoons lemon peel and lemon juice with electric mixer on medium speed 30 seconds. Gradually beat in powdered sugar. Beat 2 to 3 minutes longer or until light and fluffy.

5 Place 1 cake layer on cake plate, top side down. Spread with 1½ cups frosting. Top with second layer, top side up. Frost side and top of cake. Decorate as desired with remaining frosting. Garnish with lemon peel.

1 Serving: Calories 870; Total Fat 49g (Saturated Fat 31g; Trans Fat 2g); Cholesterol 130mg; Sodium 760mg; Total Carbohydrate 102g (Dietary Fiber 0g); Protein 5g **Exchanges:** 1½ Starch, 5½ Other Carbohydrate, 9½ Fat **Carbohydrate Choices:** 7

SWEET TIP Finely ground green tea powder can be found in health-food stores or co-ops near the other bulk teas.

Marzipan Princess Cake

Prep Time: 2 hours 5 minutes * Start to Finish: 25 hours 50 minutes * **12 SERVINGS**

marzipan covering
and decoration
    Marzipan (page 199)

cake
6	**eggs, separated**
1	**cup granulated sugar**
1½	**cups all-purpose flour**
1	**teaspoon baking powder**
½	**teaspoon salt**
¾	**cup butter, melted, slightly cooled**
1	**teaspoon vanilla**

filling
1	**box (6-serving size) vanilla pudding and pie filling mix (not instant)**
1¾	**cups half-and-half**
¼	**cup whipping cream**
1	**tablespoon powdered sugar**
½	**teaspoon vanilla**
½	**cup red raspberry preserves (not seedless jam)**

frosting
½	**cup butter, softened**
2	**cups powdered sugar**
1	**teaspoon vanilla**
2	**to 4 tablespoons milk**
	Yellow confetti sprinkles, if desired

1 At least a day before assembling, make the marzipan.

2 Heat oven to 350°F (325°F for dark or nonstick pans). Grease bottoms and sides of 2 (9-inch) round pans with shortening; lightly flour. Line pan bottoms with waxed paper or cooking parchment paper; grease again and lightly flour. In large bowl, beat egg whites with electric mixer on high speed, gradually adding ¼ cup of the granulated sugar until stiff peaks form. Set aside. In medium bowl, combine flour, baking powder and salt; set aside.

3 In another large bowl, beat egg yolks with remaining ¾ cup granulated sugar on high speed until thick and pale yellow, about 1 minute. Reduce speed to low. Gradually beat in melted butter and vanilla until smooth. Fold 1 cup of the egg whites into egg yolk mixture until well blended. Fold in remaining egg whites until blended. Sift flour over batter, one-third at a time, folding in each time. Spread one-third of batter (about 1¼ cups) into 1 pan. Spread the remaining batter (about 2½ cups) in second pan. Place both pans in oven.

4 Bake smaller cake 10 to 15 minutes; larger cake 17 to 22 minutes or until top springs back when touched lightly in center. Cool 10 minutes. Remove from pans to cooling racks. Cool completely, about 40 minutes. Refrigerate larger cake 20 minutes before assembling cake.

5 In 1½-quart saucepan, stir pudding mix and half-and-half. Bring to a boil over medium heat, stirring constantly. Pour into bowl; place plastic wrap directly on top of pudding. Cool 15 minutes; refrigerate until completely chilled, at least 2 hours. Just before assembling cake, beat pudding with electric mixer on medium speed until smooth. In small bowl, beat whipping cream, 1 tablespoon powdered sugar and ½ teaspoon vanilla on high speed until stiff peaks form. Stir whipped cream into pudding until blended.

To assemble the cake, turn to page 198.

Marzipan Princess Cake, continued

6 To assemble cake, using long, thin serrated knife, cut large cake horizontally into 2 layers. Place smaller cake on cake plate; spread top with ¼ cup of the preserves. Spread half of the pudding mixture (about 1¼ cups) over preserves, mounding slightly in center and tapering at edge. Place second layer (half of larger cake), cut side up over filling. Spread with remaining preserves. Spoon and spread remaining pudding mixture over preserves. Top with remaining cake layer, top side up. With serrated knife, trim top edge of cake so edge is slightly rounded. Refrigerate cake until ready to frost.

7 In large bowl, beat ½ cup butter, 2 cups powdered sugar, 1 teaspoon vanilla and 2 tablespoons of the milk with electric mixer on low speed until mixed. Beat on medium speed until smooth, adding milk, 1 teaspoon at a time, until spreading consistency. Place ¼ cup frosting in small bowl; cover and set aside. Spread thin layer of remaining frosting over top and side of cake. Cover and refrigerate until ready to cover with marzipan.

8 For marzipan covering for cake, generously sprinkle work surface with powdered sugar. With rolling pin, roll green marzipan to 14- to 15-inch round, adding powdered sugar and rotating disk every few rolls to prevent sticking. Roll marzipan onto rolling pin and gently unroll over cake. Press marzipan gently against top and side of cake to mold to cake and create a smooth surface. With sharp knife, trim off extra marzipan at bottom edge of cake. Roll green trimmings until ¼ inch thick; cut into ½-inch-wide strip with pastry wheel or knife. Attach to bottom of cake.

9 For daisies, generously sprinkle work surface with powdered sugar; roll marzipan to ¼-inch thickness. With sharp knife or daisy cutter, make several daisy shapes. Place daisies on top of cake, overlapping petals as desired. Place yellow confetti sprinkle in center of each daisy. Store cake in refrigerator.

1 Serving: Calories 770; Total Fat 32g (Saturated Fat 17g; Trans Fat 1g); Cholesterol 165mg; Sodium 410mg; Total Carbohydrate 111g (Dietary Fiber 1g); Protein 8g **Exchanges:** 2½ Starch, 5 Other Carbohydrate, 6 Fat **Carbohydrate Choices:** 7½

Marzipan

Prep Time: 30 minutes * Start to Finish: 24 hours 30 minutes * **16 SERVINGS**

- 1 package (7 oz) almond paste
- 3 cups powdered sugar
- 3 tablespoons light corn syrup
- 1 to 2 tablespoons water
- 2 drops green food color
  Powdered sugar

1 Marzipan needs to be made and refrigerated at least 24 hours or up to 1 week before covering cake.

2 Fit stand mixer with flat beater attachment. Crumble almond paste into large bowl; add 3 cups powdered sugar. Beat on low speed until mixture is crumbly and resembles cornmeal. Add corn syrup and 1 tablespoon water. Mix on low speed, adding water, 1 teaspoon at a time, until mixture forms a dough. Remove about one-eighth of marzipan for daisies; wrap in plastic wrap and set aside.

3 Add green food color and water, 1 teaspoon at a time, to remaining marzipan; beat on low speed until pale green and consistency of modeling clay. Sprinkle work surface generously with powdered sugar. Knead green marzipan until smooth and color is even, sprinkling with additional powdered sugar as needed to reduce stickiness. Flatten into round disk, about 6 inches in diameter. Double wrap disk in plastic wrap; refrigerate.

1 Serving: Calories 170; Total Fat 3g (Saturated Fat 0g, Trans Fat 0g); Cholesterol 0mg; Sodium 0mg; Total Carbohydrate 33g (Dietary Fiber 0g); Protein 1g **Exchanges:** ½ Starch, 1½ Other Carbohydrate, ½ Fat **Carbohydrate Choices:** 2

SWEET TIPS A heavy-duty stand mixer is a must for mixing the marzipan mixture.

You can substitute another color of food color if you like, for this recipe or to use the marzipan in another recipe.

chapter 5

Rolled, Pudding,

and Upside-Down Cakes and Cheesecakes

Mint-Chocolate Cake Roll

Prep Time: 40 minutes * Start to Finish: 1 hour 50 minutes * **12 SERVINGS**

5 **eggs, separated**

1 **cup granulated sugar**

½ **teaspoon instant coffee granules or crystals**

1 **tablespoon warm water**

6 **oz bittersweet baking chocolate, melted, cooled**

2 **tablespoons all-purpose flour**

6 **tablespoons unsweetened baking cocoa**

1 **cup whipping cream**

2 **tablespoons powdered sugar**

¼ **cup white crème de menthe Fresh mint sprigs, if desired**

1 Heat oven to 325°F (300°F for dark or nonstick pan). Grease 15 × 10 × 1-inch pan with butter. Line bottom of pan with waxed paper; grease paper with butter.

2 In large bowl, beat egg yolks with electric mixer on high speed until fluffy. Gradually add ½ cup of the granulated sugar, beating on high speed about 5 minutes or until thick and lemon colored. In small bowl, stir coffee granules in warm water until dissolved. Add cooled chocolate and coffee to egg yolk mixture; beat on low speed until blended, scraping bowl occasionally.

3 In another large bowl, beat egg whites with electric mixer on high speed until soft peaks form. Gradually add remaining ½ cup granulated sugar, 1 tablespoon at a time, beating until stiff peaks form. Fold one-quarter of the egg whites into chocolate batter to lighten. Fold in remaining egg whites. Sift flour over batter; fold in flour until blended. Pour batter into pan. With metal spatula, gently spread batter to edges of pan.

4 Bake 18 to 20 minutes or until cake springs back when lightly touched in center. Sprinkle top of cake with 3 tablespoons of the cocoa. Cover cake with a slightly damp kitchen towel; cool completely. Turn cake upside down onto kitchen towel; carefully remove waxed paper. Sprinkle cake with remaining 3 tablespoons cocoa.

5 In chilled medium bowl, beat whipping cream with electric mixer on high speed until foamy. Add powdered sugar and crème de menthe; beat until stiff peaks form. Spread over cake. Beginning at one short side, roll up cake, using towel to help roll but not incorporating towel into cake roll. Sprinkle with additional cocoa. Garnish with mint. Store covered in refrigerator.

1 Serving: Calories 290; Total Fat 17g (Saturated Fat 10g; Trans Fat 0g); Cholesterol 105mg; Sodium 40mg; Total Carbohydrate 27g (Dietary Fiber 3g); Protein 5g **Exchanges:** ½ Starch, 1½ Other Carbohydrate, ½ Medium-Fat Meat, 3 Fat **Carbohydrate Choices:** 2

SWEET TIP **This is a delicate cake roll that is melt-in-your-mouth good. Roll up gently after spreading on the mint cream and have your platter ready.**

Apple Butter Cake Roll

Prep Time: 30 minutes * Start to Finish: 1 hour 15 minutes * **10 SERVINGS**

3 **eggs**
1 **cup granulated sugar**
⅓ **cup water**
1 **teaspoon vanilla**
¾ **cup all-purpose flour**
1 **teaspoon baking powder**
½ **teaspoon ground cinnamon**
½ **teaspoon ground cloves**
¼ **teaspoon ground allspice**
¼ **teaspoon salt**
¼ **cup powdered sugar**
1½ **cups apple butter**
1 **teaspoon powdered sugar**

1 Heat oven to 375°F. Line 15 × 10 × 1-inch pan with cooking parchment paper, foil or waxed paper. In medium bowl, beat eggs with electric mixer on high speed about 5 minutes or until very thick and lemon colored.

2 Gradually beat granulated sugar into eggs. On low speed, beat in water and vanilla. Gradually beat in flour, baking powder, cinnamon, cloves, allspice and salt just until batter is smooth. Pour batter into pan; spread to corners.

3 Bake 12 to 15 minutes or until toothpick inserted in center comes out clean. Meanwhile, generously sprinkle ¼ cup powdered sugar on clean towel.

4 Immediately loosen cake from edges of pan; invert onto sugared towel. Carefully remove paper. Trim off stiff edges of cake if necessary. While hot, starting with short side, carefully roll up cake and towel. Place on cooling rack; cool at least 30 minutes.

5 Unroll cake; remove towel. Spread apple butter evenly over cake. Roll up cake; sprinkle with 1 teaspoon powdered sugar. Store covered in refrigerator.

1 Serving: Calories 240; Total Fat 2g (Saturated Fat 0.5g; Trans Fat 0g); Cholesterol 65mg; Sodium 130mg; Total Carbohydrate 53g (Dietary Fiber 2g); Protein 3g **Exchanges:** ½ Starch, 3 Other Carbohydrate, ½ Fat **Carbohydrate Choices:** 3½

SWEET TIP **If you tried to roll a regular cake, it would crack. This special kind of cake, called a sponge cake, is soft and flexible so that it can be rolled up easily.**

Cinnamon Roll Cake

Prep Time: 30 minutes * Start to Finish: 1 hour 45 minutes * **10 SERVINGS**

filling

- ½ **cup butter, softened**
- 1 **cup packed dark brown sugar**
- 2 **tablespoons all-purpose flour**
- 1 **tablespoon ground cinnamon**

cake

- 4 **eggs**
- ¾ **cup granulated sugar**
- ¼ **cup cold water**
- 2 **teaspoons clear or regular vanilla**
- 1 **cup all-purpose flour**
- 1 **teaspoon baking powder**
- ¼ **teaspoon salt**

glaze

- 2 **tablespoons butter**
- 1 **cup powdered sugar**
- ¾ **teaspoon clear or regular vanilla**
- 1 **to 2 tablespoons water**

1 Heat oven to 375°F. Line 15 × 10 × 1-inch pan with foil; generously grease foil with shortening. Sprinkle clean kitchen towel (not terry cloth) generously with powdered sugar (about ¼ cup); set aside.

2 In small bowl, mix all filling ingredients; spread evenly over foil on bottom of pan or press in with fingertips. In large bowl, beat eggs with electric mixer on high speed 5 minutes or until thick and lemon colored, scraping bowl occasionally. Gradually beat in granulated sugar until light and fluffy, scraping bowl occasionally. Beat in water and 2 teaspoons vanilla. On low speed, beat in flour, baking powder and salt just until smooth, scraping bowl occasionally. Carefully spread batter evenly over filling in pan.

3 Bake 10 to 15 minutes or until cake springs back when touched lightly in center.

4 With knife, immediately loosen cake edges from foil; turn upside down onto towel sprinkled with powdered sugar. Cool 2 minutes. Slowly peel foil away, scraping any cinnamon mixture that sticks to foil back onto cake. While cake is hot, starting with short side, carefully roll up cake using towel to aid rolling, but not incorporating towel into cake roll. Wrap outside of cake roll with towel. Place on cooling rack; cool completely, about 1 hour.

5 In 1-quart saucepan, melt butter over low heat; remove from heat. Stir in powdered sugar and ¾ teaspoon vanilla. Stir in water, 1 teaspoon at a time, until consistency of a thick glaze. Spoon glaze over top of cake roll, allowing some to flow down sides.

1 Serving: Calories 390; Total Fat 14g (Saturated Fat 8g; Trans Fat 0g); Cholesterol 105mg; Sodium 240mg; Total Carbohydrate 60g (Dietary Fiber 1g); Protein 4g **Exchanges:** 1½ Starch, 2½ Other Carbohydrate, 2½ Fat **Carbohydrate Choices:** 4

SWEET TIP **Clear vanilla only comes in imitation vanilla extract. It's used in this recipe to create the white frosting. Pure vanilla extract can be used in this recipe, but the frosting will not be as white.**

Bûche de Noël

Prep Time: 35 minutes * Start to Finish: 1 hour 35 minutes * **12 SERVINGS**

8 oz semisweet baking chocolate, chopped

1⅔ cups whipping cream

5 eggs, separated

1 cup granulated sugar

2 tablespoons vegetable oil

1 teaspoon vanilla

½ cup all-purpose flour

¼ cup unsweetened baking cocoa

½ teaspoon salt

2 tablespoons granulated sugar

2 tablespoons coffee-flavored liqueur

Powdered sugar

Sugared cranberries and rosemary sprigs, if desired

Sugared Rosemary Sprigs: Use 6 (3- to 5-inch) sprigs fresh rosemary, 2 pasteurized egg whites, slightly beaten, and 1½ cups superfine sugar. With pastry brush, brush each rosemary sprig with egg whites (do not dip into egg whites). Over waxed paper, sprinkle sugar through wire-mesh strainer over rosemary, turning to coat and shaking off excess. Place on waxed paper. Repeat with remaining rosemary sprigs. Let stand uncovered at least 8 hours or until dry.

Be sure to use pasteurized egg whites, as regular egg whites will not be food-safe. Look for them near the other eggs at the market.

1 In medium bowl, place chocolate. In 1-quart saucepan, heat ⅔ cup of the whipping cream to simmering over medium heat. Remove from heat; cool 1 minute. Pour hot cream over chocolate; stir until smooth. Let stand 30 minutes, stirring occasionally, until ganache is thickened.

2 Heat oven to 375°F. Grease 15 × 10 × 1-inch pan with shortening. Line with waxed paper; grease paper with shortening. In large bowl, beat egg yolks and ½ cup of the sugar with electric mixer on high speed until thick and lemon colored. On low speed, beat in oil and vanilla.

3 In medium bowl, beat egg whites on medium speed until soft peaks form. Gradually add remaining ½ cup sugar, beating on high speed until stiff peaks form. Gently fold egg whites into egg yolk mixture. Sift flour, ¼ cup cocoa and the salt over batter; fold gently until blended. Pour into pan, spreading batter to corners.

4 Bake 15 to 18 minutes or until cake springs back when touched lightly in center. Meanwhile, generously sprinkle clean towel with cocoa. Immediately loosen cake from edges of pan; turn upside down onto towel. Carefully remove waxed paper; trim off edges of cake if necessary. While hot, starting with long side, carefully roll up cake and towel; place on cooling rack. Cool at least 30 minutes.

5 In chilled medium bowl, beat remaining 1 cup whipping cream, 2 tablespoons sugar and liqueur on high speed with electric mixer until stiff peaks form. Unroll cake; remove towel. Spread whipped cream over cake. Roll up cake. Cut 2-inch diagonal slice from 1 end of cake roll. Place cake on serving platter; position cut piece against side of cake roll to look like a knot, using about 1 tablespoon ganache to attach to cake. Frost cake with remaining ganache. With tines of fork, make strokes in ganache to look like tree bark. Sprinkle with powdered sugar. Garnish with sugared cranberries and rosemary sprigs.

1 Serving: Calories 390; Total Fat 27g (Saturated Fat 15g; Trans Fat 0g); Cholesterol 125mg; Sodium 45mg; Total Carbohydrate 29g (Dietary Fiber 4g); Protein 6g **Exchanges:** 2 Starch, 5 Fat **Carbohydrate Choices:** 2

Sugared Cranberries: In 2-quart saucepan, heat ½ cup water, ½ cup sugar and ¾ cup fresh cranberries to boiling over medium-high heat, stirring often. (Cranberries should swell and just begin to pop.) Remove from heat; drain. Toss cranberries with ¼ cup sugar, coating well. Place in a single layer on waxed paper. Let stand uncovered 8 hours or until dry.

Lemon Cream Rolled Cake

Prep Time: 20 minutes * Start to Finish: 2 hours 55 minutes * **12 SERVINGS**

cake

- **7 eggs**
- **1 box yellow cake mix with pudding**
- **⅓ cup water**
- **2 tablespoons lemon juice**
- **2 tablespoons vegetable oil**
- **2 teaspoons grated lemon peel**
- **¼ cup powdered sugar**

filling

- **1 cup whipping cream**
- **2 tablespoons powdered sugar**
- **4 teaspoons grated lemon peel (from 2 lemons)**

garnish

- **1 tablespoon powdered sugar**

1 Heat oven to 375°F (350°F for dark or nonstick pan). Line bottom only of 15 × 10 × 1-inch pan with foil or waxed paper; spray foil and sides of pan with baking spray with flour. Place paper baking cup in each of 8 regular-size muffin cups.

2 In large bowl, beat eggs with electric mixer on high speed about 5 minutes or until thick and lemon colored. Add cake mix, water, lemon juice, oil and 2 teaspoons lemon peel. Beat on low speed 30 seconds, then on medium speed 1 minute, scraping bowl occasionally. Pour 3¼ cups batter into foil-lined pan; spread evenly. Divide remaining batter among muffin cups.

3 Bake 13 to 15 minutes or until cake (or cupcakes) springs back when lightly touched in center. If necessary, run knife around edge of pan to loosen cake. Turn cake upside down onto clean kitchen towel sprinkled with ¼ cup powdered sugar; carefully remove foil. While hot, starting with short side, carefully roll up cake and towel. Cool completely, seam side down, on cooling rack, about 1 hour 15 minutes. Remove cupcakes from pan; cool completely and freeze for another use.

4 In chilled large glass or metal bowl, beat whipping cream and 2 tablespoons powdered sugar on medium speed until foamy, then on high speed until stiff peaks form. Fold in 4 teaspoons lemon peel.

5 Unroll cake carefully and remove towel. Spread filling evenly over cake; roll up cake. On serving platter, arrange cake, seam side down; cover loosely and refrigerate at least 1 hour. Before serving, sprinkle with 1 tablespoon powdered sugar. Store covered in refrigerator.

1 Serving: Calories 220; Total Fat 12g (Saturated Fat 6g; Trans Fat 0g); Cholesterol 110mg; Sodium 200mg; Total Carbohydrate 24g (Dietary Fiber 0g); Protein 3g **Exchanges:** 1 Starch, ½ Other Carbohydrate, 2½ Fat **Carbohydrate Choices:** 1½

SWEET TIP **Make sure you spread the cake batter evenly in the corners of the pan before baking. The cake sets quickly, and you want the resulting cake roll to be even.**

Lemon Pudding Cake

Prep Time: 15 minutes * **Start to Finish:** 50 minutes * **6 SERVINGS**

3 **eggs, separated**
½ **cup fat-free (skim) milk**
¼ **cup lemon juice**
1 **teaspoon grated lemon peel**
½ **cup sugar**
⅓ **cup all-purpose flour**
⅛ **teaspoon salt**

1 Heat oven to 350°F. Grease 1-quart casserole or soufflé dish. In small bowl, beat egg yolks. Stir in milk, lemon juice and lemon peel. Add sugar, flour and salt; beat until smooth.

2 In another small bowl, beat egg whites with electric mixer on high speed until stiff peaks form. Gently fold yolk mixture into beaten egg whites. Do not overmix. Pour into casserole. Place casserole in 13 × 9-inch pan; pour hot water into pan until 1 inch deep.

3 Bake 25 to 35 minutes or until light golden brown. Serve warm or cool.

1 Serving: Calories 140; Total Fat 3g (Saturated Fat 1g; Trans Fat 0g); Cholesterol 105mg; Sodium 90mg; Total Carbohydrate 24g (Dietary Fiber 0g); Protein 4g **Exchanges:** 1 Starch, ½ Other Carbohydrate, ½ Fat **Carbohydrate Choices:** 1½

SWEET TIP **Serve this old-fashioned dessert topped with whipped cream and a lemon peel curl—yum!**

Pumpkin Pudding Cake

Prep Time: 15 minutes * Start to Finish: 1 hour 10 minutes * **9 SERVINGS**

1½ cups all-purpose flour
¾   cup granulated sugar
1   teaspoon baking powder
½   teaspoon baking soda
½   teaspoon salt
1½ teaspoons ground cinnamon
½   cup buttermilk
½   cup canned pumpkin
    (not pumpkin pie mix)
¼   cup butter, melted
⅓   cup chopped pecans
1½ cups water
¾   cup packed brown sugar

1 Heat oven to 350°F. In large bowl, mix flour, granulated sugar, baking powder, baking soda, salt and cinnamon. Add buttermilk, pumpkin and melted butter; mix well with spoon. Spread in ungreased 8- or 9-inch square pan. Sprinkle with pecans, pressing into top.

2 In small saucepan, mix water and brown sugar. Heat over medium heat until simmering, stirring until sugar is dissolved. Carefully pour over batter. (Nuts may float, but will settle as cake bakes.)

3 Bake 35 to 45 minutes or until toothpick inserted in center comes out clean. Cool 15 minutes. Serve warm, spooning sauce from bottom of pan over cake.

1 Serving: Calories 300; Total Fat 9g (Saturated Fat 3.5g; Trans Fat 0g); Cholesterol 15mg; Sodium 320mg; Total Carbohydrate 53g (Dietary Fiber 1g); Protein 3g **Exchanges:** 1 Starch, 2½ Other Carbohydrate, 1½ Fat Carbohydrate Choices: 3½

SWEET TIPS **As a pudding cake bakes, a delicious sauce forms beneath the top layer of cake. Spoon it from the pan as you would serve a crisp or a crumble.**

Spoon remaining pumpkin into a freezer container. Freeze it to use later in another pumpkin recipe.

Caramel Pudding Cake

Prep Time: 15 minutes * Start to Finish: 1 hour 10 minutes * **9 SERVINGS**

1¼ cups all-purpose flour
¾ cup granulated sugar
1½ teaspoons baking powder
½ teaspoon baking soda
¼ teaspoon salt
½ cup buttermilk
2 tablespoons butter, melted
½ cup chopped dates,
    if desired
¼ cup chopped nuts
¾ cup packed brown sugar
1½ cups very warm water
    (120°F to 130°F)
    Ice cream, if desired

1 Heat oven to 350°F. In large bowl, mix flour, granulated sugar, baking powder, baking soda and salt with spoon. Stir in buttermilk and butter. Stir in dates and nuts (batter will be thick). Spread in ungreased 8- or 9-inch square pan.

2 In small bowl, mix brown sugar and very warm water with spoon. Pour over batter.

3 Bake 45 to 55 minutes or until cake is deep golden brown and toothpick inserted in center comes out clean. Serve warm with ice cream.

1 Serving: Calories 250; Total Fat 5g (Saturated Fat 2g; Trans Fat 0g); Cholesterol 10mg; Sodium 260mg; Total Carbohydrate 49g (Dietary Fiber 0g); Protein 3g **Exchanges:** ½ Starch, 3 Other Carbohydrate, 1 Fat **Carbohydrate Choices:** 3

SWEET TIP **Spoon the caramel sauce that forms at the bottom of this dessert over the warm cake and ice cream.**

Apple Pudding Cake with Cinnamon-Butter Sauce

Prep Time: 15 minutes ✳ Start to Finish: 50 minutes ✳ **9 SERVINGS**

cake

1	**cup packed brown sugar**
¼	**cup butter, softened**
1	**egg**
1	**cup all-purpose flour**
1	**teaspoon baking soda**
1	**teaspoon ground cinnamon**
½	**teaspoon ground nutmeg**
¼	**teaspoon salt**
2	**cups chopped peeled or unpeeled cooking apples (2 medium)**

sauce

⅓	**cup butter**
⅔	**cup granulated sugar**
⅓	**cup half-and-half**
½	**teaspoon ground cinnamon**

1 Heat oven to 350°F. Grease bottom and sides of 8-inch square pan with shortening.

2 In large bowl, mix brown sugar and softened butter with spoon until light and fluffy. Beat in egg. Stir in flour, baking soda, 1 teaspoon cinnamon, the nutmeg and salt. Stir in apples. Spread batter in pan.

3 Bake 25 to 35 minutes or until toothpick inserted in center comes out clean.

4 Meanwhile, in 1-quart saucepan, heat sauce ingredients over medium heat, stirring frequently, until butter is melted and sauce is hot. Serve warm sauce over warm cake.

1 **Serving:** Calories 350; Total Fat 14g (Saturated Fat 8g; Trans Fat 0.5g); Cholesterol 60mg; Sodium 310mg; Total Carbohydrate 54g (Dietary Fiber 1g); Protein 3g **Exchanges:** 1 Starch, 2½ Other Carbohydrate, 2½ Fat **Carbohydrate Choices:** 3½

SWEET TIP You can bake the cake and make the sauce a day ahead and store them separately (refrigerate sauce). Warm the sauce in a saucepan over low heat, and heat individual pieces of cake uncovered in the microwave on High for 25 to 35 seconds or until warm.

Pear-Ginger Upside-Down Cake

Prep Time: 25 minutes * Start to Finish: 1 hour 30 minutes * **8 SERVINGS**

topping

- ¼ **cup butter**
- ⅔ **cup packed brown sugar**
- ½ **teaspoon ground ginger**
- 3 **pears, peeled, cut into ½-inch wedges**
- ¼ **cup finely chopped crystallized ginger**

cake

- 1 **tablespoon all-purpose flour**
- ¼ **cup finely chopped crystallized ginger**
- 1⅓ **cups all-purpose flour**
- 1 **teaspoon baking powder**
- ¼ **teaspoon salt**
- 1 **cup packed brown sugar**
- 6 **tablespoons butter, softened**
- 2 **eggs**
- ½ **teaspoon vanilla**
- ¼ **cup milk**

whipped cream

- 1 **cup heavy whipping cream**
- 2 **tablespoons granulated sugar**
- ¼ **teaspoon ground ginger**

1 Heat oven to 325°F. Grease bottom and sides of 8- or 9-inch square pan with shortening. In 1-quart saucepan, melt ¼ cup butter over medium heat, stirring occasionally. Stir in ⅔ cup brown sugar. Heat to boiling; remove from heat. Stir in ½ teaspoon ground ginger. Pour into pan; spread evenly. Arrange pear wedges on sugar mixture, overlapping tightly and making 2 layers if necessary. Sprinkle ¼ cup crystallized ginger over pears.

2 In small bowl, toss 1 tablespoon flour and ¼ cup crystallized ginger to coat; set aside. In another small bowl, mix 1⅓ cups flour, the baking powder and salt; set aside. In large bowl, beat 1 cup brown sugar and 6 tablespoons butter with electric mixer on medium speed, scraping bowl occasionally, until fluffy. Beat in eggs, one at a time, until smooth. Add vanilla. Gradually beat in flour mixture alternately with milk, beating after each addition until smooth. Stir in ginger-flour mixture. Spread batter over pears in pan.

3 Bake 55 to 65 minutes or until toothpick inserted in center of cake comes out clean. Cool 15 minutes on cooling rack. Meanwhile, in chilled medium bowl, beat whipping cream on high speed until it begins to thicken. Gradually add granulated sugar and ¼ teaspoon ground ginger, beating until soft peaks form.

4 Loosen edges of cake with small knife. Place heatproof plate upside down onto pan; turn plate and pan over. Serve warm with ginger whipped cream.

1 Serving: Calories 600; Total Fat 27g (Saturated Fat 15g; Trans Fat 1g); Cholesterol 135mg; Sodium 290mg; Total Carbohydrate 84g (Dietary Fiber 3g); Protein 5g Exchanges: 1½ Starch, 4 Other Carbohydrate, 5½ Fat Carbohydrate Choices: 5½

SWEET TIP **Crystallized ginger is fresh gingerroot cooked in a sugar syrup and coated with sugar. Look for it in the spice or produce section of the supermarket or in gourmet food shops.**

Upside-Down Apple-Spice Cake

Prep Time: 15 minutes * Start to Finish: 1 hour * **15 SERVINGS**

½ **cup butter**

⅔ **cup packed light brown sugar**

1 **cup chopped walnuts, toasted** *

1½ **lb apples, peeled, chopped (3 large)**

1 **box spice cake mix with pudding**

Water, vegetable oil and eggs called for on cake mix box

1 Heat oven to 350°F. In 13 × 9-inch pan, melt butter in oven. Sprinkle brown sugar and walnuts over butter; stir to combine. Sprinkle chopped apples in pan.

2 Mix cake as directed on box for 13 × 9-inch pan, using water, oil and eggs. Pour batter over apples and walnuts in pan.

3 Bake 35 to 40 minutes or until toothpick inserted in center comes out clean. Cool on cooling rack 2 minutes; run knife around sides of pan to loosen cake. Place heatproof serving plate upside down on pan; turn plate and pan over. Remove pan. Serve cake warm.

To toast walnuts, heat oven to 350°F. Spread walnuts in ungreased shallow pan. Bake uncovered 6 to 10 minutes, stirring occasionally, until light brown.

1 Serving: Calories 260; Total Fat 20g (Saturated Fat 6g; Trans Fat 0g); Cholesterol 55mg; Sodium 90mg; Total Carbohydrate 19g (Dietary Fiber 1g); Protein 2g **Exchanges:** ½ Starch, 1 Other Carbohydrate, 4 Fat **Carbohydrate Choices:** 1

"Berry Best" Upside-Down Cake

Prep Time: 15 minutes * Start to Finish: 1 hour 5 minutes * **9 SERVINGS**

⅓ cup butter

½ cup sugar

1 bag (12 oz) frozen mixed berries, thawed, drained

1⅓ cups all-purpose flour

1 cup sugar

⅔ cup milk

1 teaspoon baking powder

1 teaspoon vanilla

½ teaspoon salt

1 egg

1 Heat oven to 350°F. In 9-inch square pan or 10-inch ovenproof skillet, heat butter in oven about 2 minutes or until melted. Sprinkle ½ cup sugar over melted butter. Spoon berries evenly over sugar mixture.

2 In medium bowl, beat remaining ingredients with electric mixer on low speed 30 seconds. Beat on medium speed 2 minutes, scraping bowl frequently. Pour over berries.

3 Bake about 50 minutes or until toothpick inserted in center of cake comes out clean. Immediately place heatproof serving plate upside down over pan; turn plate and pan over. Leave pan over cake about 1 minute so sugar mixture can drizzle over cake. Serve warm.

1 Serving: Calories 300; Total Fat 8g (Saturated Fat 4g; Trans Fat 0g); Cholesterol 45mg; Sodium 250mg; Total Carbohydrate 53g (Dietary Fiber 2g); Protein 4g **Exchanges:** 1 Starch, 2½ Other Carbohydrate, 1½ Fat **Carbohydrate Choices:** 3½

SWEET TIP **Serve this delicious warm dessert topped with whipped cream.**

Strawberry-Rhubarb Upside-Down Cake

Prep Time: 25 minutes * Start to Finish: 1 hour 50 minutes * **12 SERVINGS**

¼ cup butter

1 cup packed brown sugar

2 cups sliced fresh strawberries

2 cups chopped fresh rhubarb

1 box French vanilla or yellow cake mix with pudding

1 cup water

⅓ cup vegetable oil

3 eggs

Whipped cream, if desired

1 Heat oven to 350°F (325°F for dark or nonstick pan). In 13 × 9-inch pan, melt butter in oven. Sprinkle brown sugar evenly over butter. Arrange strawberries on brown sugar; sprinkle evenly with rhubarb. Press strawberries and rhubarb gently into brown sugar.

2 In large bowl, beat cake mix, water, oil and eggs with electric mixer on low speed 30 seconds, then on medium speed 2 minutes, scraping bowl occasionally. Pour batter over strawberries and rhubarb.

3 Bake 45 to 55 minutes or until toothpick inserted in center comes out clean. Immediately run knife around sides of pan to loosen cake. Place heatproof serving plate upside down on pan; turn plate and pan over. Leave pan over cake 1 minute so brown sugar topping can drizzle over cake. Cool 30 minutes. Serve warm or cool with whipped cream. Store covered in refrigerator.

1 Serving: Calories 330; Total Fat 13g (Saturated Fat 4.5g; Trans Fat 0g); Cholesterol 65mg; Sodium 310mg; Total Carbohydrate 50g (Dietary Fiber 1g); Protein 3g Exchanges: 1 Starch, ½ Fruit, 2 Other Carbohydrate, 2½ Fat Carbohydrate Choices: 3

SWEET TIP **If fresh rhubarb is out of season, you can use frozen rhubarb. Just thaw and drain it before making the cake.**

Bittersweet Chocolate Cheesecake

Prep Time: 30 minutes * Start to Finish: 9 hours * **12 SERVINGS**

crust

- **40 thin chocolate wafer cookies (from 9-oz package), crushed (about 2½ cups)**
- **⅓ cup granulated sugar**
- **¼ cup butter, melted**

filling

- **2 packages (8 oz each) cream cheese, softened**
- **⅔ cup granulated sugar**
- **1 teaspoon vanilla**
- **1 tablespoon all-purpose flour**
- **3 eggs**
- **8 oz bittersweet baking chocolate, melted, cooled**

garnish, if desired

- **Powdered sugar**
- **Fresh raspberries**

1 Heat oven to 325°F. Wrap outside bottom and side of 9-inch springform pan with foil to prevent leaking. Lightly spray inside bottom and side of pan with cooking spray. In medium bowl, mix crust ingredients with fork until crumbly. Press mixture in bottom and 1 inch up side of pan. Bake 10 minutes or until set. Place on cooling rack; cool completely.

2 In another medium bowl, beat cream cheese, ⅔ cup granulated sugar and vanilla with electric mixer on medium speed until light and fluffy. Beat in flour. Beat in eggs, one at a time, just until blended. Beat in chocolate. Pour over crust.

3 Bake 1 hour to 1 hour 15 minutes or until edge of cheesecake is set at least 2 inches from edge of pan but center of cheesecake still jiggles slightly when moved. Turn oven off; open oven door at least 4 inches. Let cheesecake remain in oven 30 minutes. Run small metal spatula around edge of pan to loosen cheesecake. Cool on cooling rack 30 minutes. Refrigerate at least 6 hours or overnight before serving.

4 Just before serving, run small metal spatula around edge of springform pan; carefully remove foil and side of pan. Let cheesecake stand at room temperature 15 minutes before cutting. Sprinkle with powdered sugar; garnish with raspberries. Cover and refrigerate any remaining cheesecake.

1 **Serving:** Calories 480; Total Fat 31g (Saturated Fat 17g; Trans Fat 1g); Cholesterol 100mg; Sodium 340mg; Total Carbohydrate 42g (Dietary Fiber 3g); Protein 7g **Exchanges:** 2 Starch, 1 Other Carbohydrate, 6 Fat **Carbohydrate Choices:** 3

SWEET TIP **Use full-fat cream cheese for the best flavor and texture. Reduced-fat varieties will result in a softer, more watery cheesecake.**

Strawberry-Filled Cheesecake

Prep Time: 25 minutes * Start to Finish: 8 hours 55 minutes * **12 SERVINGS**

crust

- **1 cup graham cracker crumbs (about 16 squares)**
- **¼ cup sugar**
- **2 tablespoons butter, melted**

filling

- **3 packages (8 oz each) cream cheese, softened**
- **1 cup sugar**
- **1 teaspoon vanilla**
- **4 eggs**
- **1 container (8 oz) sour cream**
- **1 can (21 oz) strawberry pie filling**

1 Heat oven to 325°F. Wrap outside bottom and side of 10-inch springform pan with foil to prevent leaking. In small bowl, mix crust ingredients. Press mixture in bottom of pan. Bake 12 to 15 minutes or until set. Place on cooling rack; cool completely.

2 In large bowl, beat cream cheese, 1 cup sugar and the vanilla with electric mixer on medium speed until smooth. Beat in eggs, one at a time, just until blended. Fold in sour cream.

3 Spread half of cream cheese mixture (about 3 cups) over crust. Spoon half of pie filling by tablespoonfuls onto cream cheese mixture. Top with remaining cream cheese mixture. (Refrigerate remaining pie filling.)

4 Bake 1 hour 5 minutes to 1 hour 15 minutes or until edge of cheesecake is set at least 2 inches from edge of pan but center of cheesecake still jiggles slightly when moved. Turn oven off; open oven door at least 4 inches. Let cheesecake remain in oven 30 minutes. Run small metal spatula along edge of pan to loosen cheesecake. Cool in pan on cooling rack 30 minutes. Refrigerate at least 6 hours or overnight before serving.

5 Just before serving, run metal spatula around edge of pan; carefully remove foil and side of pan. Spoon remaining pie filling over cheesecake. Cover and refrigerate any remaining cheesecake.

1 Serving: Calories 440; Total Fat 28g (Saturated Fat 17g; Trans Fat 1g); Cholesterol 150mg; Sodium 250mg; Total Carbohydrate 40g (Dietary Fiber 0g); Protein 7g **Exchanges:** 1 Starch, 1½ Other Carbohydrate, ½ High-Fat Meat, 4½ Fat **Carbohydrate Choices:** 2½

SWEET TIP **Taking this cheesecake to a party? Leave the side on the pan to make it easier to transport.**

Caramel Cappuccino Cheesecake

Prep Time: 30 minutes   **Start to Finish:** 8 hours 50 minutes   **16 SERVINGS**

crust

1¼	**cups chocolate cookie crumbs (from 15-oz box)**
¼	**cup butter, melted**

filling

2	**tablespoons instant espresso coffee powder or granules**
2	**teaspoons vanilla**
4	**packages (8 oz each) cream cheese, softened**
1½	**cups granulated sugar**
4	**eggs**
1	**teaspoon ground cinnamon**
¼	**cup caramel topping**

topping

1	**cup whipping cream**
2	**tablespoons powdered or granulated sugar**
¼	**cup caramel topping**

1 Heat oven to 300°F. Wrap outside bottom and side of 10-inch springform pan with foil to prevent leaking. To minimize cracking, place shallow pan half full of hot water on lower oven rack.

2 In small bowl, mix cookie crumbs and melted butter with fork. Press mixture evenly over bottom of pan. Refrigerate crust while preparing filling. In another small bowl, stir espresso powder and vanilla until dissolved; set aside.

3 In large bowl, beat cream cheese and 1½ cups sugar with electric mixer on medium speed until light and fluffy. Beat in eggs, one at a time, just until blended. Add espresso mixture, cinnamon and ¼ cup caramel topping; beat about 30 seconds or until mixture is well blended. Pour over crust in pan.

4 Bake 1 hour 10 minutes to 1 hour 20 minutes or until cheesecake is set at least 2 inches from edge of pan but center of cheesecake still jiggles slightly when moved. Run small metal spatula around edge of pan to loosen cheesecake. Turn oven off; open oven door at least 4 inches. Let cheesecake remain in oven 30 minutes. Cool in pan on cooling rack 30 minutes. Refrigerate at least 6 hours or overnight.

5 Just before serving, run small metal spatula around edge of pan; carefully remove foil and side of pan. In chilled medium bowl, beat 1 cup whipping cream and 2 tablespoons sugar with electric mixer on high speed until soft peaks form. Spread whipped cream over top of cheesecake; drizzle with ¼ cup caramel topping. Cover and refrigerate any remaining cheesecake.

1 Serving: Calories 440; Total Fat 30g (Saturated Fat 18g; Trans Fat 1g); Cholesterol 140mg; Sodium 300mg; Total Carbohydrate 35g (Dietary Fiber 0g); Protein 7g **Exchanges:** ½ Starch, 2 Other Carbohydrate, 1 High-Fat Meat, 4 Fat **Carbohydrate Choices:** 2

Cherry Cheesecake with Ganache

Prep Time: 30 minutes * Start to Finish: 9 hours 35 minutes * **16 SERVINGS**

crust
1½ **cups finely crushed creme-filled chocolate sandwich cookies (about 15 cookies)**
¼ **cup butter, melted**

filling
4 **packages (8 oz each) cream cheese, softened**
1¼ **cups sugar**
4 **eggs**
½ **cup whipping cream**
1 **teaspoon almond extract**
1 **bag (16 oz) frozen dark sweet cherries, thawed, drained and patted dry (3 cups)**

ganache
½ **cup dark chocolate chips**
¼ **cup whipping cream**
3 **tablespoons corn syrup**

1 Heat oven to 325°F. Wrap outside bottom and side of 10-inch springform pan with foil to prevent leaking. Spray inside bottom and side of pan with cooking spray. In small bowl, mix crust ingredients. Press in bottom of pan. Bake 8 to 10 minutes or until set. Reduce oven temperature to 300°F. Cool crust 10 minutes.

2 Meanwhile, in large bowl, beat cream cheese and sugar with electric mixer on medium speed until fluffy. Beat in eggs, one at a time, just until blended. Beat in ½ cup whipping cream and the almond extract. Pour 4 cups filling over crust. Spoon cherries over filling. Top with remaining filling, covering cherries.

3 Bake at 300°F 1 hour 15 minutes to 1 hour 25 minutes or until edge of cheesecake is set at least 2 inches from edge of pan but center of cheesecake still jiggles slightly. Turn oven off; open door 4 inches. Let cheesecake remain in oven 30 minutes. Run small metal spatula around edge of pan to loosen cheesecake. Cool in pan on cooling rack 30 minutes. Refrigerate at least 6 hours or overnight.

4 In small microwavable bowl, microwave ganache ingredients on High 1 minute 30 seconds, stirring once, until smooth. Spread over cheesecake. Chill 30 minutes. To serve, run small metal spatula around edge of pan; carefully remove foil and side of pan. Cover; refrigerate any remaining cheesecake.

1 Serving: Calories 460; Total Fat 31g (Saturated Fat 17g; Trans Fat 1g); Cholesterol 135mg; Sodium 280mg; Total Carbohydrate 39g (Dietary Fiber 1g); Protein 6g **Exchanges:** 2 Starch, ½ Other Carbohydrate, 6 Fat **Carbohydrate Choices:** 2½

SWEET TIPS **To make cutting the cheesecake easier, dip the knife in hot water and clean it off after every cut.**

Some cracking may occur during cooling. This will not affect the quality of the cheesecake and it will not be noticeable once the cheesecake is topped with the ganache.

Salted Caramel Cheesecake

Prep Time: 50 minutes ✳ **Start to Finish:** 9 hours 20 minutes ✳ **16 SERVINGS**

crust

1¾ **cups graham cracker crumbs (about 28 squares)**

¼ **cup packed brown sugar**

½ **cup butter, melted**

filling

3 **packages (8 oz each) cream cheese, softened**

1 **cup packed brown sugar**

3 **eggs**

¾ **cup whipping cream**

¼ **cup caramel-flavored coffee syrup**

caramel sauce

½ **cup butter**

1¼ **cups packed brown sugar**

2 **tablespoons caramel-flavored coffee syrup**

½ **cup whipping cream**

1½ **teaspoons flaked sea salt**

1 Heat oven to 350°F. Wrap outside bottom and side of 9-inch springform pan with foil to prevent leaking. Grease inside bottom and side of pan with shortening. In small bowl, mix crust ingredients. Press in bottom of pan. Bake 8 to 10 minutes or until set. Reduce oven temperature to 300°F. Cool crust 10 minutes.

2 Meanwhile, in large bowl, beat cream cheese and 1 cup brown sugar with electric mixer on medium speed until smooth. Beat in eggs, one at a time, just until blended. Add ¾ cup whipping cream and ¼ cup coffee syrup; beat until blended. Pour filling over crust.

3 Bake at 300°F 1 hour 10 minutes to 1 hour 20 minutes or until edge of cheesecake is set at least 2 inches from edge of pan but center of cheesecake still jiggles slightly. Turn oven off; open door 4 inches. Let cheesecake remain in oven 30 minutes. Run small metal spatula around edge of pan to loosen cheesecake. Cool in pan on cooling rack 30 minutes. Refrigerate at least 6 hours or overnight.

4 In 2-quart saucepan, melt ½ cup butter over medium heat. Add 1¼ cups brown sugar and 2 tablespoons coffee syrup. Heat to boiling; cook and stir 1 minute until sugar dissolves. Stir in ½ cup whipping cream; return to boiling. Remove from heat. Cool 10 minutes.

5 To serve, run small metal spatula around edge of springform pan; carefully remove foil and side of pan. Cut cheesecake into slices. Drizzle caramel sauce over slices; sprinkle with salt. Cover; refrigerate any remaining cheesecake.

1 Serving: Calories 510; Total Fat 34g (Saturated Fat 20g; Trans Fat 1g); Cholesterol 140mg; Sodium 520mg; Total Carbohydrate 47g (Dietary Fiber 0g); Protein 5g **Exchanges:** 1 Starch, 2 Other Carbohydrate, 6½ Fat **Carbohydrate Choices:** 3

SWEET TIP **Caramel-flavored coffee syrup can be found by the coffees and teas in the grocery store.**

Mango-Coconut Cheesecake

Prep Time: 25 minutes * Start to Finish: 9 hours 5 minutes * **16 SERVINGS**

crust

- 2 cups crushed coconut cookies (7 to 8 oz)
- ¼ cup butter, melted

filling

- 3 packages (8 oz each) cream cheese, softened
- 1¼ cups sugar
- 2 tablespoons cornstarch
- 1 teaspoon vanilla
- 3 eggs
- 1 container (8 oz) sour cream
- 1 jar (20 oz) mango slices, drained, chopped (about 1½ cups)

garnish

- ½ cup shaved coconut, toasted*
- Additional chopped mango

1 Heat oven to 350°F. Wrap outside bottom and side of 10-inch springform pan with foil to prevent leaking. Spray inside bottom and side of pan with cooking spray. In small bowl, mix crust ingredients. Press in bottom of pan. Bake 8 to 10 minutes or until set. Reduce oven temperature to 300°F. Cool crust 10 minutes.

2 Meanwhile, in large bowl, beat cream cheese, sugar, cornstarch and vanilla with electric mixer on medium speed until light and fluffy. Beat in eggs, one at a time, just until blended. Stir in sour cream and mango. Pour filling over crust.

3 Bake at 300°F 1 hour 20 minutes to 1 hour 30 minutes or until edge of cheesecake is set at least 2 inches from edge of pan but center of cheesecake still jiggles slightly when moved. Turn oven off; open oven door at least 4 inches. Let cheesecake remain in oven 30 minutes. Run small metal spatula around edge of pan to loosen cheesecake. Cool on cooling rack 30 minutes. Refrigerate at least 6 hours or overnight.

4 To serve, run small metal spatula around edge of pan; carefully remove foil and side of pan. Sprinkle coconut and additional mango over top of cheesecake. Cover; refrigerate any remaining cheesecake.

*To toast coconut, heat oven to 350°F. Spread coconut in ungreased shallow pan. Bake uncovered 5 to 7 minutes, stirring occasionally, until golden brown.

1 Serving: Calories 370; Total Fat 25g (Saturated Fat 14g; Trans Fat 0.5g); Cholesterol 100mg; Sodium 230mg; Total Carbohydrate 31g (Dietary Fiber 0g); Protein 4g **Exchanges:** 1 Starch, 1 Other Carbohydrate, 5 Fat **Carbohydrate Choices:** 2

SWEET TIP **To make a Peach-Coconut Cheesecake instead, just use a 20-oz jar of sliced peaches for the mangoes.**

chapter 6

Party

Decorated
Cakes

Monster Cake

Prep Time: 45 minutes * Start to Finish: 2 hours * **12 SERVINGS**

cake

**1 box chocolate fudge
cake mix with pudding**

**Water, vegetable oil and
eggs called for on cake
mix box**

frosting and decorations

**1 container creamy white
ready-to-spread frosting**

Black food color

Neon green food color

**Black decorating icing
(from 4.25-oz tube)**

**2 pieces black string licorice
(5- to 6-inch)**

1 Heat oven to 350°F (325°F for dark or nonstick pan). Make and bake cake as directed on box for 13 × 9-inch pan. Cool 10 minutes. Run knife around sides of pan to loosen cake; remove from pan to cooling rack. Cool completely, about 1 hour.

2 Place cake, bottom side up, on large platter or foil-covered cookie sheet. Remove 2 tablespoons of white frosting from container; set aside. Remove one-third of the frosting (about ½ cup) to small bowl. Tint black; set aside. Tint remaining frosting neon green. Frost sides and top of cake with neon green frosting.

3 Using picture as a guide, use decorating icing with a round tip to outline hair. Add licorice pieces for eyebrows. Use reserved white frosting to form eyes. Use icing to outline remaining facial features. Spread black frosting within the outlines to fill in the hair. Store loosely covered.

1 Serving: Calories 380; Total Fat 17g (Saturated Fat 3.5g; Trans Fat 2g); Cholesterol 55mg; Sodium 410mg; Total Carbohydrate 54g (Dietary Fiber 0g); Protein 3g **Exchanges:** 1 Starch, 2½ Other Carbohydrate, 3½ Fat **Carbohydrate Choices:** 3½

SWEET TIP **To remove cake from pan, place cooling rack over pan. Carefully turn over; lift off pan.**

Stuck Santa Cake

Prep Time: 1 hour * Start to Finish: 2 hours 55 minutes * **12 SERVINGS**

1 box devil's food cake mix
with pudding

Water, vegetable oil and
eggs called for on cake
mix box

Tray or cardboard covered
with wrapping paper and
plastic food wrap or foil

1 container whipped fluffy
white frosting

1 container creamy chocolate
frosting

6 chocolate sugar wafers

Red gel food color

1 teaspoon red decorating
sugar

3 miniature marshmallows,
cut in half crosswise

2 small (1-inch) chewy
chocolate candies,
unwrapped

1 red licorice stick, cut in half

1 large marshmallow

1 roll strawberry-flavor chewy
fruit snack (from 5-oz box)

1 strip rainbow-berry flavor
sweet-sour chewy licorice

2 large peppermint candies

Powdered sugar, if desired

Coarse sugar, if desired

1 Heat oven to 325°F. Grease 9-inch square pan with shortening; coat with flour (do not use cooking spray). Lightly grease 1 muffin cup in mini muffin pan and 1 muffin cup in regular-size muffin pan.

2 Make cake batter as directed on box. Pour cake batter into 1 mini muffin cup, and 1 regular-size muffin cup, filling two-thirds full. Pour remaining batter into square pan. Bake cupcakes 11 to 14 minutes, square pan 47 to 53 minutes or until toothpick inserted in center comes out clean. Cool 10 minutes. Remove cakes from muffin cups and pan; place rounded sides up on cooling racks. Cool completely, about 1 hour. If necessary, cut off rounded tops of cakes.

3 Reserve ½ cup white frosting in small bowl and ¼ cup chocolate frosting in another small bowl. Place square cake layer, rounded side down, on plate. Frost with remaining chocolate frosting.

4 Place regular cupcake, rounded side down, on cake. Place sugar wafers around cupcake, using reserved chocolate frosting to hold in place around cupcake, to form chimney. Stack wafers, cutting as necessary to look like bricks, in 2 layers of cookies on 4 sides of cupcake.

5 Cut mini cupcake in half at angle. In small bowl, mix 2 tablespoons of the reserved white frosting with red gel food color to get deep red color. Place cupcake at angle at top of chimney; frost with red frosting. Sprinkle with red sugar. Press cut miniature marshmallows against bottom of red frosted cupcake to make Santa's behind.

6 Microwave chewy chocolate candies on High 3 to 8 seconds, just until moldable. Firmly press on ends of red licorice sticks, and shape into boots. Press licorice ends into chimney cupcake to make Santa's legs.

7 Spoon remaining reserved frosting into resealable food-storage plastic bag. Cut tiny tip from 1 corner of bag; pipe white frosting and snow on chimney, and fur around tops of boots. Generously spread remaining fluffy white frosting to look like snow drifts over cake, spreading up against the chimney.

8 For Santa's bag, wrap marshmallow with red fruit snack, pinching up at one end to form bag. Using paring knife, cut green strip out of rainbow-berry flavor sweet-sour chewy licorice. Wrap green candy strip around top of Santa's bag, and gently tie it onto the bag. Sprinkle cake with powdered sugar and then with coarse sugar to look like freshly fallen snow. Store loosely covered.

1 Serving: Calories 550; Total Fat 25g (Saturated Fat 6g, Trans Fat 4.5g); Cholesterol 45mg; Sodium 470mg; Total Carbohydrate 80g (Dietary Fiber 1g); Protein 3g **Exchanges:** 1 Starch, 4½ Other Carbohydrate, 4½ Fat **Carbohydrate Choices:** 5

Snowman Coconut Cake

Prep Time: 30 minutes * Start to Finish: 2 hours 20 minutes * **16 SERVINGS**

1 box white cake mix
with pudding

Water, vegetable oil and
egg whites called for on
cake mix box

2 candy canes, unwrapped

2 flat-bottom ice-cream
cones

Vanilla-flavored candy
coating (almond bark),
melted

1 container creamy vanilla
frosting

1 bag (7 oz) coconut
(about 2⅔ cups)

5 large black gumdrops

1 large orange gumdrop

7 small black gumdrops

1 roll chewy fruit snack
(any red flavor)

2 creme-filled chocolate
sandwich cookies

Black shoestring licorice

2 pretzel rods

1 Heat oven to 350°F (325°F for dark or nonstick pans). Make, bake and cool cake mix as directed on box for 2 (8- or 9-inch) round pans.

2 Cover 18 × 10-inch tray or cardboard with foil. To make ice skates, attach candy cane to each cone using melted candy coating; let stand until set. Arrange cake rounds with sides touching on tray. Frost with frosting. Sprinkle with coconut, pressing gently so it stays on frosting.

3 Use large black gumdrops for eyes and buttons, large orange gumdrop for nose, small black gumdrops for mouth and fruit snack roll for scarf. Place cookie on each side of head for earmuffs; attach with shoestring licorice. Arrange pretzel rods for arms and cones for ice skates. Store loosely covered.

1 Serving: Calories 260; Total Fat 10g (Saturated Fat 2g, Trans Fat 1.5g); Cholesterol 0mg; Sodium 260mg; Total Carbohydrate 41g (Dietary Fiber 0g); Protein 2g **Exchanges:** ½ Starch, 2 Other Carbohydrate, 2 Fat **Carbohydrate Choices:** 3

SWEET TIPS Use your favorite flavor of cake mix to make this cute snowman. You can also use a pretzel twist, cut in half, instead of pretzel rods for the arms and your favorite chocolate cookies for the earmuffs.

Create an attractive display by covering a piece of sturdy cardboard with wrapping paper, then plastic food wrap. Stretch and secure with tape. Or cover cardboard with foil or cooking parchment paper.

Slumber Party Cake

Prep Time: 30 minutes ✳ **Start to Finish:** 2 hours 20 minutes ✳ **12 SERVINGS**

cake

1 **box white cake mix with pudding**

Water, vegetable oil and egg whites called for on cake mix box

frosting and decorations

1 **container vanilla creamy ready-to-spread frosting**

Yellow food color

Green food color

5 **large marshmallows, flattened**

5 **creme-filled peanut butter sandwich cookies**

Decorating icing (any colors; from 6.4-oz cans)

Confetti candy sprinkles

1 Heat oven to 350°F (325°F for dark or nonstick pan). Grease or spray with cooking spray bottom only of 13 × 9-inch pan. Make and bake cake mix as directed on box. Cool 10 minutes. Run knife around sides of pan to loosen cake. Place cooling rack upside down over pan; turn rack and pan over. Remove pan. Cool cake completely, about 1 hour.

2 Spoon ⅓ cup frosting into small bowl; tint with yellow food color. Tint remaining frosting in container with green food color. With short side of cake facing you, frost the right third of cake with yellow frosting. Place flattened marshmallows on frosting for pillows; place cookies on top of pillows for faces.

3 Frost remaining cake and portion of sandwich cookies with green frosting for blanket, leaving top portions of cookies unfrosted for faces. Pipe hair and faces onto cookies, using decorating icing. Using star tip, outline blanket with decorating icing. Sprinkle with confetti candies. Store loosely covered.

1 Serving: Calories 290; Total Fat 12g (Saturated Fat 3g; Trans Fat 1g); Cholesterol 0mg; Sodium 300mg; Total Carbohydrate 44g (Dietary Fiber 0g); Protein 2g **Exchanges:** 1 Starch, 2 Other Carbohydrate, 2 Fat **Carbohydrate Choices:** 3

Baby Block Cake

Prep Time: 40 minutes * **Start to Finish:** 2 hours 25 minutes * **12 SERVINGS**

cake

- **1 box white cake mix with pudding**
- **Water, vegetable oil and egg whites called for on cake mix box**
- **½ teaspoon almond extract**
- **1 box (2.7 oz) gel food colors**

frosting and decorations

- **1 container fluffy white whipped ready-to-spread frosting**
- **Decorating icing (any colors; from 6.4-oz cans)**
- **Star-shaped candy sprinkles**

1 Heat oven to 350°F (325°F for dark or nonstick pans). Grease or spray with cooking spray bottoms only of 2 (8-inch) square pans. Make cake batter as directed on box, adding almond extract to batter. Place half of batter in separate bowl. Stir 2 drops blue food color into batter in 1 bowl; stir 2 drops red food color into remaining batter. Pour 1 color batter into each pan.

2 Bake 25 to 31 minutes or until toothpick inserted in center comes out clean. Cool 10 minutes. Run knife around pans to loosen cakes; remove cakes from pans to cooling racks. Cool completely, about 1 hour.

3 Place 1 cake layer, bottom side up, on serving plate. Spread with ½ cup frosting. Top with second cake layer, bottom side down. Spread frosting evenly on sides and top of cake. Using decorating icing, decorate cake as desired to look like baby block. Sprinkle top of cake with candy stars. Store loosely covered.

1 Serving: Calories 330; Total Fat 14g (Saturated Fat 3.5g; Trans Fat 2g); Cholesterol 0mg; Sodium 310mg; Total Carbohydrate 48g (Dietary Fiber 0g); Protein 2g **Exchanges:** 1 Starch, 2 Other Carbohydrate, 2½ Fat **Carbohydrate Choices:** 3

SWEET TIP **If you'd prefer, use green and yellow food colors, or make both of the cakes the same color. You choose!**

Bunny Butt Cake

Prep Time: 40 minutes ✳ **Start to Finish:** 3 hours 40 minutes ✳ **15 SERVINGS**

cake

1 box yellow or white cake mix with pudding

Water, vegetable oil and eggs called for on cake mix box

frosting and decorations

1 container creamy vanilla frosting

Red food color

Tray or cardboard covered with wrapping paper and plastic food wrap or foil

1 large marshmallow, cut in half

3 cups shredded coconut

Green food color

2 strawberry or cherry stretchy and tangy taffy candies (from 6-oz bag)

1 roll punch berry–flavor chewy fruit snack

3 green-colored sour candies, separated into strips

Construction paper

1 Heat oven to 325°F. Grease 1½-quart ovenproof bowl (8 inches across top) with shortening; coat with flour (do not use cooking spray). Lightly grease 3 muffin cups in regular-size muffin pan.

2 Make cake batter as directed on box. Pour cake batter into 3 muffin cups, filling two-thirds full. Pour remaining batter into 1½-quart bowl.

3 Bake cupcakes 17 to 21 minutes, bowl 47 to 53 minutes or until toothpick inserted in center comes out clean. Cool 10 minutes. Remove cakes from muffin cups and bowl; place rounded sides up on cooling racks. Cool completely, about 1 hour. If necessary, cut off rounded tops of cakes.

4 Spoon frosting into large bowl. Add red food color to make desired pink color. Place bowl cake on tray cut side down; spread ⅓ cup frosting over cake. Use frosting to adhere cupcakes to bowl cake for feet and bunny tail. Use toothpicks if necessary. Place marshmallow halves, cut sides down, on tops of 2 cupcakes to make heels of feet. Spread thin layer of frosting over side and top of cake to seal in crumbs. Freeze cake 30 to 45 minutes to set frosting.

5 Spread remaining frosting over cake. Sprinkle with 2 cups of the coconut; press gently to adhere. Shake 1 cup coconut and 3 drops green food color in tightly covered jar until evenly tinted. Surround bunny with tinted coconut. Use rolling pin to press strawberry candies into 2 large rectangles. Cut 2 large ovals and 6 small circles out of candy. Press onto bottoms of bunny feet, using frosting if needed.

6 Roll up fruit snack to make carrot shapes. Cut green sour candies in half crosswise; press into large end of each carrot to make greens on carrot. Cut ears from construction paper; wrap ends that will be inserted into cake with plastic food wrap. Insert into cake. Remove ears, plastic wrap and toothpicks before serving. Store loosely covered.

1 Serving: Calories 440; Total Fat 21g (Saturated Fat 9g, Trans Fat 2g); Cholesterol 35mg; Sodium 340mg; Total Carbohydrate 60g (Dietary Fiber 1g); Protein 2g **Exchanges:** 1 Starch, 3 Other Carbohydrate, 4 Fat **Carbohydrate Choices:** 4

SWEET TIP **Sprinkle chocolate cookie crumbs behind the feet and around the carrots to make it look like the bunny was digging.**

Panda Bear Cake

Prep Time: 1 hour 30 minutes * Start to Finish: 4 hours 30 minutes * **20 SERVINGS**

cake

- **2 boxes devil's food cake mix with pudding**
- **2 cups water**
- **1 cup vegetable oil**
- **6 eggs**

frosting and decorations

- **1½ containers chocolate creamy ready-to-spread frosting**
  Black food color
- **1 large marshmallow**
  Tray or cardboard (20 × 18 inches), covered with wrapping paper and plastic food wrap or foil
- **1½ containers vanilla creamy ready-to-spread frosting**
- **2 small round chocolate-covered creamy mints**

SWEET TIP To pipe frosting, simply place frosting in a resealable plastic freezer bag and cut off a small tip from 1 corner. Squeeze bag to pipe frosting on cake. Piping allows for good control and placement of frosting.

1 Heat oven to 350°F (325°F for dark or nonstick pans). Grease 2 (8-inch) round pans and a 13 × 9-inch pan, or spray with baking spray with flour. In large bowl, beat 1 cake mix, 1 cup of the water, ½ cup of the oil and 3 eggs with electric mixer on low speed 30 seconds, then on medium speed 2 minutes, scraping bowl occasionally. Pour evenly into round pans. Bake as directed on box. Cool cakes 10 minutes; remove from pans to cooling racks. In large bowl, beat remaining cake mix, remaining 1 cup water, ½ cup oil and 3 eggs with electric mixer on low speed 30 seconds, then on medium speed 2 minutes, stirring occasionally. Pour into 13 × 9-inch pan. Bake as directed on box. Cool cake 10 minutes; remove from pan to cooling rack. Cool completely, about 1 hour. For easier handling, refrigerate or freeze cakes about 1 hour or until firm.

2 In medium bowl, mix 1 container plus 1 cup chocolate frosting with food color to make black frosting. Cut marshmallow in half crosswise. Using serrated knife, cut off top rounded portion of each cake to level surface. Turn cakes cut sides down. Cut cakes as shown in template. Place cake pieces on tray as directed in template, attaching to tray and to each other with small amount of frosting.

3 Spread thin layer of vanilla frosting over head and thin layer of black frosting over ears, body and paws to seal in crumbs. Refrigerate or freeze cake 30 to 60 minutes to set frosting.

4 Frost head with some of remaining vanilla frosting. Frost rest of cake with some of remaining black frosting. To pipe on panda features, spoon vanilla and black frostings into separate resealable plastic freezer bags and cut small tip off 1 corner of each bag.

5 Pipe or spread vanilla frosting on body to create chest. Pipe or spread black frosting on head for patches around eyes. Place marshmallow eyes on patches. For pupils, attach 1 mint to each marshmallow slice with frosting. Pipe or spread black frosting on snout for nose and mouth. Pipe or spread vanilla frosting on back paws to create paw prints. Pipe outline around body and front legs with black frosting. Fill in outline with black frosting so front legs have thicker layer of frosting than white chest. Using metal spatula, create a different texture on the body and front legs to further define legs from chest and back paws. Store loosely covered.

1 Serving (Cake and Frosting Only): Calories 540; Total Fat 24g (Saturated Fat 6g; Trans Fat 4g); Cholesterol 65mg; Sodium 540mg; Total Carbohydrate 78g (Dietary Fiber 1g); Protein 4g **Exchanges:** 1½ Starch, 3½ Other Carbohydrate, 4½ Fat **Carbohydrate Choices:** 5

Owl with Babies Cake

Prep Time: 40 minutes * Start to Finish: 3 hours 40 minutes * **30 SERVINGS**

cake

- **2 boxes devil's food or yellow cake mix with pudding**
- **Water, vegetable oil and eggs called for on cake mix boxes**

frosting and decorations

- **2 containers creamy chocolate frosting**
- **¼ cup creamy vanilla frosting**
- **6 creme-filled chocolate sandwich cookies**
- **8 candy-coated peanut butter pieces (6 brown, 2 orange)**
- **4 banana-shaped hard candies**
- **2 banana stretchy and tangy taffy candies (from 6-oz bag)**

Cutting and Assembling Owl with Babies Cake

Top frosted cake with bowl cake layer. Cut remaining cake into owl's head and wings.

Use 2 skewers to keep ears and head up. Press cut wings against body.

1 Heat oven to 325°F. Grease 1½-quart ovenproof bowl (8 inches across top) and 2 (8-inch) round cake pans with shortening; coat with flour (do not use cooking spray). Place paper baking cups in 2 regular-size muffin cups.

2 In large bowl, make batter for both cake mixes as directed on boxes. (Two boxes of cake batter can be made at one time; do not make more than 2 boxes, and do not increase beating time.) Pour 3¾ cups batter into 1½-quart bowl. Pour 2½ cups batter in each cake pan. Divide remaining cake batter between 2 muffin cups, filling two-thirds full.

3 Bake muffin pan 17 to 21 minutes, cake pans 23 to 30 minutes and bowl 47 to 53 minutes or until toothpick inserted in center comes out clean. Cool 10 minutes. Remove cakes from pans and bowl; place rounded sides up on cooling racks. Cool completely, about 1 hour. Freeze cakes 45 minutes before cutting to reduce crumbs, if desired. If necessary, cut off rounded tops of cakes.

4 Place one 8-inch cake on serving plate; spread ⅓ cup chocolate frosting over top. Top with bowl cake layer, cut side down. Use photo as a guide to cut remaining 8-inch cake into owl's head and wings. Use 2 skewers inserted through cake layers at ears to keep head up. Press cut wing shapes against the body. Spread thin layer of chocolate frosting over sides and top of layered cake to seal in crumbs. Freeze cake 30 to 45 minutes to set frosting.

5 In small bowl, mix vanilla frosting and 2 tablespoons chocolate frosting. Spread over belly of owl with downward strokes to make ruffled look. Frost remaining owl with chocolate frosting. Twist creme-filled chocolate cookies open, leaving creme on one side of each. Discard remaining sides. Press 2 cookies onto owl cake to make eyes. Press 1 brown peanut butter candy on each cookie to make pupil. Place banana-shaped hard candies on base of owl body to make feet. Flatten banana-shaped taffy candy; cut into 2 large triangles, and press onto owl's face to make beak.

6 To make baby owls, frost cupcakes with chocolate frosting, making slight peaks for horns. Press 2 chocolate cookies on each cupcake to make eyes. Press 1 brown peanut butter candy on each cookie to make pupil. Add 1 orange peanut butter candy to each to make nose. Remove skewers before serving. Store loosely covered.

1 Serving: Calories 330; Total Fat 15g (Saturated Fat 4g, Trans Fat 2g); Cholesterol 35mg; Sodium 350mg; Total Carbohydrate 48g (Dietary Fiber 0g); Protein 2g **Exchanges:** ½ Starch, 2½ Other Carbohydrate, 3 Fat **Carbohydrate Choices:** 3

Robot Cake

Prep Time: 1 hour 45 minutes * Start to Finish: 4 hours 40 minutes * **12 SERVINGS**

cake

- 1 **box yellow cake mix with pudding**

  Water, vegetable oil and eggs called for on cake mix box

  Tray or cardboard (20 × 15 inches), covered with wrapping paper and plastic food wrap or foil

frosting and decorations

- 1½ **containers vanilla creamy ready-to-spread frosting**

  Black food color

  Blue food color

- 2 **colorful licorice twists (7-inch)**
- 2 **large black gumdrops**
- 2 **soft fruit ring candies**
- 2 **blue candy-coated chocolate candies**
- 3 **pull-apart red (cherry) licorice twists**
- 20 **candy-coated chocolate candies (any color)**
- 1 **roll chewy fruit-flavored snack (any variety)**
- 6 **thin chocolate wafer cookies**

SWEET TIP Create an attractive display by covering a piece of sturdy cardboard with wrapping paper, then plastic food wrap. Stretch and secure with tape. Or cover cardboard with foil or cooking parchment paper.

1 Heat oven to 350°F (325°F for dark or nonstick pan). Grease or spray bottom and sides of 13 × 9-inch pan. Make and bake cake as directed on box. Cool 10 minutes; remove cake from pan to cooling rack. Cool completely, about 1 hour. Refrigerate or freeze cake 1 hour until firm.

2 Tint frosting with black and blue food colors to make desired gray color. Using serrated knife, cut rounded top off cake to level surface; place cake cut side down. Cut cake in half crosswise; cut one of the halves crosswise again so that you have three pieces. The larger piece will be the robot body. For robot head, cut small portion from one narrow piece to make it same width as body piece (see photo). Trim remaining narrow piece to be base of robot. On tray, arrange cake pieces as shown in photo, attaching to tray with small amount of frosting. Spread thin layer of frosting over top and sides to seal in crumbs. Refrigerate or freeze cake 30 to 60 minutes to set frosting.

3 Frost entire cake with remaining frosting. Cut 1 colorful licorice twist into 2 (1-inch) pieces. Carefully insert licorice pieces between head and body.

4 Cut remaining colorful licorice twist in half. Using scissors, make several cuts in 1 end of each licorice piece to form antennae. Insert licorice pieces, antennae ends up, in top of head. Insert gumdrops into sides of head for ears. Arrange fruit rings on head for eyes; use 2 blue candy-coated chocolate candies for pupils. Separate 1 pull-apart red licorice twist into single strands. Trim 1 strand to 3 inches; place on head for mouth. Use remaining strands to decorate base of robot as desired, trimming to fit.

5 Tie a knot in each remaining pull-apart red licorice twist. Insert knotted licorice twists in each side of body for arms. To decorate robot body, arrange 20 candy-coated chocolate candies in desired pattern on body. Use fruit snack to form border around candy design, trimming to fit. For wheels, insert chocolate wafer cookies in base of cake. Store loosely covered.

1 Serving (Cake and Frosting Only): Calories 430; Total Fat 19g (Saturated Fat 4g; Trans Fat 3.5g); Cholesterol 50mg; Sodium 360mg; Total Carbohydrate 65g (Dietary Fiber 0g); Protein 2g **Exchanges:** 1 Starch, 3½ Other Carbohydrate, 3½ Fat **Carbohydrate Choices:** 4

Groovy Jeans Cake

Prep Time: 35 minutes ※ Start to Finish: 4 hours 15 minutes ※ **12 SERVINGS**

cake

1 box cake mix with pudding (any flavor)

Water, vegetable oil and eggs called for on cake mix box

Tray or cardboard (15 × 12 inches), covered with wrapping paper and plastic food wrap or foil

frosting and decorations

2 containers vanilla creamy ready-to-spread frosting

Yellow and blue food colors

1 roll chewy fruit-flavored snack

Assorted decorations (licorice pieces, candy decors, yellow sprinkles, candy-coated almonds)

1 Heat oven to 350°F (325°F for dark or nonstick pan). Make and bake cake as directed on box for 13 × 9-inch pan. Cool 10 minutes. Run knife around sides of pan to loosen cake; remove from pan to cooling rack. Cool completely, about 1 hour. For easier handling, refrigerate or freeze cake 30 to 60 minutes or until firm.

2 Tint ⅓ cup frosting with yellow food color. Tint remaining frosting with blue food color. Spoon yellow frosting into resealable food-storage plastic bag or disposable pastry bag; set aside. Remove cake from freezer. Using serrated knife, cut rounded top off cake to level surface; place cake cut side down. Use toothpicks to mark sections of cake to be cut (see diagram); cut cake into sections.

3 On tray, place largest piece. Place 1½-inch strip of cake along top edge of jeans; cut off excess. Place triangles along outer edges of legs. Attach cake pieces with a small amount of blue frosting. Frost with a thin layer of blue frosting to seal in crumbs. Refrigerate or freeze 30 to 60 minutes to set frosting. Frost entire cake. Use fork or decorating comb to create fabric texture, if desired.

4 To decorate cake, cut fruit snack into 8-inch length and 6-inch length. Place fruit snack on top edge of cake, overlapping in center, for belt. Cut off very small corner of yellow bag of frosting. Pipe frosting for pocket, zipper and cuff stitching. Decorate as desired with candies. Store loosely covered.

1 Serving: Calories 520; Total Fat 22g (Saturated Fat 4.5g; Trans Fat 4.5g); Cholesterol 50mg; Sodium 410mg; Total Carbohydrate 78g (Dietary Fiber 0g); Protein 2g **Exchanges:** ½ Starch, 4½ Other Carbohydrate, 4½ Fat **Carbohydrate Choices:** 5

SWEET TIP **Specialty candy stores may sell button-shaped candies for decorating this cake.**

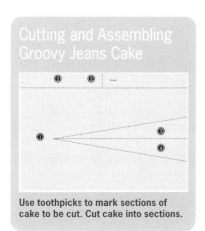

Cutting and Assembling Groovy Jeans Cake

Use toothpicks to mark sections of cake to be cut. Cut cake into sections.

Treasure Chest Cake

Prep Time: 35 minutes * Start to Finish: 4 hours 20 minutes * **15 SERVINGS**

cake

- **1 box chocolate fudge cake mix with pudding**
- **1 cup water**

  Vegetable oil and eggs called for on cake mix box

  Tray (24 × 20 inches), covered with wrapping paper and plastic food wrap or foil

frosting and decorations

- **Yellow and orange paste food colors**
- **1 container creamy white ready-to-spread frosting**

  Red pull-and-peel licorice

  Gold foil–covered chocolate coins

  Candy necklaces

  Round hard candies

  Gummy ring, halved

SWEET TIP This treasure chest can be turned into a jewelry box for a princess party. Tint the frosting pink, and use colorful hard candies for gems and strings of candy for necklaces.

1 Heat oven to 350°F (325°F for dark or nonstick pan). Spray bottom only of 13 × 9-inch pan with baking spray with flour. Make and bake cake mix as directed on box—except use 1 cup water, the oil and eggs. Cool 10 minutes; remove from pan to cooling rack. Cool completely, about 1 hour.

2 From center of cake, cut one 3-inch crosswise strip (see diagram). Cut the strip diagonally in half to make two 9-inch triangular wedges. (Discard 1 cake wedge or reserve for another use.)

3 On tray, place a 9 × 5-inch cake piece. Stir food colors into frosting to make golden yellow. Spread 1 tablespoon of frosting on 1 edge of triangular wedge of cake. Attach wedge, frosting side down, to 9 × 5-inch cake piece on tray, placing wedge along top edge of larger cake piece. Freeze all cake pieces 1 hour.

4 Spread 1 tablespoon of frosting on top edge of triangular wedge of cake. Attach remaining 9 × 5-inch cake piece to cake wedge to look like partially opened treasure chest. To seal crumbs, frost cake with a thin layer of frosting. Refrigerate or freeze 30 to 60 minutes to set frosting. Spread remaining frosting evenly over entire cake. Pull fork through frosting to look like wood grain.

5 Use pull-and-peel licorice to make handles and straps. Fill chest with chocolate coins, candy necklaces, and other hard candies. Add gummy ring half for clasp. Store loosely covered.

1 Serving (Cake and Frosting Only): Calories 400; Total Fat 25g (Saturated Fat 4.5g; Trans Fat 2g); Cholesterol 40mg; Sodium 330mg; Total Carbohydrate 43g (Dietary Fiber 0g); Protein 2g **Exchanges:** ½ Starch, 2½ Other Carbohydrate, 5 Fat **Carbohydrate Choices:** 3

Cutting and Assembling Treasure Chest Cake

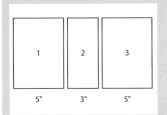

Cut one 3-inch crosswise strip.

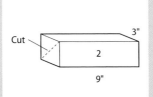

Cut the strip to make two triangular wedges.

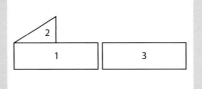

Place wedge along top edge of larger cake piece.

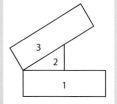

Attach cake piece to cake wedge to look like treasure chest.

Guitar Cake

Prep Time: 30 minutes ✳ **Start to Finish:** 4 hours ✳ **15 SERVINGS**

cake

- **1 box yellow cake mix with pudding**
  Water, vegetable oil and eggs called for on cake mix box
  Tray or cardboard (19 × 11 inches), covered with wrapping paper and plastic food wrap or foil

frosting and decorations

- **1 to 1½ containers vanilla creamy ready-to-spread frosting**
  Green and yellow food colors
- **10 small gumdrops**
- **1 tube (0.68 oz) orange decorating gel**
- **1 thin chocolate wafer cookie**
- **18 tart and tangy round candies**
- **1 stick gum**
  Pull-and-peel red licorice

1 Heat oven to 350°F (325°F for dark or nonstick pan). Grease or spray with cooking spray bottom and sides of 13 × 9-inch pan.

2 Make and bake cake mix as directed on box. Cool 10 minutes. Run knife around sides of pan to loosen cake; remove from pan to cooling rack. Cool completely, about 1 hour. Refrigerate or freeze cake about 1 hour or until firm.

3 Using serrated knife, cut rounded top off cake to level surface; place cake cut side down. Cut 9 × 2-inch strip of cake as shown in diagram for guitar neck. Cut body of guitar from remaining cake. Place pieces on tray.

4 Place ½ cup frosting in small bowl. Stir in 4 to 6 drops green food color. Into remaining vanilla frosting, stir 6 drops yellow food color. Attach guitar neck to body with small amount of frosting. Frost guitar neck with a thin layer of green frosting and frost top and sides of guitar body with a thin layer of yellow frosting to seal in crumbs. Refrigerate or freeze cake 30 to 60 minutes to set frosting. Frost entire cake with same colors.

5 Press 3 gumdrops on each side of neck for tuning pegs. On neck, draw crosswise lines with decorating gel, 1 inch apart, for frets. Place wafer cookie on center of body. Place tart and tangy candies around wafer cookie. Place stick of gum 1 inch under wafer cookie. Place licorice on neck for strings. Press remaining gumdrops into frosting below gum stick. Store loosely covered.

1 Serving (Cake and Frosting Only): Calories 350; Total Fat 15g (Saturated Fat 3g; Trans Fat 2.5g); Cholesterol 40mg; Sodium 290mg; Total Carbohydrate 52g (Dietary Fiber 0g); Protein 1g **Exchanges:** ½ Starch, 3 Other Carbohydrate, 3 Fat **Carbohydrate Choices:** 3½

SWEET TIP **Freezing the unfrosted cake pieces keeps crumbs in check so they won't get into the frosting.**

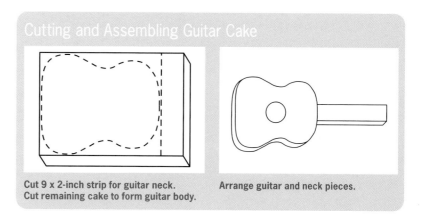

Cutting and Assembling Guitar Cake

Cut 9 x 2-inch strip for guitar neck.
Cut remaining cake to form guitar body.

Arrange guitar and neck pieces.

Flip-Flops Cake

Prep Time: 45 minutes * Start to Finish: 4 hours 20 minutes * **15 SERVINGS**

cake

1 box yellow cake mix
   with pudding

   Water, vegetable oil and eggs
   called for on cake mix box

   Tray or cardboard, covered
   with wrapping paper and
   plastic food wrap or foil

frosting and decorations

2 containers vanilla whipped
   ready-to-spread frosting

   Assorted food colors

   About 40 small round
   candy-coated fruit-flavored
   chewy candies

1 roll chewy fruit-flavored
   snack

2 edible pansy or silk daisy
   flowers

1 Heat oven to 350°F (325°F for dark or nonstick pans). Grease or spray bottom and sides of 13 × 9-inch pan. Make and bake cake as directed on box. Cool 10 minutes; remove from pan to cooling rack. Cool completely, about 1 hour. Refrigerate or freeze cake 1 hour or until firm.

2 In small bowl, mix 1 container frosting with food color to make desired color for sides of flip-flops. Reserve ⅓ cup frosting from second container. In small bowl, stir second food color into 1 cup of the remaining frosting to make desired color for top of flip-flops.

3 Using serrated knife, cut rounded top off cake to level surface; place cut side down. Cut cake lengthwise in half. Continue cutting each piece to form flip-flop shape as shown in diagram. Place pieces on tray. Spread a thin layer of frosting for "sides" over each entire flip-flop to seal in crumbs. Refrigerate or freeze cake 30 to 60 minutes to set frosting. Frost sides of flip-flops with the same remaining frosting. Frost tops of flip-flops with second color frosting.

4 Tint remaining ⅓ cup frosting with food color. To pipe frosting around top edge of flip-flops, spoon tinted frosting into small resealable food-storage plastic freezer bag and cut small tip off 1 bottom corner of bag. Pipe zigzag design. Place small candies around side edge of each flip-flop to look like jewels. Cut two 6-inch pieces from fruit roll; cut pieces lengthwise in half. Arrange on flip-flops for straps. Just before serving, top with flowers. Store loosely covered.

1 Serving: Calories 350; Total Fat 17g (Saturated Fat 4.5g; Trans Fat 3g); Cholesterol 35mg; Sodium 220mg; Total Carbohydrate 47g (Dietary Fiber 0g); Protein 1g **Exchanges:** ½ Starch, 2½ Other Carbohydrate, 3½ Fat **Carbohydrate Choices:** 3

SWEET TIP You can use paste food color to get more intense colors without diluting the frosting.

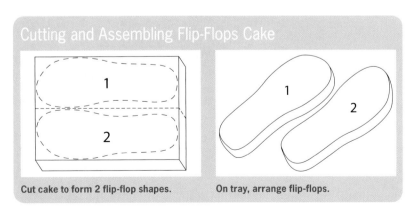

Cutting and Assembling Flip-Flops Cake

Cut cake to form 2 flip-flop shapes.   On tray, arrange flip-flops.

Butterfly Cake

Prep Time: 40 minutes ✳ Start to Finish: 3 hours 35 minutes ✳ 8 SERVINGS

cake

1 box yellow cake mix
with pudding

Water, vegetable oil and eggs
called for on cake mix box

Tray or cardboard (10 × 10
inches), covered with
wrapping paper and plastic
food wrap or foil

frosting and decorations

1 container vanilla creamy
ready-to-spread frosting

1 candy stick (8 to 10 inches
long)

Food color (in desired colors)

Decorating gel (from
0.68-oz tube) in any color

Decorating sugar crystals
(any color)

8 jelly beans or candy-coated
almonds

Small round candy
decorations

1 Heat oven to 350°F (325°F for dark or nonstick pans). Grease or spray bottoms and sides of 2 (8- or 9-inch) round pans. Make, bake and cool cake as directed on box. Wrap and freeze 1 layer for later use. Freeze remaining layer 45 minutes before cutting to reduce crumbs.

2 Cut off rounded top of cake to make flat surface; place cake cut side down. Cut cake in half crosswise; cut each half into ⅓ and ⅔ pieces (as shown in diagram). Place cake pieces on tray to form butterfly. Gently separate cake pieces to form wings.

3 Reserve ½ cup frosting; set aside. Spread top and sides of cake with thin layer of frosting to seal in crumbs. Refrigerate or freeze 30 to 60 minutes to set frosting. Frost cake with remaining frosting. Place candy stick between cake pieces for butterfly body.

4 Stir food color into reserved frosting until well blended. Spread over cake in desired pattern on wings. Outline wing patterns with gel. Sprinkle with sugar crystals. Place jelly beans on corners of wings. Decorate butterfly with candy decorations. Store loosely covered.

1 Serving (Cake and Frosting Only): Calories 400; Total Fat 17g (Saturated Fat 3.5g; Trans Fat 3.5g); Cholesterol 40mg; Sodium 320mg; Total Carbohydrate 60g (Dietary Fiber 0g); Protein 1g **Exchanges:** ½ Starch, 3½ Other Carbohydrate, 3½ Fat **Carbohydrate Choices:** 4

SWEET TIP Turn the extra cake layer into a trifle! Cut the cake into 1-inch cubes, and layer them with chocolate pudding and fresh strawberries in a large glass bowl. Top with whipped cream.

Cutting and Assembling Butterfly Cake

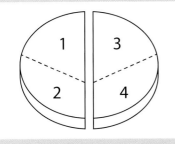

Cut cake crosswise in half; cut each half into ⅓ and ⅔ pieces.

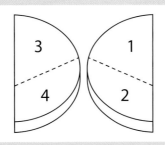

On tray, arrange cake pieces to form butterfly.

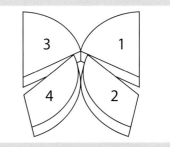

Separate cake pieces to form wings.

Building Blocks Cakes

Prep Time: 35 minutes * Start to Finish: 4 hours 10 minutes * **12 SERVINGS**

1 box yellow cake mix
  with pudding

  Water, vegetable oil and
  eggs called for on cake
  mix box

2 containers vanilla creamy
  ready-to-spread frosting

  Red, yellow and blue gel
  or paste food colors

  Tray or cardboard (15 × 12
  inches), covered with
  wrapping paper and plastic
  food wrap or foil

12 large marshmallows,
  cut in half crosswise

1 Heat oven to 350°F (325°F for dark or nonstick pan). Grease or spray bottom and sides of 13 × 9-inch pan. Make and bake cake mix as directed on box. Cool in pan 10 minutes; remove from pan to cooling rack. Cool completely, about 1 hour. Refrigerate or freeze cake about 1 hour or until firm.

2 Meanwhile, in small bowl for each color, tint 1 cup frosting red, 1 cup frosting yellow and ⅔ cup frosting blue with food colors. Leave remaining frosting white.

3 Using serrated knife, cut rounded dome from top of cake to make flat surface; place cake cut side down. Cut cake crosswise into thirds. Cut one of the thirds in half crosswise to make 2 squares. Place cake pieces on tray.

4 To seal in crumbs, frost top and sides of 1 square cake with thin layer of blue frosting and 1 square cake with thin layer of white frosting. Frost 1 rectangular cake with thin layer of yellow frosting and 1 rectangular cake with thin layer of red frosting. Refrigerate or freeze 30 to 60 minutes to set frosting.

5 Add final coat of frosting to each cake. Frost 4 marshmallow halves with blue frosting; place in square design on blue cake. Frost 4 marshmallow halves with white frosting; place in square design on white cake. Frost 8 marshmallow halves with yellow frosting; place on yellow cake. Frost 8 marshmallow halves with red frosting; place on red cake. Store loosely covered.

1 Serving: Calories 560; Total Fat 23g (Saturated Fat 5g; Trans Fat 4.5g); Cholesterol 55mg; Sodium 430mg; Total Carbohydrate 86g (Dietary Fiber 0g); Protein 2g **Exchanges:** ½ Starch, 5 Other Carbohydrate, 4½ Fat **Carbohydrate Choices:** 6

SWEET TIPS Use kitchen scissors to cut marshmallows. Spray blades of scissors with cooking spray to keep them from getting sticky.

Stick fork in side of marshmallow halves to hold while frosting. Use metal spatula or knife to slide marshmallow from fork onto cake. Smooth frosting on marshmallow with spatula.

Sailboat Cake

Prep Time: 25 minutes * Start to Finish: 3 hours * **15 SERVINGS**

cake

1   **box cake mix with pudding (any flavor)**

   Water, oil and eggs called for on cake mix box

   Tray or cardboard (24 × 24 inches), covered with wrapping paper and plastic food wrap, or foil

frosting and decorations

1   **container fluffy white whipped ready-to-spread frosting**

1   **tablespoon unsweetened baking cocoa**

   Red pull-and-peel licorice

1   **roll chewy fruit-flavored snack (any flavor)**

   Ring-shaped hard candies

   Tiny star candies

   Miniature candy-coated chocolate baking bits

1   Heat oven to 350°F (325°F for dark or nonstick pan). Spray bottom only of 13 × 9-inch pan with baking spray with flour. Make and bake cake mix as directed on box. Cool 10 minutes. Run knife around side of pan to loosen cake; remove from pan to cooling rack. Cool completely, about 1 hour.

2   Cut cake (as shown in diagram). If desired, freeze pieces uncovered about 1 hour for easier frosting.

3   On tray, arrange cake pieces to form sailboat (as shown in diagram), leaving space between sails for mast. Frost sails with 1 cup of the frosting.

4   Gently fold cocoa into remaining frosting until blended. Frost hull of sailboat with cocoa frosting. Place piece of licorice on cake between sails for mast. Cut flags from fruit snack and press on mast. Decorate cake with candies and baking bits. Store loosely covered at room temperature.

1 Serving (Cake and Frosting Only): Calories 300; Total Fat 13g (Saturated Fat 3g; Trans Fat 2g); Cholesterol 40mg; Sodium 260mg; Total Carbohydrate 41g (Dietary Fiber 0g); Protein 3g **Exchanges:** 1 Starch, 2 Other Carbohydrate, 2½ Fat **Carbohydrate Choices:** 3

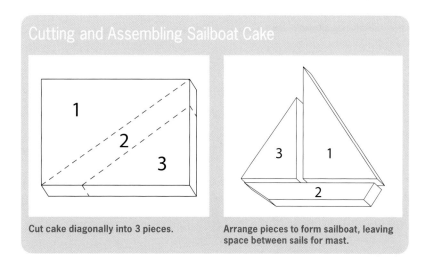

Cutting and Assembling Sailboat Cake

Cut cake diagonally into 3 pieces.

Arrange pieces to form sailboat, leaving space between sails for mast.

Party-Time Purse Cake

Prep Time: 40 minutes * Start to Finish: 3 hours * **15 SERVINGS**

cake

1 box white cake mix with pudding

Water, vegetable oil and egg whites called for on cake mix box

frosting and decorations

1½ containers creamy white ready-to-spread frosting

Blue paste food color

Decorating bag with tips

1 plastic plate

Candy-coated chocolate candies

1 or 2 large marshmallows

Colored sugar

SWEET TIP To keep scissors from sticking to marshmallow, spray lightly with cooking spray.

1 Heat oven to 350°F (325°F for dark or nonstick pan). Make, bake and cool cake as directed on box for 13 × 9-inch pan.

2 Cut cake crosswise in half. On serving plate, place 1 cake piece; spread top with 2 tablespoons white frosting from ½ container. Top with second cake piece. Stand cake pieces on end with cut sides down (see diagram). Freeze 1 hour.

3 Stir food color into 1 container of frosting to tint light blue. Spread entire cake with light blue frosting.

4 Along front and top of cake, mark outline of an elongated V-shape with toothpick for purse flap. Stir food color into remaining ½ container of frosting to tint dark blue; frost purse flap with dark blue frosting. Place remaining dark blue frosting in decorating bag fitted with writing tip #7 or #8; pipe shell border along purse flap and edges of purse.

5 Cut rim from plastic plate; cut rim in half. Insert into top of cake for handle. Decorate purse with candies. Cut marshmallow with kitchen scissors into slices; sprinkle with colored sugar. Arrange marshmallow slices on purse for clasp. Press candy onto center of clasp. Store loosely covered.

1 Serving (Cake and Frosting Only): Calories 350; Total Fat 13g (Saturated Fat 3g; Trans Fat 2.5g); Cholesterol 0mg; Sodium 320mg; Total Carbohydrate 56g (Dietary Fiber 0g); Protein 2g **Exchanges:** ½ Starch, 3 Other Carbohydrate, 2½ Fat **Carbohydrate Choices: 4**

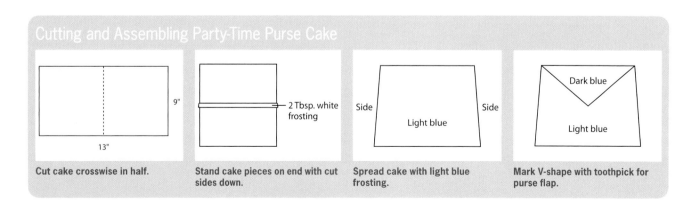

Cutting and Assembling Party-Time Purse Cake

Cut cake crosswise in half.

Stand cake pieces on end with cut sides down.

Spread cake with light blue frosting.

Mark V-shape with toothpick for purse flap.

Sports Party Cake

Prep Time: 35 minutes * Start to Finish: 4 hours 25 minutes * 15 SERVINGS

1 box cake mix with pudding (any flavor)

Water, vegetable oil and eggs called for on cake mix box

1½ containers fluffy white whipped ready-to-spread frosting

Food colors

Tray or cardboard (15 × 12 inches), covered with wrapping paper and plastic food wrap or foil

1 Heat oven to 350°F (325°F for dark or nonstick pan). Spray bottom only of 13 × 9-inch pan with baking spray with flour. Make and bake cake as directed on box. Cool 10 minutes; remove from pan to cooling rack. Cool completely, about 1 hour. For easier handling, refrigerate or freeze cake 30 to 60 minutes or until firm.

2 Meanwhile, tint 2¼ cups of the frosting with food color as desired for your favorite team's jersey color. Tint ½ cup frosting as desired for team name and numbers. Remove cake from freezer. Using serrated knife, cut rounded top off cake to level surface; place cake cut side down on cutting board.

3 Place short side of cake toward you. Poke toothpick in cake at a point 4 inches from top and 1 inch from outside edge, on both sides. Poke toothpick in cake at bottom, 1 inch from outside edge, on both sides. Cut 1 × 8-inch piece (marked with toothpicks) from outer edge of each side. Cut each piece in half crosswise, forming 4 (1 × 4-inch) pieces. Cut neck hole from top of cake.

4 On tray, place largest piece of cake. Using small amount of jersey-colored frosting, attach 2 small rectangular pieces on each side of top of cake to lengthen sleeves. Frost with a thin layer of frosting to seal in crumbs. Refrigerate or freeze 30 to 60 minutes to set frosting.

5 Frost entire cake with jersey-colored frosting. Pipe other color frosting onto cake to create team name, numbers and shirt trim. Store loosely covered.

1 Serving: Calories 340; Total Fat 16g (Saturated Fat 4g; Trans Fat 2g); Cholesterol 40mg; Sodium 250mg; Total Carbohydrate 45g (Dietary Fiber 0g); Protein 2g **Exchanges:** 1 Starch, 2 Other Carbohydrate, 3 Fat **Carbohydrate Choices:** 3

Automobile Cake

Prep Time: 1 hour 5 minutes ❋ Start to Finish: 3 hours 30 minutes ❋ **12 SERVINGS**

cake

2	cups all-purpose flour
1	cup granulated sugar
3	teaspoons baking powder
½	teaspoon salt
¼	cup butter, softened
¼	cup shortening
¾	cup milk
1	teaspoon vanilla
2	eggs

frosting

⅔	cup butter, softened
5½	cups powdered sugar
2	teaspoons vanilla
	About 3 tablespoons milk
	Desired food color

decorations

	Tray or cardboard (13 × 9½ inches), covered with wrapping paper and plastic food wrap or foil
4	creme-filled chocolate sandwich cookies
1	tube (.68 oz) black or brown decorating gel
	Black and yellow licorice beans
1	white and 2 red gum balls
	Silver nonpareils

1 Heat oven to 300°F. Grease bottoms and sides of 2 (9 × 5-inch) loaf pans with shortening; lightly flour. In large bowl, beat all cake ingredients with electric mixer on medium speed 30 seconds, scraping bowl constantly. Beat on high speed 2 minutes, scraping bowl occasionally. Pour batter into pans.

2 Bake 40 to 45 minutes or until toothpick inserted in center comes out clean. Cool 10 minutes; remove cakes from pans to cooling racks. Cool completely, about 1 hour.

3 Cut and remove 3-inch piece from end of one loaf; discard or save for another use. Freeze remaining piece uncovered about 1 hour for easier frosting, if desired.

4 In large bowl, beat ⅔ cup butter and the powdered sugar with electric mixer on medium speed until smooth. Gradually beat in 2 teaspoons vanilla and 2 tablespoons milk, adding more milk if necessary for spreading consistency. Reserve ½ cup frosting. Tint remaining frosting with food color.

5 Place whole loaf on tray. Frost top with ⅓ cup colored frosting. Top with cut piece of loaf, positioning as shown in photo; trim front and back as desired to resemble car front and back. Attach cookies with small amount of frosting for wheels. Draw outline of windows with sharp knife. Frost windows and hubcaps with reserved white frosting. Frost sides and top of car with remaining colored frosting, building up around wheels for fenders.

6 Using decorating gel, outline windows, hood, doors and bumpers. Use licorice beans for grille, door handles and signal lights. Cut gum balls in half; use for headlights and taillights. Make spoke markings on wheel with knife. Press 1 silver nonpareil in center of each wheel. Use silver nonpareils for hood ornament if desired. Remove nonpareils before serving cake.

1 Serving: Calories 640; Total Fat 23g (Saturated Fat 11g; Trans Fat 1.5g); Cholesterol 75mg; Sodium 400mg; Total Carbohydrate 102g (Dietary Fiber 1g); Protein 4g **Exchanges:** 1½ Starch, 5½ Other Carbohydrate, 4½ Fat **Carbohydrate Choices:** 7

chapter 7

Tiny
Cakes

Bittersweet Baby Cakes

Prep Time: 20 minutes * **Start to Finish:** 55 minutes * **8 SERVINGS**

½ teaspoon unsweetened baking cocoa
1½ cups bittersweet chocolate chips
1 cup butter, cut into pieces
¾ cup granulated sugar
8 eggs
2 teaspoons instant espresso coffee powder or granules
Powdered sugar, if desired

1 Heat oven to 325°F. Spray 8 (6-oz) individual baking dishes (ramekins) or custard cups with cooking spray. Sprinkle sides of dishes with cocoa. Place on cookie sheet with sides.

2 In 1-quart saucepan, melt chocolate chips and butter over low heat, stirring frequently. Remove from heat; cool completely.

3 In large bowl, beat granulated sugar, the eggs and coffee powder with electric mixer on high speed 3 minutes. Add cooled chocolate mixture, beating on low speed just until blended. Divide batter evenly among baking dishes.

4 Bake 25 minutes, rotating cookie sheet after 10 minutes (edges should be set but center of cakes should look unbaked). Cool 10 minutes. Run knife around edges of dishes to loosen cakes. Sprinkle with powdered sugar. Serve warm.

1 Serving: Calories 530; Total Fat 38g (Saturated Fat 22g; Trans Fat 1g); Cholesterol 250mg; Sodium 270mg; Total Carbohydrate 38g (Dietary Fiber 2g); Protein 8g **Exchanges:** ½ Starch, 2 Other Carbohydrate, 1 Medium-Fat Meat, 6½ Fat **Carbohydrate Choices:** 2½

SWEET TIP Spoon warmed dark chocolate ice cream topping onto dessert plates, then invert cakes onto plates. Garnish with a dollop of sweetened whipped cream.

Molten Butterscotch Cakes

Prep Time: 15 minutes * Start to Finish: 35 minutes * **6 SERVINGS**

6 teaspoons graham cracker crumbs

1 cup butterscotch chips (6 oz)

⅔ cup butter

3 whole eggs

3 egg yolks

¾ cup packed brown sugar

½ cup all-purpose flour

1 Heat oven to 450°F. Spray sides and bottoms of 6 (6-oz) custard cups with baking spray with flour. Sprinkle 1 teaspoon cracker crumbs onto bottom and around side of each cup.

2 In 1-quart saucepan, melt butterscotch chips and butter over medium heat, stirring constantly. Remove from heat; cool slightly, about 5 minutes.

3 Meanwhile, in large bowl, beat whole eggs and egg yolks with whisk until well blended. Beat in brown sugar. Beat in butterscotch mixture and flour until well blended. Divide batter evenly among custard cups. Place cups on cookie sheet with sides.

4 Bake 12 to 14 minutes or until sides are set and centers are still soft (tops will be puffed and cracked). Let cakes stand 3 minutes. Run small knife or metal spatula along sides of cups to loosen cakes. Immediately place dessert plate upside down on top of each cup; turn plate and cup over. Remove cup. Serve cakes warm.

1 Serving: Calories 550; Total Fat 34g (Saturated Fat 21g; Trans Fat 1g); Cholesterol 260mg; Sodium 220mg; Total Carbohydrate 56g (Dietary Fiber 0g); Protein 6g **Exchanges:** 2 Starch, 1½ Other Carbohydrate, 6½ Fat **Carbohydrate Choices:** 4

SWEET TIP Don't be tempted to overbake these! When these individual cakes are served, the centers should be soft and have a pudding-like texture.

Maple-Walnut Mini Cupcakes

Prep Time: 20 minutes * Start to Finish: 55 minutes * **36 MINI CUPCAKES**

cupcakes

1⅓	cups all-purpose flour
½	teaspoon baking powder
⅛	teaspoon salt
½	cup butter, softened
¾	cup granulated sugar
2	eggs
½	cup milk
¾	cup chopped walnuts, toasted*
1	teaspoon maple flavor

frosting

4	oz (half of 8-oz package) cream cheese, softened
¼	cup butter, softened
1¾	cups powdered sugar
½	teaspoon maple flavor

garnish

Turbinado sugar (raw sugar) or maple sugar, if desired

Chopped walnuts or walnut halves, if desired

1 Heat oven to 350°F. Place mini paper baking cup in each of 36 mini muffin cups.

2 In medium bowl, mix flour, baking powder and salt; set aside. In large bowl, beat ½ cup butter and the granulated sugar with electric mixer on medium speed 2 to 4 minutes or until light and fluffy. Add eggs, one at a time, beating well after each addition. Beat in flour mixture alternately with milk. Stir in ¾ cup walnuts and 1 teaspoon maple flavor. Divide batter evenly among muffin cups, filling each almost full.

3 Bake 17 to 18 minutes or until toothpick inserted in center comes out clean. Remove from pans to cooling racks; cool completely, about 15 minutes.

4 In medium bowl, beat cream cheese and ¼ cup butter until blended. Gradually add powdered sugar and ½ teaspoon maple flavor, beating until smooth. Frost cupcakes. Garnish with turbinado sugar and walnuts.

To toast walnuts, heat oven to 350°F. Spread walnuts in ungreased shallow pan. Bake uncovered 6 to 10 minutes, stirring occasionally, until light brown.

1 Mini Cupcake: Calories 130; Total Fat 7g (Saturated Fat 3.5g; Trans Fat 0g); Cholesterol 25mg; Sodium 65mg; Total Carbohydrate 14g (Dietary Fiber 0g); Protein 1g **Exchanges:** ½ Starch, ½ Other Carbohydrate, 1½ Fat **Carbohydrate Choices:** 1

Chipotle Devil's Food Mini Cupcakes

Prep Time: 35 minutes * Start to Finish: 1 hour 15 minutes * **32 MINI CUPCAKES**

cupcakes

- 1 **cup all-purpose flour**
- ¾ **cup granulated sugar**
- ⅓ **cup unsweetened dark baking cocoa**
- ½ **teaspoon baking soda**
- ½ **teaspoon salt**
- ½ **teaspoon ground cinnamon**
- ¼ **teaspoon chipotle chile powder**
- ½ **cup buttermilk**
- ⅓ **cup butter, softened**
- 1 **egg**
- ½ **teaspoon vanilla**

frosting

- 6 **oz cream cheese, softened**
- 3 **cups powdered sugar**
- ½ **to 1 teaspoon milk**
  Red gel or paste food color
  Green food color

1 Heat oven to 350°F. Place mini paper baking cup in each of 32 mini muffin cups. In large bowl, combine all cake ingredients. Beat with electric mixer on low speed until moistened. Beat on medium speed 2 minutes. Fill muffin cups two-thirds to three-quarters full, about 1 tablespoon per cup.

2 Bake 15 to 18 minutes or until toothpick inserted in center comes out clean. Let stand 10 minutes; remove from pans to cooling racks. Cool completely, about 20 minutes.

3 In small bowl, combine cream cheese and powdered sugar. Beat with electric mixer on low speed until mixed. Beat at medium speed until creamy. Spoon 2 tablespoons into one custard cup and 2 tablespoons into another custard cup; set aside. To remaining frosting, gradually beat in enough milk to make frosting smooth and spreadable. Frost cupcakes.

4 Stir small amount of red food color into 2 tablespoons of the frosting, or until bright red. Stir 1 drop green food color into remaining 2 tablespoons frosting or until medium green. Spoon each colored frosting into a small resealable food-storage plastic bag. Cut ¼-inch opening in one corner of red frosting bag. Pipe a small chile pepper on top of each cupcake, curving slightly and tapering to a soft point. Snip a tiny opening in one corner of the green frosting bag. Squiggle a little frosting at the wide end of the pepper for stem. Store in refrigerator.

1 Mini Cupcake: Calories 120; Total Fat 4g (Saturated Fat 2.5g; Trans Fat 0g); Cholesterol 15mg; Sodium 95mg; Total Carbohydrate 20g (Dietary Fiber 0g); Protein 1g **Exchanges:** ½ Starch, 1 Other Carbohydrate, ½ Fat **Carbohydrate Choices:** 1

SWEET TIPS The chipotle chile powder gives these chocolaty treats a slightly smoky flavor plus a bit of heat. You can use regular chili powder, which will provide less heat, or ancho chile powder, which will provide some heat but no smoky flavor. Look for these specialty items with the other spices at the supermarket.

Gel or paste food color will provide a vibrant red color without softening the frosting. You can use liquid food color, but the frosting might not hold its shape as well.

Only have 2 mini muffin pans? Refrigerate the remaining batter. Once the muffins have been removed from pan, line with paper baking cups and bake batter as directed.

Boozy Bourbon Chocolate Cupcakes

Prep Time: 40 minutes * Start to Finish: 1 hour 45 minutes * **24 CUPCAKES**

cupcakes

- **1 box devil's food cake mix with pudding**
- **1 cup water**
- **⅓ cup vegetable oil**
- **¼ cup bourbon**
- **3 eggs**
- **1 teaspoon vanilla**

filling

- **¾ cup whipping cream**
- **6 oz semisweet baking chocolate, finely chopped**
- **⅓ cup butter, softened**
- **3 tablespoons coffee-flavored liqueur**

frosting

- **1 jar (7 oz) marshmallow creme (1¾ cups)**
- **1 cup butter, softened**
- **2 tablespoons vanilla-flavored vodka**
- **3 cups powdered sugar**

garnish

- **¼ cup coffee-flavored liqueur**

1 Heat oven to 350°F (325°F for dark or nonstick pan). Generously spray 24 regular-size muffin cups with cooking spray. Make cake batter as directed on box, using cake mix, water, oil, bourbon, eggs and vanilla. Divide batter evenly among muffin cups (about two-thirds full).

2 Bake 20 to 22 minutes or until toothpick inserted in center comes out clean. Cool in pans 10 minutes; remove from pans to cooling rack. Cool completely, about 30 minutes.

3 Meanwhile, for filling, in medium microwavable bowl, microwave whipping cream uncovered on High 1 minute 30 seconds or until boiling. Stir in remaining filling ingredients until chocolate is melted and smooth. If necessary, microwave on High an additional 15 to 30 seconds until mixture can be stirred smooth. Cover; refrigerate about 60 minutes or until spreading consistency.

4 For frosting, in large bowl, beat marshmallow creme, 1 cup butter and the vodka with electric mixer on medium speed until blended. Beat in powdered sugar until fluffy. If necessary, beat additional powdered sugar until piping consistency.

5 To assemble, cut tops off each cupcake horizontally. Spread about 1 tablespoon filling onto bottom of each cupcake; add cupcake top. Pipe frosting on cupcake tops. Just before serving, drizzle each cupcake with ½ teaspoon coffee liqueur.

1 Cupcake: Calories 340; Total Fat 19g (Saturated Fat 10g; Trans Fat 0g); Cholesterol 55mg; Sodium 230mg; Total Carbohydrate 38g (Dietary Fiber 1g); Protein 3g **Exchanges:** 1 Starch, 1½ Other Carbohydrate, 3½ Fat **Carbohydrate Choices:** 2½

SWEET TIP **For the full tipsy effect, place the cupcake top at a slight angle.**

Pecan-Bourbon-Crunch Italian Cream Cups

Prep Time: 40 minutes * Start to Finish: 1 hour 40 minutes * **20 CUPCAKES**

cupcakes

4	**eggs**
½	**cup water**
4½	**teaspoons bourbon or apple cider**
1	**teaspoon vanilla**
2¼	**cups cake flour**
1½	**cups granulated sugar**
2	**teaspoons baking powder**
1	**bag (5 oz) glazed pecans, finely chopped**
15	**tablespoons butter, slightly softened**
1	**package (8 oz) cream cheese, softened**

frosting

9	**tablespoons butter, slightly softened**
2	**tablespoons bourbon or apple cider**
½	**teaspoon finely grated lemon peel**
⅛	**teaspoon salt**
4½	**cups powdered sugar**
¾	**cup flaked coconut**

1 Heat oven to 350°F. Place paper baking cup in each of 20 regular-size muffin cups.

2 In 2-cup glass measure, mix eggs, water, 4½ teaspoons bourbon and the vanilla with wire whisk. In medium bowl, mix flour, granulated sugar and baking powder. Remove 1 tablespoon of the flour mixture to small bowl; add ¾ cup of the glazed pecans and toss to coat. Set aside. Reserve remaining glazed pecans for frosting.

3 Cut butter into tablespoon-size pieces. Cut 3 tablespoons of the cream cheese into cubes; reserve remaining cream cheese for frosting. Add butter pieces and cream cheese cubes, a few at a time, to flour mixture in medium bowl, beating with electric mixer on low speed. Pour in all but ½ cup of the egg mixture. Beat on low for 30 seconds, then medium for 30 seconds, scraping bowl occasionally. Add remaining egg mixture in a slow stream; beat 30 seconds longer. Stir in reserved pecan mixture.

4 Spoon into muffin cups. Bake 20 to 25 minutes or until tops spring back when lightly touched. Cool 5 minutes; remove from pans to cooling racks. Cool completely, about 30 minutes.

5 Meanwhile, in large bowl, beat 9 tablespoons butter, 2 tablespoons bourbon, the lemon peel, salt and reserved cream cheese with electric mixer on low speed until smooth. Gradually beat in powdered sugar, 1 cup at a time, on low speed until smooth. Stir in ½ cup of the reserved glazed pecans and the coconut.

6 Pipe or spread frosting on top of each cupcake; sprinkle with remaining glazed pecans.

1 Cupcake: Calories 480; Total Fat 25g (Saturated Fat 13g; Trans Fat 0.5g); Cholesterol 90mg; Sodium 250mg; Total Carbohydrate 57g (Dietary Fiber 1g); Protein 4g **Exchanges:** 1½ Starch, 2½ Other Carbohydrate, 5 Fat **Carbohydrate Choices:** 4

SWEET TIPS **Lightly spray lined muffin pan with cooking spray to help prevent cupcake crowns from sticking to pan.**

Look for the glazed pecans in the produce or snack section of your grocery store.

Vanilla Bean Cupcakes

Prep Time: 30 minutes * Start to Finish: 1 hour 20 minutes * **24 CUPCAKES**

cupcakes

- **2 vanilla beans, each cut in half lengthwise**
- **1½ cups milk**
- **2½ cups all-purpose flour**
- **3 teaspoons baking powder**
- **½ teaspoon salt**
- **¾ cup unsalted butter, softened**
- **1 cup granulated sugar**
- **4 eggs**

frosting

- **4 cups powdered sugar**
- **1 cup unsalted butter, softened**
- **⅛ teaspoon salt**
- **Reserved ¼ cup milk-vanilla seed mixture**

1 Scrape vanilla bean seeds into microwavable bowl; add beans to bowl, cover beans with ¾ cup milk. Microwave on High 1 minute or until mixture boils. Let stand 15 minutes. Remove beans. Add remaining milk to warm milk mixture, stir well. Reserve ¼ cup milk mixture.

2 Heat oven to 350°F (325°F for dark or nonstick pans). Place paper baking cup in each of 24 regular-size muffin cups. In medium bowl, mix flour, baking powder and ½ teaspoon salt. In large bowl, beat ¾ cup butter with electric mixer on medium speed 30 seconds. Gradually add sugar, beating after each addition. Beat 2 minutes longer. Add eggs, one at a time, beating well after each addition. Beat 2 minutes longer. On low speed, alternately add flour mixture and milk mixture, beating just until blended. Divide batter evenly among muffin cups.

3 Bake 17 to 22 minutes or until toothpick comes out clean. Cool 5 minutes; remove from pans to cooling racks. Cool completely. In large bowl, beat frosting ingredients on low speed until blended, adding 1 tablespoon reserved milk mixture at a time. Frost cupcakes.

1 Cupcake: Calories 300; Total Fat 15g (Saturated Fat 9g; Trans Fat 0.5g); Cholesterol 70mg; Sodium 140mg; Total Carbohydrate 39g (Dietary Fiber 0g); Protein 3g **Exchanges:** 2½ Other Carbohydrate, 3 Fat **Carbohydrate Choices:** 2½

SWEET TIP **To remove seeds from a vanilla bean, cut the bean in half lengthwise. Run the blade of a knife across the inside of the bean, gathering seeds on the edge of the knife.**

Sauvignon Blanc Wine Cupcakes

Prep Time: 30 minutes * Start to Finish: 1 hour 15 minutes * **24 CUPCAKES**

cupcakes

- **1** box yellow cake mix with pudding
- **½** cup water
- **½** cup Sauvignon Blanc wine
- **½** cup vegetable oil
- **3** eggs
- **2** teaspoons grated lemon peel

frosting

- **6** cups powdered sugar
- **⅓** cup butter, softened
- **⅛** teaspoon salt
- **⅓** cup Sauvignon Blanc wine
- **1** teaspoon grated lemon peel

garnish

Yellow decorator sugar crystals

Edible yellow pearls

1 Heat oven to 350°F (325°F for dark or nonstick pans). Place paper baking cup in each of 24 regular-size muffin cups. Make cake batter as directed on box, using cake mix, water, ½ cup wine, oil, eggs and 2 teaspoons lemon peel. Divide batter evenly among muffin cups (about two-thirds full).

2 Bake 20 to 22 minutes or until toothpick inserted in center comes out clean. Cool in pans 10 minutes; remove from pans to cooling rack. Cool completely, about 30 minutes.

3 In large bowl, beat powdered sugar, butter and salt with electric mixer on low speed until blended. Beat in ⅓ cup wine and 1 teaspoon lemon peel. If frosting is too thick, beat in more wine a few drops at a time. Frost cupcakes. Sprinkle with yellow sugar and pearls.

1 Cupcake: Calories 260; Total Fat 8g (Saturated Fat 3g; Trans Fat 0g); Cholesterol 35mg; Sodium 170mg; Total Carbohydrate 45g (Dietary Fiber 0g); Protein 1g **Carbohydrate Choices:** 3

SWEET TIP **For yellow decorator sugar crystals, edible yellow pearls and decorative cupcake liners, check out www.fancyflours.com.**

Zinfandel Wine Cupcakes

Prep Time: 30 minutes * Start to Finish: 1 hour 20 minutes * **24 CUPCAKES**

cupcakes

- **1 box devil's food cake mix with pudding**
- **¾ cup water**
- **½ cup Zinfandel wine**
- **⅓ cup vegetable oil**
- **3 eggs**
- **1 cup miniature semisweet chocolate chips**

frosting

- **6 cups powdered sugar**
- **⅓ cup butter, softened**
- **⅓ cup unsweetened baking cocoa**
- **⅛ teaspoon salt**
- **½ cup Zinfandel wine**

garnish

- **Chocolate curls**

1 Heat oven to 350°F (325°F for dark or nonstick pan). Place paper baking cup in each of 24 regular-size muffin cups. Make cake batter as directed on box, using cake mix, water, ½ cup wine, oil and eggs. Stir in chocolate chips. Divide batter evenly among muffin cups (about two-thirds full).

2 Bake 20 to 22 minutes or until toothpick inserted in center comes out clean. Cool in pans 10 minutes; remove from pans to cooling rack. Cool completely, about 30 minutes.

3 In large bowl, beat powdered sugar, butter, cocoa and salt with electric mixer on low speed until blended. Beat in ½ cup wine. If frosting is too thick, beat in more wine a few drops at a time. Frost cupcakes. Garnish with chocolate curls.

1 Cupcake: Calories 290; Total Fat 9g (Saturated Fat 4g; Trans Fat 0g); Cholesterol 35mg; Sodium 190mg; Total Carbohydrate 50g (Dietary Fiber 1g); Protein 2g **Carbohydrate Choices:** 3

SWEET TIP **To make chocolate curls, warm a chocolate bar by holding it in your hands for several minutes till slightly soft. Using vegetable peeler, shave chocolate in long strands along smooth side of chocolate. Transfer curls with toothpick to cupcakes.**

Tiramisu Cupcakes

Prep Time: 35 minutes * Start to Finish: 1 hour 55 minutes * **24 CUPCAKES**

1 box white cake mix
   with pudding

1 cup water

⅓ cup vegetable oil

¼ cup brandy

3 egg whites

3 tablespoons instant
   espresso coffee powder
   or granules

⅓ cup boiling water

2 tablespoons corn syrup

1 package (8 oz) cream
   cheese, softened

½ cup powdered sugar

2 cups whipping cream

   Unsweetened baking cocoa,
   if desired

   Chocolate-covered
   espresso beans, if desired

1 Heat oven to 350°F (325°F for dark or nonstick pans). Place paper baking cup in each of 24 regular-size muffin cups. In large bowl, beat cake mix, water, oil, brandy and egg whites with electric mixer on low speed 30 seconds, then on medium speed 2 minutes. Divide batter evenly among muffin cups. Bake 18 to 23 minutes or until toothpick inserted in center comes out clean.

2 Meanwhile, in small bowl, stir espresso powder and boiling water. Stir in corn syrup. Cool 10 minutes. Pierce top of warm cupcakes with large-tined fork. Slowly spoon about 1 teaspoon espresso mixture over top of each cupcake, allowing it to soak into holes. Cool completely, about 30 minutes. Remove cupcakes from pans.

3 In medium bowl, beat cream cheese and powdered sugar with electric mixer on low speed until mixed. Beat on high speed until smooth. On high speed, gradually beat in whipping cream until stiff peaks form, about 2 minutes. Spoon in dollops on cupcakes. Sprinkle with cocoa and top with espresso beans. Store covered in refrigerator.

1 Cupcake: Calories 220; Total Fat 13g (Saturated Fat 7g; Trans Fat 0g); Cholesterol 35mg; Sodium 180mg; Total Carbohydrate 21g (Dietary Fiber 0g); Protein 2g **Exchanges:** ½ Starch, 1 Other Carbohydrate, 2½ Fat **Carbohydrate Choices:** 1½

SWEET TIPS To easily sprinkle baking cocoa over cupcakes, place cocoa in a fine strainer and tap gently.

If you have only 1 pan and a recipe calls for more cupcakes than your pan will make, cover and refrigerate the rest of the batter while baking the first batch. Cool the pan about 15 minutes, then bake the rest of the batter, adding 1 to 2 minutes to the bake time.

Orange-Thyme Mini Cupcakes

Prep Time: 25 minutes * **Start to Finish:** 50 minutes * **24 MINI CUPCAKES**

cupcakes

- ¾ **cup all-purpose flour**
- 1 **teaspoon baking soda**
- ⅛ **teaspoon salt**
- ⅓ **cup granulated sugar**
- ¼ **cup butter, softened**
- 1 **egg plus 1 egg white**
- 2 **tablespoons milk**
- 2 **teaspoons grated orange peel**
- 1½ **teaspoons chopped fresh thyme leaves**

garnish

- 1 **tablespoon granulated sugar**
- 2 **teaspoons grated orange peel**

glaze

- 1 **cup powdered sugar**
- 4 **to 6 teaspoons orange juice**

1 Heat oven to 350°F. Grease 24 mini muffin cups with shortening or spray with cooking spray.

2 In small bowl, mix flour, baking soda and salt; set aside. In medium bowl, beat ⅓ cup granulated sugar and the butter with electric mixer on medium speed until creamy. Add egg and egg white, milk, 2 teaspoons orange peel and the thyme; beat on medium speed 1 minute, scraping bowl occasionally. On low speed, beat in flour mixture, just until blended.

3 Fill muffin cups about two-thirds full. Bake 9 to 12 minutes or until toothpick inserted in center comes out clean. Cool in pan 5 minutes; remove cupcakes from pans to cooling racks. Cool completely, about 20 minutes.

4 In small bowl, combine 1 tablespoon granulated sugar and 2 teaspoons orange peel; set aside. In another small bowl, mix powdered sugar and enough orange juice for drizzling consistency. Using fork or spoon, drizzle glaze over top of cupcakes. Sprinkle with orange peel mixture. To serve, place cupcakes in mini paper baking cups.

1 Mini Cupcake: Calories 70; Total Fat 2g (Saturated Fat 1.5g; Trans Fat 0g); Cholesterol 15mg; Sodium 85mg; Total Carbohydrate 12g (Dietary Fiber 0g); Protein 1g **Exchanges:** ½ Starch, ½ Fat **Carbohydrate Choices:** 1

SWEET TIP **Wait a minute—thyme in a little cake? Adding savory flavors to typically sweet items is a growing trend. Try these tasty little cakes; we think you'll like them.**

Neapolitan Cupcakes

Prep Time: 45 minutes ✳ **Start to Finish:** 1 hour 45 minutes ✳ **24 CUPCAKES**

cupcakes

- **1 box white cake mix with pudding**

  Water, vegetable oil and egg whites called for on cake mix box
- **½ teaspoon almond extract**
- **½ teaspoon vanilla**
- **¼ cup unsweetened baking cocoa**
- **½ cup miniature semisweet chocolate chips**

frosting and decorations

- **1 container (12 oz) chocolate whipped ready-to-spread frosting**
- **1 container (12 oz) fluffy white whipped ready-to-spread frosting**
- **1 container (12 oz) strawberry mist whipped ready-to-spread frosting**

  Assorted candy sprinkles

  Additional miniature semisweet chocolate chips

1 Heat oven to 350°F (325°F for dark or nonstick pans). Place white paper baking cup in each of 24 regular-size muffin cups.

2 Make cake mix as directed on box for cupcakes, using water, oil and egg whites and adding almond extract and vanilla. Pour half of batter into small bowl; stir in cocoa and ½ cup chocolate chips. Divide chocolate batter evenly among muffin cups. Carefully spoon white batter evenly over chocolate batter.

3 Bake as directed on box. Cool 10 minutes. Remove cupcakes from pans to cooling racks. Cool completely, about 30 minutes.

4 Frost cupcakes with a layer of chocolate frosting, white frosting and strawberry frosting. Decorate with candy sprinkles and additional chocolate chips.

1 Cupcake (Cupcake and Frosting Only): Calories 300; Total Fat 13g (Saturated Fat 4g; Trans Fat 2.5g); Cholesterol 0mg; Sodium 210mg; Total Carbohydrate 44g (Dietary Fiber 0g); Protein 1g **Exchanges:** 1 Starch, 2 Other Carbohydrate, 2½ Fat **Carbohydrate Choices:** 3

Strawberries and Cream Cake Pops

Prep Time: 40 minutes * Start to Finish: 2 hours 10 minutes * **36 CAKE POPS**

cake

- **1 box white cake mix with pudding**
- **Water, vegetable oil and egg whites called for on cake mix box**

filling

- **½ cup powdered sugar**
- **2 oz cream cheese, softened**
- **¼ cup butter, softened**
- **¼ cup strawberry jam**
- **1 cup dried strawberries, chopped**

coating and decorations

- **1 cup red candy melts (from 14-oz bag), melted**
- **2 bags (14 oz each) pink candy melts or coating wafers, melted**
- **36 paper lollipop sticks**
- **1 large block white plastic foam**
- **½ cup pink sugar**

1 Heat oven to 350°F. Spray 13 × 9-inch pan with cooking spray. Make and bake cake mix as directed on box, using water, oil and egg whites. Cool completely.

2 Line cookie sheet with waxed paper. In large bowl, beat powdered sugar, cream cheese, butter and jam with electric mixer on medium speed until blended. Crumble cake into cream cheese mixture; mix well. Stir in dried strawberries. Shape into 2-inch balls; place on cookie sheet. Freeze until firm. When cake balls are firm, transfer to refrigerator.

3 Spoon about 2 tablespoons melted red candy into pink candy; swirl gently. Remove several cake balls from refrigerator at a time. Dip tip of 1 lollipop stick about ½ inch into melted candy and insert stick into 1 cake ball no more than halfway. Dip each cake ball into swirled candy to cover; tap off excess. (Spoon more red candy into pink candy as needed.) Poke opposite end of stick into foam block. Sprinkle with pink sugar. Let stand until set.

1 Cake Pop: Calories 278; Total Fat 13g (Saturated Fat 7g; Trans Fat 0g); Cholesterol 0mg; Sodium 118mg; Total Carbohydrate 40g (Dietary Fiber 0g); Protein 1g **Exchanges:** ½ Starch, 2 Other Carbohydrate, 2½ Fat **Carbohydrate Choices:** 2½

Spring Chicks Cake Pops

Prep Time: 1 hour * Start to Finish: 2 hours 30 minutes * **48 CAKE POPS**

cake

1 box cake mix with pudding (any flavor)

Water, vegetable oil and eggs called for on cake mix box

filling

1 cup creamy ready-to-spread frosting (any flavor without chips or nuts)

coating and decorations

3 bags (14 oz each) yellow candy melts

48 paper lollipop sticks

Block of white plastic foam

48 orange heart sprinkles

96 yellow heart sprinkles

96 orange wildflower sprinkles

96 blue or green mini confetti sprinkles

1 Make and bake cake mix in 13 × 9-inch pan as directed on box using water, oil and eggs. Cool completely. In large bowl, crumble cake. Add frosting; mix well. Roll into 1-inch balls; place on waxed paper–lined cookie sheet. Freeze until firm. Keep refrigerated.

2 In microwavable bowl, microwave 1 bag of candy melts uncovered on Medium (50%) 1 minute, then in 15-second intervals, until melted; stir until smooth. Remove several cake balls at a time from refrigerator. Dip tip of 1 lollipop stick about ½ inch into melted candy and insert stick into 1 cake ball no more than halfway. Dip into melted candy to cover; tap off any excess. (Reheat candy in microwave or add vegetable oil if too thick to coat.) Poke opposite end of stick into foam block. Let stand until set. Repeat with remaining candy melts and cake balls.

3 With toothpick, dot small amount of leftover melted candy on each cake pop for beak; attach 1 orange heart sprinkle, pointed side out. With same technique, attach 2 yellow sprinkles for wings, pointed side out, on sides of pop; attach 2 orange wildflower sprinkles at bottom of pop for feet; and attach 2 blue sprinkles for eyes.

1 Cake Pop: Calories 220; Total Fat 11g (Saturated Fat 6g; Trans Fat 0g); Cholesterol 20mg; Sodium 110mg; Total Carbohydrate 27g (Dietary Fiber 0g); Protein 2g **Exchanges:** 2 Other Carbohydrate, 2 Fat **Carbohydrate Choices:** 2

SWEET TIP **You don't have to make 48 cake pops at one time. Cut the cake into 3 equal pieces. One piece will make about 16 cake pops, and you can freeze the rest of the cake for another time. Use 1 bag of candy melts to coat the 16 cake pops. Remember to also use only ⅓ cup frosting.**

Make Your Own Cake Pops!

It's not hard to achieve the perfect cake pop or cake ball, but there are some tips that will help.

Here's just a little info to get you started. These little morsels are simply a mixture of crumbled baked cake and frosting rolled into balls and dipped in candy coating—what could be yummier than that? You can choose to use a convenient cake mix to start, or why not try one of our new scratch recipes for making these tasty treats? You'll want lollipop sticks for cake pops, or if you are making cake balls, look for decorative mini cupcake liners to serve them in.

✳ Bake the cake the night before and let it cool completely.

✳ To crumble the cake, cut it into four sections and rub two of the sections together over a large bowl. Then crumble the last small pieces by hand. Roll the cake mixture into 1-inch balls.

✳ Before dipping the cake balls in the melted candy, chill them for 10 to 15 minutes in the freezer, then move them to the refrigerator.

✳ Place candy-dipped cake pops into a block of plastic foam to dry.

✳ Store the cake pops in small bags tied with decorative ribbon. If the pops contain cream cheese, be sure to store them in the refrigerator.

Cappuccino Cake Pops

Prep Time: 1 hour 40 minutes * **Start to Finish:** 3 hours 45 minutes * **50 CAKE POPS**

cake

½	**cup hot water**
6	**tablespoons instant espresso coffee powder or granules**
1	**cup plus 2 tablespoons all-purpose flour**
½	**teaspoon baking soda**
¼	**teaspoon salt**
⅔	**cup sugar**
¼	**cup butter, softened**
2	**eggs**
2	**tablespoons coffee-flavored liqueur**
¼	**cup buttermilk**

filling

2	**containers (12 oz each) milk chocolate whipped ready-to-spread frosting**

coating and decorations

50	**paper lollipop sticks**
2	**blocks white plastic foam**
½	**cup fluffy white whipped ready-to-spread frosting (from 12-oz container)**
50	**chocolate-covered coffee beans (about 1 cup)**
2	**tablespoons unsweetened baking cocoa**

1 Heat oven to 350°F. Grease bottom and sides of 8-inch square pan with shortening; lightly flour. In small bowl, stir hot water and coffee powder until coffee is dissolved; set aside. In medium bowl, mix flour, baking soda and salt; set aside.

2 In large bowl, beat sugar and butter with electric mixer on medium speed until light and fluffy. Beat in eggs, one at a time, just until blended. Beat in liqueur and coffee mixture. On low speed, alternately add flour mixture and buttermilk, beating just until blended after each addition. Pour into pan.

3 Bake 28 to 30 minutes or until toothpick inserted in center comes out clean. Cool 10 minutes; remove from pan to cooling rack. Cool completely, about 45 minutes.

4 Line cookie sheet with waxed paper. With fingers, crumble cake into large bowl. Add ½ cup of the chocolate frosting; mix well with spoon. Roll cake mixture into 1-inch balls; place on cookie sheet. Freeze about 30 minutes or until firm; when firm, transfer to refrigerator.

5 In medium microwavable bowl, microwave remaining chocolate frosting uncovered on Medium (50%) 30 seconds or until melted; stir until smooth. Remove several cake balls from refrigerator at a time. For each pop, dip tip of 1 lollipop stick about ½ inch into melted frosting and insert stick into 1 cake ball no more than halfway. Dip cake ball into melted frosting to cover; tap off any excess. Poke opposite end of stick into foam block. Let stand until set.

6 In small microwavable bowl, microwave white frosting uncovered on Medium (50%) 10 to 20 seconds or until melted; stir until smooth. Spoon ½ teaspoon frosting on top of each cake pop, letting it drip down side slightly. Immediately top with coffee bean. Let stand until set. Sprinkle lightly with cocoa. Store loosely covered in refrigerator.

1 Cake Pop: Calories 109; Total Fat 5g (Saturated Fat 2g; Trans Fat 0g); Cholesterol 0mg; Sodium 78mg; Total Carbohydrate 15g (Dietary Fiber 0g); Protein 1g **Exchanges:** 1 Other Carbohydrate 1 Fat **Carbohydrate Choices:** 1

Lemon Meringue Cake Pops

Prep Time: 50 minutes * Start to Finish: 2 hours 55 minutes * **48 CAKE POPS**

cake

3	cups all-purpose flour
4½	teaspoons baking powder
½	teaspoon salt
1	cup milk
2	teaspoons vanilla
1	teaspoon grated lemon peel
5	egg whites
1¾	cups granulated sugar
1	cup butter, softened

filling

1	jar (10 oz) lemon curd (about 1 cup)

coating and decorations

1	box fluffy white ready-to-spread frosting mix
½	cup boiling water
48	paper lollipop sticks
2	blocks white plastic foam
¼	cup coarse yellow sparkling sugar

1 Heat oven to 350°F. Grease bottom and sides of 13 × 9-inch pan with shortening; lightly flour. In medium bowl, mix flour, baking powder and salt; set aside. In small bowl, mix milk, vanilla, lemon peel and egg whites; set aside.

2 In large bowl, beat granulated sugar and butter with electric mixer on medium speed until light and fluffy. On low speed, alternately add flour mixture and milk mixture, beating just until blended after each addition. Pour into pan.

3 Bake 30 to 35 minutes or until toothpick inserted in center comes out clean. Cool completely in pan on cooling rack, about 1 hour.

4 Line cookie sheet with waxed paper. With fingers, crumble cake into large bowl. Add lemon curd; mix well with spoon. Roll cake mixture into 1-inch balls; place on cookie sheet. Freeze about 30 minutes or until firm; keep frozen.

5 In medium deep bowl, beat frosting mix and boiling water with electric mixer on low speed 30 seconds, scraping bowl constantly. Beat on high speed 5 to 7 minutes, scraping bowl occasionally, until stiff glossy peaks form.

6 Remove several cake balls at a time from freezer. For each pop, insert 1 lollipop stick halfway into 1 cake ball. Dip cake ball into frosting, swirling to coat. Poke opposite end of stick into foam block. Sprinkle pops with sparkling sugar.

1 Cake Pop: Calories 133; Total Fat 5g (Saturated Fat 3g; Trans Fat 0g); Cholesterol 0mg; Sodium 121mg; Total Carbohydrate 22g (Dietary Fiber 0g); Protein 1g **Exchanges:** ½ Starch, Fruit1 Other Carbohydrate, 1 Fat **Carbohydrate Choices:** 1½

SWEET TIP **A mock meringue coats these cake balls infused with tangy lemon curd. Store them loosely covered in the refrigerator.**

Cookies 'n' Cream Sports Ball Cake Pops

Prep Time: 1 hour 35 minutes * Start to Finish: 4 hours * 28 CAKE POPS

cake

- 1 cup all-purpose flour
- ½ teaspoon baking soda
- ½ teaspoon baking powder
- ¼ teaspoon salt
- ¾ cup granulated sugar
- ¼ cup butter, softened
- ½ cup sour cream
- 2 egg whites
- 1 teaspoon vanilla
- ¼ cup milk

filling

- 2 cups powdered sugar
- 3 tablespoons butter, softened
- 1 tablespoon milk
- 1 teaspoon vanilla
- 8 creme-filled chocolate sandwich cookies, coarsely crushed (about 1 cup)

coating and decorations

- 2 bags (12 oz each) candy melts of desired color
- 28 paper lollipop sticks
- 2 blocks white plastic foam Icing writer or food decorating pen of desired color

1 Heat oven to 350°F. Grease 8- or 9-inch round pan with shortening; lightly flour. In medium bowl, mix flour, baking soda, baking powder and salt; set aside.

2 In large bowl, beat granulated sugar and ¼ butter with electric mixer on medium speed about 2 minutes or until light and fluffy, scraping bowl occasionally. Beat in sour cream. Beat in egg whites, one at a time, beating well after each addition. Beat in 1 teaspoon vanilla. On low speed, alternately add flour mixture, about one-third at a time, and milk, about half at a time, beating just until blended. Pour into pan.

3 Bake 33 to 38 minutes or until top springs back when touched lightly in center. Cool 15 minutes.

4 Meanwhile, in medium bowl, mix powdered sugar and 3 tablespoons butter with electric mixer on low speed until blended. Beat in 1 tablespoon milk and 1 teaspoon vanilla. With fingers, crumble warm cake into medium bowl. Stir powdered sugar mixture into crumbled cake until well blended. Stir in crushed cookies. Cover; refrigerate 1 to 2 hours or until firm enough to shape. Roll cake mixture into 28 (1½-inch) balls; place on waxed paper–lined cookie sheet. Freeze 30 minutes.

5 In 2-cup microwavable measuring cup, microwave 12 oz of the candy melts as directed on package until melted. Coating must be at least 3 inches deep; add more candy melts as necessary to reach and/or maintain 3-inch depth. Remove several cake balls at a time from freezer. To make each cake pop, dip tip of lollipop stick ½ inch into melted candy and insert 1 inch into cake ball. Dip into melted candy to cover; very gently tap off excess. (Reheat candy in microwave or add vegetable oil if too thick to coat.) Poke opposite end of stick into foam block. With icing writer, decorate cake pops to resemble desired sports balls. Let stand until set.

1 Cake Pop: Calories 130; Total Fat 4.5g (Saturated Fat 2.5g; Trans Fat 0g); Cholesterol 10mg; Sodium 105mg; Total Carbohydrate 20g (Dietary Fiber 0g); Protein 1g **Exchanges:** ½ Starch, 1 Other Carbohydrate, 1 Fat **Carbohydrate Choices:** 1

SWEET TIPS Look for icing writers in the cake decorating section of craft stores.

Crush the cookies quickly by placing them in a resealable food-storage plastic bag and crushing them with a rolling pin.

If you'd like to make footballs, simply shape cake balls into football shapes instead of rolling into balls.

Trix® Cereal Cake Pops

Prep Time: 1 hour 15 minutes * Start to Finish: 5 hours 45 minutes * **48 CAKE POPS**

cake
1 box yellow or white cake mix with pudding

Water, vegetable oil and eggs or egg whites called for on cake mix box

filling
1 container vanilla creamy ready-to-spread frosting

coating and decorations
4 cups Trix® cereal

36 oz vanilla-flavored candy coating (almond bark)

48 paper lollipop sticks

1 Heat oven to 350°F (325°F for dark or nonstick pan). Make and bake cake as directed on box for 13 × 9-inch pan. Cool completely, about 1 hour.

2 With fingers, crumble cake into large bowl. Stir in frosting until well blended. Refrigerate about 2 hours or until firm enough to shape.

3 Roll cake mixture into 48 (1½-inch) balls; place on cookie sheet. Freeze 1 to 2 hours or until firm. Meanwhile, coarsely crush cereal. Line cookie sheet with waxed paper.

4 In 1-quart microwavable bowl, microwave 12 oz of the candy coating uncovered on High 1 minute 30 seconds; stir. Continue microwaving and stirring in 15-second intervals until melted; stir until smooth. Remove one-third of the balls from freezer. Using 2 forks, dip and roll each ball in coating. Place on waxed paper–lined cookie sheet. Immediately sprinkle with crushed cereal. Melt remaining candy coating in 12-oz batches; dip remaining balls and sprinkle with cereal. Place in refrigerator.

5 To serve, carefully insert sticks into cake balls. Store any remaining cake balls in airtight container in refrigerator.

1 Cake Pop: Calories 220; Total Fat 11g (Saturated Fat 5g; Trans Fat 0.5g); Cholesterol 20mg; Sodium 125mg; Total Carbohydrate 29g (Dietary Fiber 0g); Protein 2g **Exchanges:** 1 Starch, 1 Other Carbohydrate, 2 Fat **Carbohydrate Choices:** 2

SWEET TIP **To display, insert cake pop sticks into a foam block.**

Tequila Sunrise Cake Pops

Prep Time: 1 hour 5 minutes ✳ **Start to Finish:** 3 hours 10 minutes ✳ **18 CAKE POPS**

cake

- **1 cup all-purpose flour**
- **⅓ cup granulated sugar**
- **1 tablespoon grated orange peel**
- **1 teaspoon baking powder**
- **¼ teaspoon baking soda**
- **¼ teaspoon salt**
- **¼ cup orange juice**
- **¼ cup vegetable oil**
- **2 tablespoons orange-flavored liqueur**
- **1 tablespoon grenadine syrup**
- **2 eggs**

filling

- **¼ cup butter, softened**
- **1½ cups powdered sugar**
- **3 tablespoons tequila**

coating

- **1 bag (12 oz) yellow candy melts**
- **18 paper lollipop sticks**
- **2 blocks white plastic foam (each about 12 × 3 × 2 inches)**
- **1 bag (12 oz) orange candy melts**
- **Red colored sugar**

1 Heat oven to 350°F (325°F for dark or nonstick pan). Spray bottom only of 8 × 4-inch loaf pan with cooking spray. In large bowl, combine all cake ingredients. Beat with electric mixer on low speed until mixed. Beat on medium speed 2 minutes. Pour into pan.

2 Bake 30 to 35 minutes or until toothpick inserted in center comes out clean. Cool in pan 10 minutes; remove from pan to cooling rack. Cool completely, about 50 minutes. Trim browned edges from sides and bottom of cake.

3 In food processor with metal blade, crumble half of cake. Cover; process with on-and-off pulses until cake is fine crumbs. Place in large bowl; repeat with remaining cake.

4 In small bowl, combine all filling ingredients; beat on low speed until mixed. Beat on medium speed until creamy. Add to cake crumbs and mix until all crumbs are moistened and mixture holds together. Roll into 18 (1½-inch) balls onto waxed paper–lined cookie sheet. Freeze 30 minutes.

5 In 2-cup microwavable measuring cup, microwave yellow candy melts as directed on package until melted. Remove several cake balls at a time from freezer. Dip top ½ inch of each lollipop stick into melted coating and insert 1 inch into each cake ball. Dip into melted candy to cover; very gently tap off excess. (Reheat candy in microwave or add vegetable oil if too thick to coat.) Poke opposite end of stick into foam block. Let stand until set.

6 In another 2-cup microwavable measuring cup, microwave orange candy melts as directed on package until melted. Dip bottom half of each yellow-coated cake pop into orange melted candy. Dip tops into red colored sugar. Place in foam block. Let stand until set.

1 Cake Pop: Calories 350; Total Fat 17g (Saturated Fat 12g; Trans Fat 0g); Cholesterol 30mg; Sodium 150mg; Total Carbohydrate 46g (Dietary Fiber 0g); Protein 1g **Carbohydrate Choices:** 3

SWEET TIPS The cake balls are actually better the second day, as the flavors have a chance to mellow. They will keep at room temperature for several days.

You can find the candy melts at your local craft store in the candy-making and cake-decorating section.

Raspberry-Chocolate Cake Pops

Prep Time: 1 hour 30 minutes * Start to Finish: 6 hours 15 minutes * 28 CAKE POPS

cake

1¼   **cups all-purpose flour**
1¾   **teaspoons baking powder**
½   **teaspoon salt**
¼   **cup butter, softened**
¾   **cup granulated sugar**
3   **egg whites**
½   **teaspoon vanilla**
½   **cup milk**

truffles

8   **oz semisweet baking chocolate, finely chopped**
4   **teaspoons raspberry-flavored vodka**
¼   **cup heavy whipping cream**
2   **tablespoons butter**

filling

⅓   **cup butter, softened**
2½   **cups powdered sugar**
2   **tablespoons raspberry-flavored vodka**

coating

1   **bag (12 oz) dark chocolate candy melts**
28   **paper lollipop sticks**
1   **bag (12 oz) light cocoa candy melts**

SWEET TIP Raspberry vodka adds a nice berry flavor without turning the cake and filling purple-gray, like black raspberry liqueur would.

1   Heat oven to 350°F. Grease 8- or 9-inch round pan with shortening; lightly flour. In small bowl, mix flour, baking powder and salt. In medium bowl, beat ¼ cup butter with electric mixer on medium speed 30 seconds. Beat in granulated sugar, ¼ cup at a time, beating well after each addition. Beat 2 minutes longer, scraping bowl occasionally. Add egg whites, one at a time, beating well after each addition. Beat in vanilla. On low speed, alternately add flour mixture, one-third at a time, and milk, about half at a time, beating just until blended. Spread in pan.

2   Bake 35 to 40 minutes or until toothpick inserted in center comes out clean. Cool 20 minutes. With fingers, crumble cake into medium bowl. Line 2 cookie sheets with waxed paper. In small bowl, place chopped chocolate and 4 teaspoons raspberry vodka. In small microwavable bowl, microwave whipping cream and 2 tablespoons butter on High 1 minute or until boiling. Stir until butter is melted. Pour over chocolate mixture; stir until chocolate is melted and smooth. If necessary, microwave on High 10 to 15 seconds until mixture can be stirred smooth. Pour into 8-inch square glass baking dish; cover and refrigerate 1 hour. When firm, use melon baller to make 28 round truffle centers. Place on cookie sheet; refrigerate.

3   In medium bowl, beat ⅓ cup butter with electric mixer on medium speed until smooth. Gradually beat in powdered sugar and 2 tablespoons raspberry vodka on low speed until smooth. Stir into crumbled cake until blended. Cover; refrigerate 1 to 2 hours or until firm enough to shape.

4   Roll cake mixture into 28 (1½-inch) balls. On waxed paper, flatten each into 3-inch round; place truffle in center of each. Quickly shape round up and around truffle, pinching round together to seal any cracks. Place on cookie sheet. Freeze 30 minutes.

5   In 2-cup microwavable measuring cup, microwave dark chocolate candy melts as directed on package until melted. Dip top of each of 14 lollipop sticks ½ inch into melted dark chocolate and insert 1 inch into each of 14 cake balls. Dip into melted candy to cover; tap off excess. (Heat candy in microwave if too thick to coat.) Place each cake ball in mini cupcake liner. Reserve remaining coating. Repeat with light cocoa candy melts and remaining cake balls. Let stand until set. Use remaining melted candy to drizzle dark chocolate over light cocoa cake pops and light cocoa over dark chocolate cake pops. Let stand until set, about 15 minutes.

1 Cake Pop: Calories 320; Total Fat 17g (Saturated Fat 12g; Trans Fat 0g); Cholesterol 15mg; Sodium 150mg; Total Carbohydrate 40g (Dietary Fiber 1g); Protein 2g **Carbohydrate Choices:** 2½

Mango-Lime Mini Cupcake Bites

Prep Time: 30 minutes * Start to Finish: 1 hour 20 minutes * **24 MINI CUPCAKE BITES**

cupcakes

- 1 cup all-purpose flour
- 1 teaspoon baking powder
- ⅛ teaspoon salt
- ¼ cup unsalted butter, softened
- ⅓ cup granulated sugar
- 2 eggs
- ⅓ cup milk
- 1 teaspoon grated lime peel
- ½ cup finely chopped mango (½ medium)

frosting

- ¼ cup unsalted butter, softened
- 2 cups powdered sugar
- ½ teaspoon grated lime peel
- 2 tablespoons fresh lime juice

1 Heat oven to 350°F. Place mini paper baking cup in each of 24 mini muffin cups; spray paper cups with cooking spray. In small bowl, mix flour, baking powder and salt; set aside.

2 In medium bowl, beat ¼ cup butter and the granulated sugar with electric mixer on medium speed 1 minute. On low speed, add eggs, one at a time, beating well after each addition. Alternately add flour mixture and ⅓ cup milk, beating after each addition until smooth. Beat in 1 teaspoon lime peel. Stir in mango. Divide batter evenly among baking cups.

3 Bake 12 minutes or until toothpick comes out clean. Cool 10 minutes. Remove from pans to cooling racks. Cool completely, about 30 minutes.

4 In medium bowl, beat frosting ingredients with electric mixer on medium speed until smooth. Spoon frosting into decorating bag fitted with star tip; pipe onto each mini cupcake. Sprinkle with additional grated lime peel.

1 Mini Cupcake Bite: Calories 120; Total Fat 4.5g (Saturated Fat 2.5g; Trans Fat 0g); Cholesterol 30mg; Sodium 40mg; Total Carbohydrate 18g (Dietary Fiber 0g); Protein 1g **Exchanges:** 1 Other Carbohydrate, 1 Fat **Carbohydrate Choices:** 1

SWEET TIP **You can replace the lime with lemon in this recipe, but do not remove citrus entirely as it balances the sweetness of the mango.**

Mini Chocolate Chunk–Filled Cupcakes

Prep Time: 40 minutes * Start to Finish: 1 hour 50 minutes * **72 MINI CUPCAKES**

cupcakes

1 **box dark chocolate cake mix with pudding**

 Water, vegetable oil and eggs called for on cake mix box

½ **cup semisweet chocolate chunks (from 12-oz bag)**

frosting and decorations

2 **containers (12 oz each) vanilla whipped ready-to-spread frosting**

72 **walnut halves (2 cups), toasted***

4 **tubes (0.68 oz each) red decorating gel**

1 Heat oven to 350°F. Place mini paper baking cup in each of 72 mini muffin cups. Make cake mix as directed on box for cupcakes, using water, oil and eggs. Divide batter evenly among muffin cups. Gently press 1 chocolate chunk into center of each muffin cup.

2 Bake 11 to 12 minutes or until toothpick inserted in center comes out clean. Cool 5 minutes; remove from pans to cooling racks. Cool completely, about 30 minutes.

3 Frost cupcakes with vanilla frosting. Top each with 1 walnut half. Using red gel, pipe along edges of walnut halves to look like brains. Store cupcakes loosely covered at room temperature.

To toast walnuts, heat oven to 350°F. Spread walnuts in ungreased shallow pan. Bake uncovered 6 to 10 minutes, stirring occasionally, until light brown.

1 Mini Cupcake: Calories 100; Total Fat 6g (Saturated Fat 1.5g; Trans Fat 0.5g); Cholesterol 10mg; Sodium 65mg; Total Carbohydrate 12g (Dietary Fiber 0g); Protein 1g **Exchanges:** ½ Starch, ½ Other Carbohydrate, 1 Fat **Carbohydrate Choices:** 1

SWEET TIP Swap out chocolate chunks for raspberry slice candies. Cut raspberry slice candies into thirds and place one in center of each cupcake before baking to create a red center.

Apricot Petits Fours

Prep Time: 1 hour 20 minutes * Start to Finish: 5 hours 10 minutes * **54 PETITS FOURS**

cake

- 1 **box yellow cake mix with pudding**
- 1 **cup apricot nectar or juice**
- ⅓ **cup vegetable oil**
- 1 **teaspoon grated orange peel**
- 2 **eggs**
- 2 **tablespoons orange-flavored liqueur or apricot nectar**

icing

- 9 **cups powdered sugar**
- ¾ **cup apricot nectar or water**
- ½ **cup corn syrup**
- ⅓ **cup butter, melted**
- 2 **teaspoons almond extract**

decorations, if desired

Sliced almonds

Orange peel

1 Heat oven to 350°F (325°F for dark or nonstick pan). Spray bottom and sides of 15 × 10 × 1-inch pan with baking spray with flour.

2 In large bowl, beat all cake ingredients except liqueur with electric mixer on low speed 30 seconds, then on medium speed 2 minutes, scraping bowl occasionally. Pour batter into pan.

3 Bake 22 to 28 minutes or until cake springs back when touched lightly in center. Brush liqueur over top of cake. Cool completely, about 20 minutes. To avoid cake crumbs when adding icing, freeze cake 1 hour before cutting.

4 In large bowl, beat icing ingredients on low speed until powdered sugar is moistened. Beat on high speed until smooth. If necessary, add 2 to 3 teaspoons more apricot nectar until icing is pourable.

5 Place cooling rack on cookie sheet or waxed paper to catch icing drips. Cut cake into 9 rows by 6 rows. Working with 6 pieces at a time, remove cake pieces from pan and place on cooling rack. Spoon icing evenly over top and sides of cake pieces, letting icing coat sides. (Icing that drips off can be reused.) Let stand until icing is set, about 2 hours.

6 Decorate with almonds and orange peel. Store in single layer in airtight plastic container.

1 Petit Four: Calories 150; Total Fat 3g (Saturated Fat 1g; Trans Fat 0g); Cholesterol 10mg; Sodium 70mg; Total Carbohydrate 30g (Dietary Fiber 0g); Protein 0g **Exchanges:** 2 Other Carbohydrate, ½ Fat **Carbohydrate Choices:** 2

SWEET TIPS You can make the cakes up to 2 weeks ahead and freeze, but wait to add the icing until shortly before you serve them.

Apricot nectar sounds like an exotic ingredient, but you're likely to find it in the juice aisle of the supermarket.

Mini Royal Fruitcakes

Prep Time: 1 hour 30 minutes * Start to Finish: 28 hours * **96 MINI CAKES**

1 cup dried currants
1 cup golden raisins
½ cup sweetened dried cranberries
1 orange
1 lemon
½ cup brandy
1 cup butter, softened
¼ cup molasses
1 cup packed brown sugar
4 eggs, lightly beaten
1½ cups all-purpose flour
3 tablespoons brandy
4 containers white or vanilla creamy ready-to-spread frosting
Edible fresh flowers and mint leaves, if desired

1 In large bowl place currants, golden raisins and dried cranberries. Zest and juice orange; add to bowl. Zest and juice lemon; add to bowl. Pour in ½ cup brandy, mix well. Cover with plastic wrap and let stand overnight. Drain extra liquid off soaked fruit, if needed.

2 Heat oven to 325°F. Grease and flour 13 x 9-inch cake pan. To make cake, beat butter, molasses and sugar in large bowl with electric mixer on medium speed, scraping bowl occasionally until blended. Gradually add the eggs and flour, alternating until both are incorporated. Stir in soaked fruit. Spread into pan.

3 Bake 50 to 55 minutes or until toothpick inserted in center comes out clean and surface is deep golden brown. Let cool in pan, about 2 hours. Brush with remaining 3 tablespoons brandy. Remove from pan.

4 To decorate, cut cake into 12 rows by 8 rows. Place 24 squares, leaving space between each, on cooling rack. Set over waxed paper to catch drips.

5 In medium microwave-safe bowl, place frosting from one container. Microwave on High in 30-second intervals, stirring until smooth and pourable. Quickly spoon about 1 tablespoon frosting over each of 24 mini cakes, covering tops and letting frosting drip over sides. Reheat frosting as needed, if necessary. Repeat with remaining frosting and mini cakes. Let stand about 30 minutes or until frosting is set. Decorate with edible fresh flowers and mint. Store loosely covered.

1 Mini Cake: Calories 130; Total Fat 5g (Saturated Fat 2g; Trans Fat 1g); Cholesterol 15mg; Sodium 60mg; Total Carbohydrate 20g (Dietary Fiber 0g); Protein 0g **Exchanges:** 1½ Other Carbohydrate, 1 Fat **Carbohydrate Choices:** 1

SWEET TIP **For extra brandy flavor, wrap the undecorated cake in foil and let stand for up to 2 weeks. Unwrap and sprinkle with 1 tablespoon additional brandy each week.**

Almond Petits Fours

Prep Time: 1 hour * Start to Finish: 1 hour 50 minutes * 58 PETITS FOURS

cake

- 1 box white cake mix with pudding
  Water, vegetable oil and egg whites called for on cake mix box
- 1 teaspoon almond extract

glaze

- 1 bag (2 lb) powdered sugar
- ½ cup water
- ½ cup corn syrup
- 2 teaspoons almond extract
- 1 to 3 teaspoons hot water

decoration

- Assorted colors decorating icing (in 4.25-oz tubes), fresh edible flowers or purchased candy flowers

1 Heat oven to 350°F (325°F for dark or nonstick pans). Spray bottoms only of 58 mini muffin cups with baking spray with flour.

2 Make cake batter as directed on box, adding 1 teaspoon almond extract with the water. Divide batter evenly among muffin cups (about half full).

3 Bake 10 to 15 minutes or until toothpick inserted in center comes out clean. Cool 5 minutes; remove from pan to cooling rack. Cool completely, about 30 minutes.

4 Place cooling rack on cookie sheet or waxed paper to catch glaze drips. In 3-quart saucepan, stir powdered sugar, ½ cup water, the corn syrup and 2 teaspoons almond extract. Heat over low heat, stirring frequently, until sugar is dissolved; remove from heat. Stir in hot water, 1 teaspoon at a time, until glaze is pourable. Turn each mini cake on cooling rack so top side is down. Pour about 1 tablespoon glaze over each cake, letting glaze coat the sides. Let stand 15 minutes.

5 With decorating icing, pipe designs on cakes, or garnish cakes with flowers just before serving. Store loosely covered.

1 Petit Four: Calories 110; Total Fat 1.5g (Saturated Fat 0g; Trans Fat 0g); Cholesterol 0mg; Sodium 60mg; Total Carbohydrate 24g (Dietary Fiber 0g); Protein 0g **Exchanges:** ½ Starch, 1 Other Carbohydrate **Carbohydrate Choices:** 1½

SWEET TIPS **You can make the cakes up to 2 weeks ahead and freeze, but wait to add the glaze until shortly before you serve them.**

If you have only 1 pan and a recipe calls for more cupcakes than your pan will make, cover and refrigerate the rest of the batter while baking the first batch. Cool the pan about 15 minutes, then bake the rest of the batter, adding 1 to 2 minutes to the bake time.

Butterfly Cupcake Petits Fours

Prep Time: 2 hours 30 minutes ✳ Start to Finish: 3 hours 20 minutes ✳ 72 PETITS FOURS

cupcakes

2¾	cups all-purpose flour
3	teaspoons baking powder
½	teaspoon salt
¾	cup shortening
1⅔	cups granulated sugar
5	egg whites
2½	teaspoons vanilla
1¼	cups milk

glaze

8	cups powdered sugar
½	cup water
½	cup light corn syrup
2	teaspoons almond extract

decorations

Pastel-colored candy-coated chocolate candies

Small yogurt-covered pretzel twists

Black string licorice, cut into ½-inch pieces

1 Heat oven to 350°F. Place mini paper baking cup in each of 24 mini muffin cups.

2 In medium bowl, mix flour, baking powder and salt; set aside. In large bowl, beat shortening with electric mixer on medium speed 30 seconds. Gradually add granulated sugar, about ⅓ cup at a time, beating well after each addition. Beat 2 minutes longer. Add egg whites, one at a time, beating well after each addition. Beat in vanilla. On low speed, alternately add flour mixture, about a third at a time, and milk, about half at a time, beating just until blended.

3 Fill each muffin cup two-thirds full with batter. (Cover and refrigerate remaining batter until ready to bake; cool pan before reusing.)

4 Bake 12 to 16 minutes or until golden brown and toothpick inserted in center comes out clean. Cool 5 minutes; remove cupcakes from pans to cooling racks. Cool completely, about 15 minutes. Repeat with remaining batter to make additional 48 cupcakes.

5 In 2½-quart saucepan, beat glaze ingredients until smooth. Heat over low heat just until lukewarm. Remove from heat. If necessary, add hot water, a few drops at a time, until glaze is pourable.

6 Remove paper baking cups from cooled cupcakes; turn cupcakes upside down on cooling rack over large bowl. Working with 1 cupcake at a time, pour enough glaze over top to cover top and sides. (Glaze can be reheated, if necessary, to make it pourable.) Place 4 pastel candies in a row in center of cupcake. Place 2 pretzels, 1 on each side of the row of candies, to look like wings. Add 2 licorice pieces for antennae.

1 Petit Four: Calories 120; Total Fat 2.5g (Saturated Fat 0.5g; Trans Fat 0g); Cholesterol 0mg; Sodium 45mg; Total Carbohydrate 24g (Dietary Fiber 0g); Protein 1g **Exchanges:** ½ Starch, 1 Other Carbohydrate, ½ Fat **Carbohydrate Choices:** 1½

SWEET TIP **For sparkly butterfly wings, brush pretzels with a little of the glaze, then sprinkle with colored sugar.**

Espresso Petits Fours

Prep Time: 1 hour * Start to Finish: 2 hours 20 minutes * **35 PETITS FOURS**

cake

- **3** eggs, separated
- **¾** cup granulated sugar
- **½** cup butter, melted
- **1⅓** cups all-purpose flour
- **1** teaspoon baking powder
- **¼** teaspoon salt
- **⅓** cup water
- **1** teaspoon instant espresso coffee powder or granules

filling

- **3** tablespoons coffee-flavored liqueur
- **½** cup butter, softened
- **1½** cups powdered sugar
- **½** teaspoon vanilla
- **½** cup toasted* sliced almonds

icing

- **2** cups powdered sugar
- **3** tablespoons coffee-flavored liqueur
- **2** tablespoons cornstarch
- **1** tablespoon butter, melted
- **1** to 2 teaspoons water

garnish

- **35** small espresso coffee beans
- **35** toasted sliced almonds

SWEET TIPS The cake is easier to split if it is cold.

Toast a few extra almonds, about ¾ cup. Pick out the prettiest slices for the top garnish; chop ½ cup of the remaining almonds, and keep the rest for topping salads or other desserts.

1 Heat oven to 350°F. Grease 13 × 9-inch pan with shortening; lightly flour. In medium bowl, beat egg whites with electric mixer on high speed until stiff peaks form, gradually adding ¼ cup of the granulated sugar. Set aside.

2 In large bowl, beat egg yolks, remaining ½ cup granulated sugar and ½ cup melted butter at medium speed until creamy. Add flour, baking powder and salt. Mix on low speed until moistened. (Batter will be thick.) In small bowl, mix ⅓ cup water and the espresso powder; add to batter. Beat on low speed until blended. Beat on medium speed until smooth. Fold in beaten egg whites. Spread in pan.

3 Bake 18 to 23 minutes or until top springs back when touched lightly in center. Cool in pan 10 minutes. Run knife around edges to loosen; turn cake upside down onto cooling rack. Place another cooling rack on cake and turn upside down so top of cake is upright. Cool completely, about 30 minutes. Cover loosely and freeze 15 minutes or refrigerate 30 minutes.

4 With long, thin serrated knife, cut cake horizontally in half. Brush 3 tablespoons liqueur over cut side of bottom half. In small bowl, beat ½ cup butter, 1½ cups powdered sugar and vanilla with electric mixer on low speed until mixed. Beat on medium speed until smooth. Process ½ cup almonds in food processor 10 to 15 seconds or until finely chopped. Stir into filling. Spread filling evenly over bottom half of cake. Place top of cake over filling, cut side down. Press down firmly. Cover with plastic wrap; freeze 15 minutes.

5 In medium bowl, beat all icing ingredients on low speed until smooth, adding water if necessary for drizzling consistency. Trim outside edges of cake to create 10½ × 7½-inch rectangle. Cut into 7 rows by 5 rows, forming 35 squares. Place on 2 large cooling racks set over waxed paper. Using fork or spoon, drizzle and slightly spread each cake with icing. Top each with coffee bean and 1 sliced almond. Let stand until set, about 15 minutes. Flatten 35 mini paper baking cups slightly. Place 1 cake bite on each paper. Store loosely covered.

To toast almonds, heat oven to 350°F. Spread almonds in ungreased shallow pan. Bake uncovered 6 to 10 minutes, stirring occasionally, until light brown.

1 Petit Four: Calories 160; Total Fat 7g (Saturated Fat 3.5g; Trans Fat 0g); Cholesterol 30mg; Sodium 85mg; Total Carbohydrate 22g (Dietary Fiber 0g); Protein 1g **Carbohydrate Choices:** 1½

Engagement Ring Mini Cupcakes

Prep Time: 20 minutes * Start to Finish: 1 hour * **58 MINI CUPCAKES**

1 **box white cake mix with pudding**

Water, vegetable oil and egg whites called for on cake mix box

2 **cups powdered sugar**

3 **to 4 tablespoons milk**

Assorted colored rock candy

1 Heat oven to 350°F (325°F for dark or nonstick pans). Place paper baking cup in each of 58 mini muffin cups.

2 Make cake batter as directed on box, using water, oil and egg whites. Divide batter evenly among muffin cups, each about two-thirds full. If necessary, refrigerate any remaining batter until ready to use.

3 Bake 11 to 14 minutes or until toothpick inserted in center comes out clean. Cool 5 minutes; remove from pan to cooling rack. Cool completely, about 30 minutes.

4 In small bowl, stir powdered sugar and 3 tablespoons milk until smooth. Add additional milk 1 teaspoon at a time, until desired spreading consistency. Frost cupcakes. Top with rock candy pieces. Store loosely covered.

1 Mini Cupcake: Calories 70; Total Fat 1.5g (Saturated Fat 0g; Trans Fat 0g); Cholesterol 0mg; Sodium 60mg; Total Carbohydrate 13g (Dietary Fiber 0g); Protein 0g **Exchanges:** ½ Starch, ½ Other Carbohydrate **Carbohydrate Choices:** 1

SWEET TIPS Using a scoop makes spooning cupcake batter quick, less messy and also ensures cupcakes will be the same size. Use a #70 or small-sized spring-loaded ice-cream scoop that is equal to about 1 tablespoon.

If you have only 1 pan and a recipe calls for more cupcakes than your pan will make, cover and refrigerate the rest of the batter while baking the first batch. Cool the pan about 15 minutes, then bake the rest of the batter, adding 1 to 2 minutes to the bake time.

Double Dark Chocolate–Coconut Vegan Cupcakes

Prep Time: 40 minutes ✳ **Start to Finish:** 1 hour 20 minutes ✳ **12 SERVINGS**

cupcakes

- 1½ **cups all-purpose flour**
- 1 **cup granulated sugar**
- ½ **cup unsweetened baking cocoa**
- 1 **teaspoon baking soda**
- ½ **teaspoon salt**
- 1 **cup original- or vanilla-flavored soymilk**
- ½ **cup canola oil or vegetable oil**
- 1 **tablespoon cider vinegar**
- 1½ **teaspoons vanilla**
- ½ **cup miniature vegan chocolate chips**

frosting

- ½ **cup vegan vegetable oil spread stick, softened**
- ⅓ **cup virgin unrefined coconut oil (solid, not melted)**
- 1 **teaspoon vanilla**
- 2 **to 4 teaspoons water**
- 3 **tablespoons unsweetened baking cocoa**
- 3 **cups sifted powdered sugar**

garnish, if desired

- **Chocolate curls**
- **Shredded or shaved coconut**

1 Heat oven to 350°F. Line 12 mini and 12 regular-size muffin cups with paper baking cups. In large bowl, using wire whisk, mix flour, granulated sugar, ½ cup cocoa, the baking soda and salt. In medium bowl, using whisk, mix soymilk, canola oil, vinegar and 1½ teaspoons vanilla. Pour wet mixture into dry mixture; beat with whisk until well mixed. Stir in chocolate chips. Fill each mini muffin cup with 1 level measuring tablespoon batter. Divide remaining batter among regular-size muffin cups.

2 Bake mini cupcakes 12 to 16 minutes or until toothpick inserted in center comes out clean. Bake regular-size cupcakes 22 to 26 minutes or until toothpick inserted in center comes out clean. Cool in pans 10 minutes; remove from pans to cooling rack. Cool completely, about 30 minutes.

3 In large bowl, beat vegan spread stick, coconut oil, 1 teaspoon vanilla and 2 teaspoons of the water with electric mixer on low speed until smooth. Beat in 3 tablespoons cocoa and the powdered sugar, 1 cup at a time. Gradually beat in just enough remaining water until smooth and spreadable.

4 To assemble cupcake stacks, remove paper baking cups. Pipe frosting on top of 1 regular-size cupcake. Top with 1 mini cupcake; frost top of mini cupcake. Repeat with remaining cupcakes and frosting. Garnish with chocolate curls and coconut.

1 Serving: Calories 490; Total Fat 24g (Saturated Fat 9g; Trans Fat 0g); Cholesterol 0mg; Sodium 280mg; Total Carbohydrate 66g (Dietary Fiber 2g); Protein 3g **Exchanges:** 1 Starch, 3½ Other Carbohydrate, 4½ Fat **Carbohydrate Choices:** 4½

SWEET TIP This recipe is geared for vegans but can be enjoyed by anyone. When you are cooking or baking a vegan recipe, always read labels to make sure each recipe ingredient is vegan. If you're unsure about any ingredient or product, check with the manufacturer.

Pun...   ...snap Cheesecakes

Prep Time... ...ours 20 minutes * **24 MINI CHEESECAKES**

cakes

26	gingersnap cookies
3	packages (8 oz each) cream cheese, softened
1	cup sugar
3	eggs
¾	cup canned pumpkin (not pumpkin pie mix)
1	teaspoon pumpkin pie spice
1	cup miniature semisweet chocolate chips

topping

½	cup whipping cream
1	tablespoon sugar

1 Heat oven to 350°F. Place paper baking cup in each of 24 regular-size muffin cups. Place 1 gingersnap, flat side down, in bottom of each cup.

2 In large bowl, beat cream cheese and 1 cup sugar with electric mixer on medium speed until light and fluffy. Beat in eggs, one at a time, just until blended. Add pumpkin and pumpkin pie spice; beat just until blended. Stir in chocolate chips. Pour into muffin cups, filling full.

3 Bake 30 to 35 minutes or until almost firm. Cool 20 minutes. Remove from pans. Refrigerate cheesecakes in paper baking cups at least 2 hours before serving.

4 Place remaining 2 gingersnaps in resealable food-storage plastic bag; seal bag and crush with rolling pin or meat mallet (or crush in food processor). In chilled small bowl, beat whipping cream and 1 tablespoon sugar with electric mixer on high speed until stiff peaks form. Remove cheesecakes from paper baking cups. Spoon 1 teaspoon whipped cream on each cheesecake. Sprinkle with gingersnap crumbs.

1 Mini Cheesecake: Calories 230; Total Fat 15g (Saturated Fat 8g; Trans Fat 0g); Cholesterol 60mg; Sodium 150mg; Total Carbohydrate 21g (Dietary Fiber 1g); Protein 3g **Exchanges:** ½ Starch, 1 Other Carbohydrate, 3 Fat **Carbohydrate Choices:** 1½

SWEET TIP **You'll have some leftover canned pumpkin. Stir it into plain pancake batter to make pumpkin pancakes.**

Chocolate-Almond Cheesecake Bites

Prep Time: 50 minutes * **Start to Finish:** 3 hours 30 minutes * **48 CHEESECAKE BITES**

crust

16	**thin chocolate wafer cookies (from 9-oz package), crushed (1 cup)**
¼	**cup butter, melted**

filling

1	**package (8 oz) cream cheese, softened**
¼	**cup sour cream**
¼	**cup sugar**
1	**egg**
¼	**teaspoon almond extract**

coating

2⅓	**cups semisweet chocolate chips**
3	**tablespoons shortening**
2	**oz vanilla-flavored candy coating (almond bark), chopped**
1	**teaspoon vegetable oil**

1 Heat oven to 300°F. Cut 14 × 12-inch sheet of heavy-duty foil; line 8-inch square pan with foil so foil extends over sides of pan. Spray foil with cooking spray. In small bowl, mix crust ingredients. Press in bottom of pan.

2 In large bowl, beat cream cheese, sour cream and sugar with electric mixer on medium speed until fluffy. Beat in egg and extract, scraping bowl if necessary. Pour over crust.

3 Bake 30 to 40 minutes or until edges are set (center will be soft but will set when cool). Cool on cooling rack 1 hour. Cover; refrigerate 1 hour. Meanwhile, cover 2 cookie sheets with waxed paper.

4 Using foil, lift cheesecake out of pan. Cut into 8 rows by 6 rows, making 48 oblong cheesecake bites. In 1-quart microwavable bowl, microwave chocolate chips and shortening uncovered on Medium (50%) 3 minutes. Stir; microwave in 15-second increments, stirring after each, until melted and smooth.

5 Work with half of bites at a time (24 bites); refrigerate other half until needed. Place 1 bite on fork and dip fork into chocolate to coat. Lift fork from chocolate and allow excess chocolate to drain off. Place on cookie sheet. Repeat with remaining cheesecake bites.

6 In small microwavable bowl, microwave candy coating and oil uncovered on High 1 minute. Stir; microwave in 15-second increments, stirring after each, until melted. Spoon into small resealable food-storage plastic bag. Seal bag; cut tiny hole in corner of bag. Squeeze bag to pipe melted coating over dipped bites. Store covered in refrigerator.

1 Cheesecake Bite: Calories 100; Total Fat 7g (Saturated Fat 4g; Trans Fat 0g); Cholesterol 15mg; Sodium 40mg; Total Carbohydrate 9g (Dietary Fiber 0g); Protein 1g **Exchanges:** ½ Other Carbohydrate, 1½ Fat **Carbohydrate Choices:** ½

SWEET TIP **If the chocolate coating cools and starts to get thick, microwave on High for 10 to 15 seconds to soften it.**

Metric Conversion Guide

Volume

U.S. UNITS	CANADIAN METRIC	AUSTRALIAN METRIC
¼ teaspoon	1 mL	1 ml
½ teaspoon	2 mL	2 ml
1 teaspoon	5 mL	5 ml
1 tablespoon	15 mL	20 ml
¼ cup	50 mL	60 ml
⅓ cup	75 mL	80 ml
½ cup	125 mL	125 ml
⅔ cup	150 mL	170 ml
¾ cup	175 mL	190 ml
1 cup	250 mL	250 ml
1 quart	1 liter	1 liter
1½ quarts	1.5 liters	1.5 liters
2 quarts	2 liters	2 liters
2½ quarts	2.5 liters	2.5 liters
3 quarts	3 liters	3 liters
4 quarts	4 liters	4 liters

Weight

U.S. UNITS	CANADIAN METRIC	AUSTRALIAN METRIC
1 ounce	30 grams	30 grams
2 ounces	55 grams	60 grams
3 ounces	85 grams	90 grams
4 ounces (¼ pound)	115 grams	125 grams
8 ounces (½ pound)	225 grams	225 grams
16 ounces (1 pound)	455 grams	500 grams
1 pound	455 grams	0.5 kilogram

Note: The recipes in this cookbook have not been developed or tested using metric measures. When converting recipes to metric, some variations in quality may be noted.

Measurements

INCHES	CENTIMETERS
1	2.5
2	5.0
3	7.5
4	10.0
5	12.5
6	15.0
7	17.5
8	20.5
9	23.0
10	25.5
11	28.0
12	30.5
13	33.0

Temperatures

FAHRENHEIT	CELSIUS
32°	0°
212°	100°
250°	120°
275°	140°
300°	150°
325°	160°
350°	180°
375°	190°
400°	200°
425°	220°
450°	230°
475°	240°
500°	260°

Index

Recipe Testing and Calculating Nutrition Information

RECIPE TESTING:

❋ Large eggs and 2% milk were used unless otherwise indicated.

❋ Fat-free, low-fat, low-sodium or lite products were not used unless indicated.

❋ No nonstick cookware and bakeware were used unless otherwise indicated. No dark-colored, black or insulated bakeware was used.

❋ When a pan is specified, a metal pan was used; a baking dish or pie plate means ovenproof glass was used.

❋ An electric hand mixer was used for mixing only when mixer speeds are specified.

CALCULATING NUTRITION:

❋ The first ingredient was used wherever a choice is given, such as ⅓ cup sour cream or plain yogurt.

❋ The first amount was used wherever a range is given, such as 3- to 3½-pound whole chicken.

❋ The first serving number was used wherever a range is given, such as 4 to 6 servings.

❋ "If desired" ingredients were not included.

❋ Only the amount of a marinade or frying oil that is absorbed was included.